TCP/IP

TCP/IP

Accelerated MCSE Study Guide

Dave Kinnaman

McGraw-Hill
New York • San Francisco • Washington, D.C. • Auckland
Bogotá • Caracas • Lisbon • London • Madrid • Mexico City
Milan • Montreal • New Delhi • San Juan • Singapore
Sydney • Tokyo • Toronto

Library of Congress Cataloging-in-Publication Data

Kinnaman, Dave.
    TCP/IP / Dave Kinnaman.
        p.   cm.—(Accelerated MCSE study guide)
    Includes index.
    ISBN 0-07-067686-0
    1. Electronic data processing personnel—Certification.
2. Microsoft software—Examinations—Study guides. 3. TCP/IP
(Computer network protocol) I. Title. II. Series.
    QA76.3.K59 1998
    005.7'1376—dc21   98-33235
                                        CIP

McGraw-Hill

A Division of The McGraw-Hill Companies

1 2 3 4 5 6 7 8 9 0 AGM/AGM 9 0 3 2 1 0 9 8

ISBN 0-07-067686-0

The sponsoring editor for this book was Michael Sprague and the production supervisor was Tina Cameron. It was set by D & G Limited, LLC.

Printed and bound by Quebecor/Martinsburg.

McGraw-Hill books are available at special quantity discounts to use as premiums and sales promotions, or for use in corporate training programs. For more information, please write to Director of Special Sales, McGraw-Hill, 11 West 19th Street, New York, NY 10011. Or contact your local bookstore.

 This book is printed on recycled, acid-free paper containing a minimum of 50% recycled de-inked fiber.

Contents

CHAPTER 1

Introduction to
the Study Guide

So you want to become a *Microsoft Certified Systems Engineer* (MCSE), do you? Purchasing this book is a good first step, because it's specifically designed to prepare you for your vital MCSE examinations. This first chapter will help you plan for the entire process of becoming an MCSE and assist you in outlining what it takes to pass all the MCSE exams.

According to Microsoft, "Microsoft Certified Systems Engineers design, install, support, and troubleshoot information systems. MCSEs are network gurus, support technicians, and operating system experts." That's a central information technology role with major responsibilities in today's computer networking world.

Plan Your MCSE Process

To prepare for such a major role, it takes a solid plan. You must know all your options. Let's begin the planning with a discussion of the components of the objective: the core exams and elective exams that lead toward the MCSE certificate. After identifying the core and elective exams, the remainder of this section is devoted to dispelling several myths about MCSE exams that could derail your plan if you believed them.

Core and Elective Exams

Two possible paths toward the MCSE exist at this writing, but the vast majority of candidates concentrate on the more recent one. The older path is based on Windows NT 3.51 and the newer one is based on Windows NT 4.0. Because the exams for Windows NT 3.51 have been scheduled for retirement, little more will be said about Windows NT 3.51.

MICROSOFT WINDOWS NT 4.0 TRACK

This track consists of mastering four core exams and two elective exams. All the many current elective exams are presented after the core exams.

You must choose four core exams from these eight:

- 70-030: Microsoft Windows 3.1 (retired September 1998)
- 70-048: Microsoft Windows for Workgroups 3.11 (retired September 1998)
- 70-058: Networking Essentials
- 70-064: Implementing and Supporting Microsoft Windows 95
- 70-067: Implementing and Supporting Microsoft Windows NT Server 4.0
- 70-068: Implementing and Supporting Microsoft Windows NT Server 4.0 in the Enterprise
- 70-073: Microsoft Windows NT Workstation 4.0
- 70-098: Implementing and Supporting Microsoft Windows 98

You Must Choose Two Elective Exams

A great number of elective exams are available. You can choose to become an expert on any two of these 10 software products:

- SNA Server
- Systems Management Server
- SQL Server
- TCP/IP on Microsoft Windows NT
- Exchange Server
- Internet Information Server
- Proxy Server

- Microsoft Mail for PC Networks—Enterprise
- Site Server
- Explorer 4.0 by Using the Internet Explorer Administration Kit

CAUTION

Microsoft allows you to use exams as electives one or two or three versions of several software products. Only one exam per product, regardless of the version, can be counted toward the two elective requirement. For example, if you pass both 70-013: Implementing and Supporting Microsoft SNA Server version 3.0 and 70-085: Implementing and Supporting Microsoft SNA Server version 4.0, these two exams only count for one elective. *The point is that passing exams on two versions of one product won't count as two electives—just one counts as an elective.*

One of these:

70-013: Implementing and Supporting Microsoft SNA Server 3.0

70-085: Implementing and Supporting Microsoft SNA Server 4.0

Or

70-014: Implementing and Supporting Microsoft Systems Management Server 1.0 (retired)

70-018: Implementing and Supporting Microsoft Systems Management Server 1.2

70-086: Implementing and Supporting Microsoft Systems Management Server 2.0

Or

70-021: Microsoft SQL Server 4.2 Database Implementation

70-027: Implementing a Database Design on Microsoft SQL Server 6.5

70-029: Implementing a Database Design on Microsoft SQL Server 7.0

Or

70-022: Microsoft SQL Server 4.2 Database Administration for Microsoft Windows NT

70-026: System Administration for Microsoft SQL Server 6.5

70-028: System Administration for Microsoft SQL Server 7.0

Or
70-053: Internetworking Microsoft TCP/IP on Microsoft Windows NT (3.5-3.51)

70-059: Internetworking with Microsoft TCP/IP on Microsoft Windows NT 4.0

Or
70-075: Implementing and Supporting Microsoft Exchange Server 4.0 (retired June 1, 1998)*

70-076: Implementing and Supporting Microsoft Exchange Server 5

70-081: Implementing and Supporting Microsoft Exchange Server 5.5

Or
70-077: Implementing and Supporting Microsoft Internet Information Server 3.0 and Microsoft Index Server 1.1

70-087: Implementing and Supporting Microsoft Internet Information Server 4.0

Or
70-078: Implementing and Supporting Microsoft Proxy Server 1.0

70-088: Implementing and Supporting Microsoft Proxy Server 2.0

Or
70-037: Microsoft Mail for PC Networks 3.2-Enterprise

Or
70-056: Implementing and Supporting Web Sites Using Microsoft Site Server 3.0

Or
70-079: Implementing and Supporting Microsoft Internet Explorer 4.0 by Using the Internet Explorer Administration Kit

With all these options available, MCSE candidates can surely find elective exams that fit their own career and workplace goals.

*Exam 70-075: for Exchange Server 4.0 retired on June 1, 1998. If you have already passed this elective exam, you will be required to take a replacement elective exam on or before September 1, 1999. Replacement exams include all current MCSE electives listed here.

Required Software and Hardware

Many current MCSE holders earned their certificates at little or no expense to themselves because their employers paid the costs for both training and exams. Many of them also did all or almost all their exam preparation on the clock, so that their employers actually paid them to get an MCSE certificate. These fortunate MCSEs didn't even have to pay for software or equipment because their employers also supplied appropriate software and hardware needed to practice all the skills necessary for their MCSE exams. If your employer offers this kind of comprehensive support, wonderful. On the other hand, if your employer expects you to pay your way to the MCSE entirely by yourself, here are some thoughts on what you'll need.

REQUIRED SOFTWARE

In most cases, you'll need at least one copy of both the server and the client software, because most MCSE exams are about *administering networks* that contain the software in question. You'll need to know how the product works from both the client and administrator points of view, even if the exam is specifically about a client software, such as Windows NT 4.0 Workstation. As just mentioned, the MCSE exams are usually from the system support and administrator's point of view, rather than the client user's point of view.

Installing a Microsoft client software may, of course, require a pre-existing operating system or a previous version of the client software, depending on the product involved. Similarly, several Microsoft server operating systems require you to have *other* server operating systems already available on the network, or installed and underlying on the server computer. This means that more than one server software program may be required in order for you to use and become familiar with all the tested features of the server software required for the exam.

MINIMUM REQUIRED HARDWARE

For one or more Windows NT Workstation computers:

- 12 MB RAM
- VGA video
- Keyboard
- IDE, EIDE, SCSI, or ESDI hard disk
- 486/25 processor or faster

- 124 MB free hard drive space (Recommended minimum: over 300 MB, including a copy of the entire I386 installation directory [223 MB] plus Windows 95 or DOS 6.22). For hard disk controllers using translation mode to address the drive, increase these minimum sizes by 80 MB.

- CD-ROM drive, or a floppy disk drive and an active network connection

For one or more Windows NT Server computers:

- 16 MB RAM (32 MB or more recommended)

- VGA video

- Keyboard

- IDE, EIDE, SCSI, or ESDI hard disk

- 486/25 processor (486DX2/50 or better preferred)

- 124 MB free hard drive space (Recommended minimum: over 300 MB, including a copy of the entire I386 installation directory [223 MB] plus Windows 95 or DOS 6.22). For hard disk controllers using translation mode to address the drive, increase these minimum sizes by 80 MB.

- CD-ROM drive (Windows NT compatible recommended), or a floppy disk drive and an active network connection

- Recommended: 28.8 v.34 (or faster) external modem, for remote debugging and troubleshooting

COSTS TO OBTAIN AN MCSE

As mentioned above, the costs of an MCSE certificate are invisible to many current certificate holders because the costs are entirely supported by their employers. Because these advanced skills are of great value to the workplace, it's appropriate that employers provide this support, in exchange for more efficient and more productive work skills.

Some supportive employers do require a contract to assure themselves that the newly trained MCSE will not change jobs to another employer shortly after obtaining the MCSE certificate—presumably before the current employer has had time to recoup the costs of the MCSE for their former employee. These contracts typically require the employee to repay MCSE costs on a pro-rated basis, depending on how long the MCSE candidate remained with the former employer. Often the new employer picks up the costs of buying-out the former employer's training contract as a part of the new and more advantageous employment agreement.

Note that MCSE holders are considered more employable, and therefore more mobile in their employment. The cost efficiency of information technology workplaces has been hard hit by a mercenary, contract-worker mentality that drains the spirit from workers. In contrast, employers who provide an environment of mutual trust and employment security, by fostering loyalty and good will in all employees, will obtain the best return on their investment in employee MCSE training.

MCSE Expense Budget	Costs
Examinations—$600 (retests at $100 each)	
Training, seminars, workshops	
Study time	
Books and materials	
Practice examination software	
Network hardware, network analysis equipment	
Server and client hardware	
Server and client software	

MCSE Myth #1: Everyone Must Take Six Exams to Earn the MCSE

Reality: Some People Are Exempt from One Exam

Some networking professionals are exempt from taking the Networking Essentials exam because they have already passed a similarly rigorous exam through Novell, Banyan, Sun, or Microsoft. These professionals are already skilled and possess certificates to prove it; thus, Microsoft grants them MCSE certificates after they pass only five additional Microsoft exams.

Specifically, Microsoft automatically grants credit for the Networking Essentials exam once you've passed a *Microsoft Certified*

Professional (MCP) exam and provide evidence that you hold one of these exact certificates:

NOVELL

CNE—Certified Novell Engineer

CNI—Certified Novell Instructor

ECNE—Enterprise Certified Novell Engineer

MCNE—Master Certified Novell Engineer

BANYAN

CBE—Certified Banyan CBE

CBS—Certified Banyan Specialist

SUN

CNA—Sun Certified Network Administrators for Solaris 2.5

CNA—Sun Certified Network Administrators for Solaris 2.6

So if you already hold one of the above certificates, just pass one MCP exam, and provide proof of your previous networking certificate, and you'll receive credit for two exams for the price of one.

What's an MCP Exam?

An MCP exam is a Microsoft exam first of all. Passing an MCP exam makes you a Microsoft Certified Professional and automatically enrolls you in the Microsoft MCP program. But not all Microsoft exams are MCP exams. Networking Essentials, specifically, is not an MCP exam. The sidebar has more information about the MCP designation.

Microsoft Certified Professional

MICROSOFT CERTIFIED PROFESSIONALS (MCPS)

Microsoft Certified Professionals get their certificates by passing a Microsoft exam based on a Windows server or desktop operating system. Please note: Not all MCP exams contribute to an MCSE certificate! In fact, not very many do! Be sure to check the official Microsoft requirements when you make your MCSE plans to assure yourself that requirements have not changed since this study guide was written. Here are all the MCP exams which, as of this writing, contribute toward an MCSE certification:

MCP Exams in the Windows NT 4.0 MCSE Track

- 70-030: Microsoft Windows 3.1 (retired September 1998)
- 70-048: Microsoft Windows for Workgroups 3.11-Desktop (retires September 1998)
- 70-064: Implementing and Supporting Microsoft Windows 95
- 70-067 Implementing and Supporting Microsoft Windows NT Server 4.0
- 70-073 Implementing and Supporting Microsoft Windows NT Workstation 4.0

MCP Exams in the Windows NT 3.51 MCSE Track

- 70-030: Microsoft Windows 3.1 (retired September 1998)
- 70-042: Implementing and Supporting Windows NT Workstation 3.51 (retires as Windows NT Workstation 5.0 exam is released)
- 70-043: Implementing and Supporting Windows NT Server 3.51 (retires as Windows NT Server 5.0 exam is released)
- 70-048: Microsoft Windows for Workgroups 3.11-Desktop (retired September 1998)
- 70-064: Implementing and Supporting Microsoft Windows 95

Every MCSE certificate holder has multiple MCP designations because of the nature of the MCSE requirements. There is also a *premium* MCP certificate called MCP+Internet available. MCP certificates are considered the basic Microsoft certificate that leads to a premium MCP certificate or, in many cases, to MCSE status. MCPs have a private Microsoft Web site, a free magazine, other benefits, and a special logo of their own. The Microsoft MCP Web site is located at http://www.microsoft.com/mcp.

TWO RETIRED MICROSOFT EXAMS CAN SUBSTITUTE FOR NETWORKING ESSENTIALS

In addition to the networking certificates listed above from Banyan, Novell, and Sun that can substitute for passing the Networking Essentials exam, there are two more ways to achieve an MCSE with only five (additional) exams. If you happen to have taken and passed one of the following two retired Microsoft exams, you can use that previous exam to have the Networking Essentials exam MCSE requirement waived:

- Exam 70-046: Networking with Microsoft Windows for Workgroups 3.11 (retired)

- Exam 70-047: Networking with Microsoft Windows 3.1 (retired).

  Retired Microsoft exams are explained in detail later in this chapter.

MCSE Myth #2: Only One Year to Finish

Reality: Take As Long As You Like To Finish Your MCSE

Take as much time as you need to be prepared for each test. There is no stated time limit for completion of the MCSE certificate. Begin and then take examinations when you are ready. Although there is a popular misconception that you have only one year (or two years or *whatever*) to complete your MCSE certificate, there is, in fact, no time limit. The only limits are your own motivation and the time available in your life. As an adult, you can decide for yourself how much more of your life you want to spend working as something other than an MCSE.

So you should plan to progress at your own deliberate or expeditious speed, depending on your needs, your personal learning style, and the amount of time, money, and concentration you can devote to this project. Everyone starts their MCSE studies with different personal backgrounds, different circumstances, and different knowledge. Each reader brings different expectations for this book. Some readers will want a guide for the following reasons:

- To confirm they already know enough to be certified.

- To accompany a class or even a crash course.

- To study on their own, reading and applying the concepts as they go.

  Not having an MCSE time limit is also consistent with good educational design because adults learn best at their own rates and in their own ways. It also keeps Microsoft away from the *bad guy* enforcer role. This way Microsoft never has to say, *"Sorry, all your work was for nothing, you're too late. You must start over."*

WHAT IF IT TAKES TOO LONG?

There is a possible downside to extending your MCSE studies. The longer you take, the more likely it is that one of the exams you've already passed will be retired *before* you finish your MCSE studies. If an exam you've passed is retired while you are still pursuing your MCSE, you'll need to replace the retired exam with a current exam, causing you more work to accomplish the same original goal.

Another reason to progress toward your MCSE with all due dispatch is in recognition of your own personal learning style. Many adults learn best if they concentrate heavily on learning, passing exams as a kind of punctuation in their study cycle. Also, each exam has areas of overlap with other exams. What you learn for one exam will help with other exams as well. Taking Exam B soon after taking Exam A, while Exam A's information is still fresh in your memory, can be ideal for some adult learners. Adjust your exam strategy to accommodate your own learning style.

Also establish a timeline for yourself. The longer you take to complete the MCSE track, the less likely you are to finish. Establish a study and examination schedule for yourself and make a serious effort to stick to the schedule and complete the exams in a timely manner. People generally work better if *the end is in sight*, so help yourself by creating a game plan for your certification.

MCSE Myth #3: There's a Two-Week Wait for a Retest

Reality: The First Retest Is Anytime, The Second Retest After Two Weeks

Although there have been several changes instituted to improve security around the MCSE exams, it is still okay to retake a failed exam as soon as you want. So if it happens that you fell asleep during the exam, you just had a bad day and only missed passing by one question, you were coming down with the flu the day of the exam, or you otherwise failed an exam in a fluke event that did not represent your true level of mastery of the material, then you can reschedule the same exam and retest as soon as you please—at full price, of course. If you fail twice, however, you will be required to wait at least two weeks before trying a third time.

TEST TIP

Many MCSE candidates and MCSE certificate holders are convinced that certain questions appear on more than one exam. It seems to others that one or two questions are pulled from their *mother* exam and placed at random on other exams without a discernible pattern. They claim that questions they expected on the TCP/IP exam turned up on the Windows NT Server or the Enterprise exam, for instance. Building a strong personal foundation of knowledge and experience is the only defense against this sort of random substitution if it occurs.

It is clear that the exams are at least quasi-hierarchical in that almost all Windows NT Workstation questions are legitimate fodder for the Windows NT Server exam, and all Windows NT Server exam questions are fair game for the Windows NT Server in the Enterprise exam, for instance. Likewise, all Networking Essentials questions are also fair game on the TCP/IP exam. This is another reason to take the exams in a deliberate, thoughtful order that makes sense with your own experience and knowledge.

MCSE Myth #4: You Must Pass Exam A *Before* Exam B

Reality: There Is No Required Exam Sequence

Please understand that there is no required sequence at all. You can literally take the MCSE exams in any order you please and achieve your certificate with no prejudice based on the order of your exams. However, there are good reasons why you might want to consider a purposeful sequence, rather than a random sequence of tests.

Which Exam Should You Take First?

Here is a sample way to plan your studies. It's based on three assumptions that may or may not be true for you. First, the assumptions are:

1. You aren't already certifiable in one or more exam areas.

2. You don't have more extensive experience and knowledge in some exam areas than the others.

3. You've decided to take these six exams, for example, to satisfy the requirements for the MCSE.

EXAMPLE CORE REQUIREMENTS

70-058 Networking Essentials

70-067 Implementing and Supporting Microsoft Windows NT Server 4.0

70-068 Implementing and Supporting Microsoft Windows NT Server 4.0 in the Enterprise

70-073 Implementing and Supporting Microsoft Windows NT Workstation 4.0

EXAMPLE ELECTIVE REQUIREMENTS

70-059 Internetworking with Microsoft TCP/IP on Windows NT 4.0

70-077 Implementing and Supporting Microsoft Internet Information Server 3.0 and Microsoft Index Server 1.1

If these exams and givens fit your case, you might want to proceed in one of the exam sequences suggested below. First, check out the sidebar for basic suggestions for sequencing all MCSE exams:

SUGGESTIONS FOR MCSE EXAM SEQUENCING

Take the exam(s) you are *already* better prepared for first, if possible, to get things rolling and to begin your benefits as a MCP. Current Microsoft MCP benefits are summarized in another sidebar.

Take the more fundamental exam first, if one exam is a building block for another exam. This allows you to begin laying the conceptual and learning foundation for more complex ideas.

Take exams which have Fair to High overlaps in Table 1.1 one after the other, if possible.

Take exams that will be easiest for you either at the beginning or at the end of the sequence, or as a deliberate break between tougher exams that are more challenging to you.

Table 1.1

Perceived Exam Overlaps	Networking Essentials	Windows NT Workstation	Windows NT Server	NT Server in the Enterprise	TCP/IP
Networking Essentials					
NT Workstation	Low				
NT Server	Low	High			
NT Server/Enterprise	Fair	Low	High		
TCP/IP	High	Low	Low	Low	
IIS and Index Server	Low	Low	Fair	Fair	High
Windows 95	Low	Low	Low	Low	Fair
Exchange Server 5.0	Low	Low	Fair	Fair	Fair

Some exams overlap more than others. The Windows NT Server and the Windows NT Server in the Enterprise exams have a high degree of overlap.

Enterprise, Server, Workstation

Table 1.1 estimates the overlap of content and knowledge areas between several popular exams. Of these, the three most closely related exams are the:

- Windows NT Workstation
- Windows NT Server
- Windows NT Server in the Enterprise exams

It makes sense to take these three exams in that order (Workstation, Server, and Enterprise) unless you already have an extensive or special expertise in Windows NT Server or Windows NT Server in the Enterprise.

Of the exams listed in Table 1.1, these four are generally considered to be the toughest exams:

- Windows NT Server in the Enterprise
- TCP/IP on Microsoft Windows NT (any version)
- Windows 95 (retired version)
- Exchange Server 5.0

TCP/IP, Networking Essentials, IIS and Index Server

The next strongest relationship among the exams is the high degree of overlap between TCP/IP and both the Networking Essentials exams and the IIS and Index Server exam. Because Networking Essentials is considered the foundation of standards and definitions needed for networking concepts used in other exams, Networking Essentials is often taken early in the exam sequence.

As said, TCP/IP is judged to be one of the more difficult exams, even after the exam was redesigned to moderate the impact of subnetting.

IIS and Index Server is commonly considered one of the most straightforward MCSE exams, largely because MCSE candidates are familiar with how to prepare for Microsoft exams by the time they attempt IIS and Index Server. IIS and Index Server also covers a more limited amount of material than the other exams, making it a quicker study.

So, combining all these information sources, here are some acceptable proposed exam sequences:

EXAM SEQUENCE A

1. Networking Essentials

2. Workstation

3. Server

4. Enterprise

5. TCP/IP

6. IIS and Index Server

EXAM SEQUENCE B

1. Networking Essentials

2. TCP/IP

3. Workstation

4. Server

5. IIS and Index Server

6. Enterprise

EXAM SEQUENCE C

1. Workstation

2. Networking Essentials

3. Server

4. Enterprise

5. TCP/IP

6. IIS and Index Server

If you selected other exams for your MCSE, rather than the six used in these examples, use these same principles to find your own ideal exam sequence.

SOME NETWORKING EXPERTS FIND MICROSOFT EXAMS DIFFICULT

It is not uncommon for networking professionals with years of actual experience to fail the Networking Essentials exam. Likewise, it is often heard that the TCP/IP exam is considered tough by seasoned Internet experts. Why is this so?

The most satisfying explanation is that these professionals already *know too much* about real-world networking and they *read into* the exams real-world facts that are not stated in the question. Many Microsoft exam questions are stated ambiguously and the resultant vagueness seems to force these professionals to make assumptions. They assume that if the question says X, and they know that X is almost always because of Y, that Z must be true—only to find that Z is not even an available answer!

Network professionals advise that, for their colleagues taking the Networking Essentials or TCP/IP exams from Microsoft, nothing from the real world should be assumed. Read the questions at face value only in order to avoid reading anything real into the question. Often the questions that are the most troubling to these experts are the ones that test their factual knowledge, rather than testing their troubleshooting expertise and network design experience.

Therefore, networking professionals with extensive prior experience often wait to take these two exams (Networking Essentials and TCP/IP) until the end of their exam sequence, hoping to get into the flow of the Microsoft tests before encountering these too-familiar topics.

BETA EXAMS ARE HALF-PRICE!

When a new exam is under construction, Microsoft *tests* the exam questions on folks like you and me. For $50, rather than the regular, full price of $100, you or I can take, and possibly pass, an exam while it is still in its *beta* stage.

You should expect beta exams to have between 150 and 200 questions because they contain all the questions being considered for all versions of that exam. On a beta exam, you'll have *only* three hours to answer all the questions. This means that on a beta exam you must work at least at the same rapid pace you would use on a regular exam, if not faster.

Although beta exams can save you some money, they can also be frustrating because you won't get your scores back from Microsoft until the real exam is released. Waiting that long can be quite a trauma when you're used to having immediate results as you leave the testing room!

Important—Please Note: Beta Exams are designated with a *71* at the beginning of the exam code number, rather than the regular exam codes that begin with a 70.

To find out if any beta exams are available, you can check this MCP Exam Information Web site:

http://www.microsoft.com/mcp/examinfo/exams.htm

Another point should be made about the MCP Exam Information Web site. The dynamic links on the page jump to the official Microsoft Preparation Guides for each upcoming examination. Notice that the Preparation Guides become available *even before* the beta exams. This means you can actually start studying for an exam at the same time that they're preparing the exam to test your skills.

However, studying before the beta exam exists usually requires that you have access to the beta software product the exam will be based on. One of the many benefits of obtaining an MCSE certificate is a one-year subscription to the Microsoft Beta Evaluation program with free monthly CDs containing Microsoft beta software. As of April 1998, these exams were *expected soon* in beta form:

Beta Exam Expected July 1998

Beta Exam 71-098 Implementing and Supporting Microsoft Windows 98 for

Exam 70-098 Implementing and Supporting Microsoft Windows 98

Exam Preparation Guide for exam 70-098 at:
http://www.microsoft.com/mcp/exam/stat/SP70-098.htm

Beta Exam Expected Summer 1998

Beta Exam 71-028 System Administration for Microsoft SQL Server 7.0 for

Exam 70-028 System Administration for Microsoft SQL Server 7.0

Exam 70-028: System Administration for Microsoft SQL Server 7.0 Status Page and Preparation Guide located at:
http://www.microsoft.com/mcp/exam/stat/SP70-028.htm

Beta Exam Expected Summer 1998

Beta Exam 71-055 Developing Solutions with Microsoft FrontPage98 for

Exam 70-055 Developing Solutions with Microsoft FrontPage98

Exam 70-055: Developing Solutions with Microsoft FrontPage 98 Status Page and Preparation Guide located at:

`http://www.microsoft.com/mcp/exam/stat/SP70-055.htm`

Beta Exam Expected Fall 1998

Beta Exam 71-086 Implementing and Supporting Microsoft Systems Management Server 2.0 for

Exam 70-086 Implementing and Supporting Microsoft Systems Management Server 2.0

Exam Preparation Guide for exam 70-086 located at:

`http://www.microsoft.com/mcp/exam/stat/SP70-086.htm`

Beta Exam Expected Fall 1998

Beta Exam 71-029 Implementing a Database Design on Microsoft SQL Server 7.0 for

Exam 70-029 Implementing a Database Design on Microsoft SQL Server 7.0

Exam 70-029: Implementing a Database Design on Microsoft SQL Server 7.0 Status Page and Preparation Guide located at:

`http://www.microsoft.com/mcp/exam/stat/SP70-029.htm`

Old Exams Are Eventually Retired

Yes, Microsoft retires old exams. However, they take several specific measures to mollify the effect of obsolete exams on certified professionals, including giving six months advance warning in writing and substantially cutting the cost of replacement exams for at least six months *after* the former exam is retired. Read on for the details.

When an *Operating System* (OS) is no longer commonly in use, supporting the old operating system becomes increasingly expensive. If new and better operating systems are available at reasonable prices and the migration path for the majority of users is not too burdensome, it stands to reason that the manufacturer would want to withdraw the old OS from support. Similarly, Microsoft examinations are withdrawn and retired when their use has waned, especially when the OS they are based upon is becoming obsolete.

In explaining Microsoft's policy on retirement of exams, it's useful to know that they highly value the relevance of the *skills measured by the exams*. If your skills are still good in the marketplace, there is less reason to retire the exam that certified those skills. Microsoft explains that their exam retirement decisions are based on several factors, including:

- Total number of copies of the product ever sold (the customer base).
- Total number of exams ever taken (the MCP base).
- Ongoing sales of corresponding Microsoft products.
- Ongoing sales of corresponding Microsoft courseware.

By considering this broad framework, Microsoft can retire only exams that have fallen from use and truly become obsolete. Microsoft announces which exams are being withdrawn and retired at the Microsoft Certified Professional Web site. Retired MCP Exam Information is found at:

```
http://www.microsoft.com/mcp/examinfo/retired.htm
```

If your MCSE certificate is based on an exam that is being or has been retired, you'll probably need to find a replacement exam to prepare for and pass in order to position your certificate for renewal.

WHAT HAPPENS WHEN ONE OF MY EXAMS IS RETIRED?

Although there are no guarantees that these policies will always be the same, here are the current Microsoft policies on exam retirements:

- First, you'll be mailed a notification in writing at least six months *before* your certification is affected.
- You'll be given a date deadline to pass specific replacement exam(s).
- You can take all replacement exams at a 50 percent discount until at least six months after the exam retirement date.

For any questions or comments about Microsoft exam retirements, or if you ever want to check your certification status or ask about the MCSE program in general, just send an e-mail to mcp@msprograms.com or call one of the following regional education centers:

Microsoft Regional Education Centers	
North America	800-636-7544
Asia and Pacific	61-2-9870-2250
Europe	353-1-7038774
Latin America	801-579-2829

In addition, many more toll-free numbers for Microsoft International Training & Certification Customer Service Centers in several dozen countries worldwide can be found at:

```
http://www.microsoft.com/train_cert/resc.htm
```

One more thought on retiring exams: Because an MCSE certificate is good for life, or until exams are retired, the *only way* to be sure that MCSE professionals are keeping up with the real world information technology market is for Microsoft to retire exams. For the MCSE to continue to signify the highest level of professional skills, old exams must be retired and replaced with more current exams based on skills currently in demand.

EARLY WARNING OF EXAM RETIREMENT

One of the earliest warnings that an exam you've taken may become obsolete is that the development of a new exam is announced for the next version of the software, or a beta exam is announced for a new version of the exam. Once beta software or a beta exam has appeared, watch for further signs more closely.

Usually there is advanced warning that an exam is being withdrawn many months before the event. If you subscribe to the following monthly mailing lists and read the Web pages mentioned, you'll have the longest forewarning to choose how you'll prepare for any changes:

- *MCP News Flash* (monthly): Includes exam announcements and special promotions.

- *Training and Certification News* (monthly): Contains info about training and certification at Microsoft.

To subscribe to either newsletter, visit the Personal Information Center Web page at: http://207.46.130.169/regwiz/forms/PICWhyRegister. htm, register with Microsoft, and then subscribe.

Don't be caught off guard. Stay in touch with the status of the MCSE exams you've invested in mastering!

FREE SAMPLE EXAM SOFTWARE CD-ROM

Microsoft will ship a CD-ROM containing a dated snapshot of the *Microsoft Certified Professional* (MCP) Web site and sample examination software called *Personal Exam Prep* (PEP) exams (it comes through UPS, so an ordinary U.S. post office box address won't work). By calling Microsoft in the United States or Canada at (800) 636-7544, you can request the most recent CD-ROM of the MCP Web site. Ask for the *Roadmap CD-ROM*. They may protest greatly— don't worry. They'll say the Roadmap to Certification CD-ROM is no longer available and that you would be much better off to check the Microsoft Web site for more up-to-date information. However, they'll also still ship a CD-ROM if you insist (as of this writing) and if you provide an address other than a post office box. Of course, if you're in a hurry, you can always download the free sample exam software directly from the Microsoft Web site (mspep.exe, 561K) at http://www.microsoft.com/mcp/examinfo/practice.htm.

The free PEP exam download currently covers these Microsoft tests:

- 70-018 Implementing and Supporting Microsoft Systems Management Server 1.2

- 70-026 System Administration of Microsoft SQL Server 6

- 70-058 Networking Essentials

- 70-059 Internetworking with Microsoft TCP/IP on Windows NT 4.0

- 70-063 Implementing and Supporting Microsoft Windows 95 (retired)

- 70-067 Implementing and Supporting Microsoft Windows NT Server 4.0

- 70-068 Implementing and Supporting Microsoft Windows NT Server 4.0 in the Enterprise

- 70-073 Implementing and Supporting Microsoft Windows NT Workstation 4.0

- 70-075 Implementing and Supporting Microsoft Exchange Server 4.0

- 70-077 Implementing and Supporting Microsoft Internet Information Server 3.0 and Microsoft Index Server 1.1

- 70-160 Microsoft Windows Architecture

- 70-165 Developing Application with Microsoft Visual Basic 5.0

FREE PERSONAL EXAM PREP (PEP) TEST SOFTWARE

The PEP sample exam software has many values. First, you should take the appropriate PEP exam as the *beginning* of your studies for each new exam. This mere act commits you to the course of study for that exam and offers you a valid taste of the depth and breadth of the real exam. Seeing what kind of material is on the exams also lets you recognize the actual level of detail expected on the exams so that you can avoid studying too much or too little to pass the exam.

Later, by taking the PEP examination again from time to time, you can generally gauge your progress through the material. The PEP exam also gives you practice at taking an exam on a computer. Perhaps best of all, it allows you to print the questions and answers for items you may have missed so that you can concentrate on areas where your understanding is weakest.

Although the PEP tests are written by Self Test Software, they are distributed free by Microsoft to assist MCP candidates in preparing for the real exams. Take advantage of this generous offer!

Several other sources of practice exam software, including several more free samples, are provided in a sidebar later in this chapter.

Prepare For Each Exam with the Free TechNet CD-ROM

The value of this offer cannot be overestimated. The free TechNet Trial CD-ROM includes the entire Microsoft knowledge base, plus many evaluation and deployment guides, white papers, and all the text from the Microsoft resource kits. This information is straight from the horse's mouth and is therefore indispensable to your successful studies for the MCSE certificate. And the price can't be beat. Do not delay; get this free TechNet CD-ROM today!

Of course, Microsoft is hoping you'll actually subscribe to Tech-Net. TechNet can help you solve obscure problems more quickly, it can help you keep up to date with fast paced technology developments inside and outside of Microsoft, and it can help you keep your bosses and your users happy. Once you have earned the MCSE certificate, you may convince your employer to subscribe, if you don't subscribe yourself. For a free TechNet Trial Subscription, go to `http://204.118.129.122/giftsub/Clt1Form.asp`. On the same Web page, you can also register for free newsletters.

Remember, Microsoft exams generally don't require you to recall obscure information. Common networking situations and ordinary administrative tasks are the real focus. Exam topics include common circumstances, ordinary issues, and popular network problems that networking and operating system experts are confronted with every day.

USE PRACTICE EXAMS

Taking a practice exam early helps you focus your study on the topics and level of detail appropriate for the exam. As mentioned, taking another practice exam later can help you gauge how well your studies are progressing. Many professionals wait until their practice exams scores are well above the required passing score for that exam; then they take the real exam.

There are many sources of practice exams and most of the vendors offer free samples of some kind. Microsoft supplies free sample exams from Self Test Software and the MCSE mailing lists on the Internet often recommend products from Transcender. Both of these and several other practice exam sources are listed in the sidebar.

PRACTICE EXAMS AVAILABLE—FREE SAMPLES!

BeachFrontQuizzer

E-Mail: `info@bfq.com`
`http://www.bfq.com/`
Phone: 888/992-3131
A free practice exam (for Windows NT 4.0 Workstation) is available for download.

LearnKey
http://www.learnkey.com/
Phone: 800/865-0165
Fax: 435/674-9734
1845 W. Sunset Blvd
St. George, UT 84770-6508
MasterExam simulation software at $800 for six exam simulations or $150 each.

NetG
info@netg.com
support@netg.com
http://www.netg.com/
800/265-1900 (in United States only)
630/369-3000
Fax: 630/983-4518

NETg International
info@uk.netg.com
1 Hogarth Business Park
Burlington Lane
Chiswick, London
England W4 2TJ
Phone: 0181-994-4404
Fax: 0181-994-5611
Supporting Microsoft Windows NT 4.0 Core Technologies Part 1 (course 71410, Unit 1, 7.7 MB) and Microsoft FrontPage Fundamentals (course 71101, Unit 2, 8.1 MB) are available as free sample downloads.

Prep Technologies, Inc.
Sales@mcpprep.com
Support@mcpprep.com
http://www.mcpprep.com/
1-888/627-7737 (1-888/MCP-PREP)
1-708/478-8684 (outside U.S.)
CICPreP (Computer Industry Certification Preparation from ITS, Inc.)
A free 135-question practice exam is available (5+ MB).

Self Test Software

feedback@stsware.com
http://www.stsware.com/

Americas:
Toll-Free: 1-800/244-7330 (Canada and USA)
Elsewhere: 1-770/641-1489
Fax: 1-770/641-9719

Self Test Software, Inc.

4651 Woodstock Road
Suite 203, M/S 384
Roswell, GA 30075-1686

Australia/Asia:
stsau@vue.com
Phone: 61-2-9320-5497
Fax: 61-2-9323-5590
Sydney, Australia

Europe/Africa
Phone: 31-348-484646
Fax: 31-348-484699

$79 for the first practice exam, $69 for additional practice exams ordered at the same time.

Twelve free practice exams are available for download. These are the same free practice exams that Microsoft distributes by download or CD-ROM.

Transcender

Product Questions: sales@transcender.com
Technical Support Questions: support@transcender.com
Demo download problems: troubleshooting@transcender.com
http://www.transcender.com/
Phone: 615/726-8779
Fax: 615/726-8884
621 Mainstream Drive Suite 270
Nashville, TN 37228-1229
Fifteen free practice exams are available for download.

VFX Technologies, Inc

sales@vfxtech.com
support@vfxtech.com
http://www.vfxtech.com/

Phone: 610/265.9222
Fax: 610/265.6007
PO Box 80222
Valley Forge, PA 19484-0222 USA
Twenty-two free practice MCP Endeavor exam preparation modules
are available for download.

ORGANIZE BEFORE THE DAY OF EXAM

Make sure you have plenty of time to study before each exam. You
know yourself—give yourself enough time to both study *and* get
plenty of sleep for at least two days before the exam. Make sure
coworkers, family and friends are aware of the importance of this
effort so that they give you the time and space to devote to your
studies.

Once you have the materials and equipment you need, as well as
study times and locations properly selected, force yourself to study
and practice. Reward yourself when you finish a segment or unit of
studying. Pace yourself so that you complete your study plan on time.

SURVEY TESTING CENTERS

Call each testing center in your area to find out what times they
offer Microsoft exams. Jot down the center's name, address, and
phone number along with the testing hours and days of the week.
Once you've checked the testing hours at all the centers in your
local area, you're in a better position to schedule an exam at Center B if Center A is already booked for the time you wanted to take
your next exam.

The Sylvan technician taking your registration may not easily
find all other testing centers near you, so be prepared to suggest
alternative testing center names for the technician to locate in the
event your first choice is not available.

Plan to take your MCSE exams at a time of your own choice after
you know when exams are available in your area. This puts you in
control and allows you to take into account your own life situation
and your own style. If you are sharpest in the early morning, take
the exams in the morning. If you can't get calm enough for an
exam until late afternoon, schedule your exams for whatever time
of day or phase of the moon that best suits you. If you really need
to have a *special* time slot, schedule your exam well in advance.

SAME DAY AND WEEKEND TESTING

You may be able to schedule an exam on the same day that you call to register if you're lucky. This special service requires the test vendor, Sylvan or VUE, to download the exam or store the exam at the testing site especially for you, and it requires the testing site to have an open slot at a time acceptable to your needs. Sometimes this works out and sometimes it doesn't. Most testing centers are interested in filling all available exam time slots, so if you get a wild hair to take an exam *today,* why not give it a try? VUE testing centers can schedule exams for you, and they store exams onsite, so they are especially well positioned for same day testing.

SHOP AROUND FOR THE BEST TESTING CENTER AVAILABLE

Shop around your area for the best testing center. Some testing centers are distractingly busy and noisy at all times. Some official testing centers have slow 25 MHz computers, small 12-inch monitors, cramped seating conditions, or distracting activity outside the windows of the testing rooms. Some centers occasionally even have crabby, uninformed staff. Some centers actually limit testing to certain hours or certain days of the week, rather than allowing testing during all open hours.

Because these MCSE exams are important to your career, you deserve to use the best testing environment available. The best center costs the same $100 that a less pleasant center does. Shop around and find out exactly what is available in your area.

If you are treated improperly or if appropriate services or accommodations were not available when they should have been, let Sylvan or VUE and Microsoft know by e-mail and telephone.

CHECK FOR AVIATION TESTING CENTERS

Some of the best testing centers are actually at airports. Aviation training centers, located at all major airports to accommodate pilots, are frequently well equipped and pleasant environments. Aviation training centers participate in Microsoft testing in order to better use their investment in computer testing rooms and to broaden their customer base.

The best thing about aviation training centers is that they are regularly open all day on weekends, both Saturday and Sunday. One verified example of an aviation training center and an excellent Microsoft testing center that is available all day every weekend is Wright Flyers in San Antonio, Texas (210-820-3800), Wflyers@Flash.Net.

OFFICIAL EXAM REGISTRATION AND SCHEDULING

VUE exam scheduling and rescheduling services are available on weekends and evenings; in fact, they're open on the Web 24 hours, 365 days a year. Sylvan's telephone hours are Monday through Friday 7:00 A.M. through 7:00 P.M. central time, and the new Saturday telephone hours are 7:00 A.M. through 3:00 P.M.

As mentioned, many testing centers are open weekends on both Saturday and Sunday. If something goes horribly wrong at a Sylvan testing center after 3:00 P.M. on Saturday, or anytime on Sunday, you'll have to wait to talk to Sylvan when they open on Monday morning. As has happened, if a testing center simply fails to open its doors for your scheduled exam while Sylvan is closed for the weekend, you can do nothing until Monday morning.

Install the Software and Try Each Option

Make sure you know the layout of the various options in the software's *Graphical User Interface* (GUI) and the popular configuration options that are set on each menu. Become *GUI familiar* with each software product required in your next exam by opening and studying and trying each and every option on each and every menu. Also, for whatever they're worth, read the Help files, especially any context-sensitive Help!

Commonly tested, everyday network features, like controlling access to sensitive resources, printing over the network, client and server software installation, configuration, troubleshooting, load balancing, fault tolerance, and combinations of these topics (such as security-sensitive printing over the network) are especially important. Remember that the exams are from the network administrator's point of view. Imagine what issues network designers, technical support specialists, and network administrators are faced with every day—those are the issues that will be hit hardest on the exams.

MCSE candidates are expected to be proficient at planning, renovating, and operating Microsoft networks that are well integrated with Novell networks, IBM LANs, IBM mainframes, network printers (with their own network interface cards), and other common network services. Microsoft expects you to be able to keep older products, especially older Microsoft products, running as long as possible, as well as to know when they finally must be upgraded and how to accomplish the upgrade or migration with the least pain and expense.

Pass One Exam at a Time

Microsoft exams are experience-based and require real know-how, not just book learning. Don't be fooled by anyone—you must have real experience with the hardware and software involved to excel on the exams, or to excel as an MCSE holder in the workplace.

Passing a Microsoft exam is an accomplishment that proves you have the experience and knowledge that is required, yet it also shows that you know how to deal with the exam situation, one question at a time. This section describes the various kinds of questions you'll encounter on the MCSE exams and gives you tips about successful strategies for dealing with each kind of question. This section then walks you through the process of scheduling an exam, arriving at the test center, and taking the exam. A brief resource list of additional information related to topics in this chapter is also provided.

Choose The Best Answer

These questions are the most popular because they are seemingly simple questions. *Choose the best answer* means *one* answer, but the fact that there is only one answer doesn't make the question easy—unless you know the material.

First, try to eliminate at least two obviously wrong answers. This narrows the field so that you can choose among the remaining options more easily.

SOME QUESTIONS INCLUDE EXHIBITS

Briefly look at the exhibit when you *begin* to read the question. Note important features in the exhibit and finish a careful reading of the whole question. Then return to the exhibit after you've read the entire question to check on any relevant details revealed in the question. Some exhibits have nothing to do with answering the question correctly, so don't waste your time on the exhibit if it has no useful information for finding the solution.

Choose All That Apply

The most obvious tough questions are those with an uncertain number of multiple choices: *Choose all that apply.* Here you should use the same procedure to eliminate wrong answers first. Select only the items that you have confidence in—don't be tempted to take a wild guess. Remember, the Microsoft exams do not allow partial credit for partial answers, so any wrong answer is deadly, even if you got the rest of it right!

Really Read the Scenario Questions!

There is no better advice for these killer questions: Read the scenario questions carefully and completely. These seemingly complex questions are composed of several parts, generally in this pattern:

1. First, there are a few short paragraphs describing the situation, hardware, software, and the organization involved, possibly including one or two exhibits that must be opened, studied, and then minimized or closed again.
2. The required results.
3. Two or three optional desired results.
4. The proposed solution.
5. Four multiple choice answers you must choose from.

Pay close attention to the number of optional results specified in answer B.

Most scenario questions have an opening screen, warning you to *Pay close attention to the number of optional results specified in answer B.* This instruction accommodates the fact that there are two and sometimes three optional results. It also accommodates occasional proposed solutions that satisfy the required result and only some of the optional results.

Often two scenario questions in a row differ only in their proposed solution. They'll have the same test, the same exhibit, the same results, but different solutions are proposed. Sometimes some other slight differences might be introduced in the second scenario, so compare those similar questions, noting the differences to see what's missing or what's new in the second question. If the second question satisfies all the required and desired results, that at least tends to imply that the *previous* scenario did not satisfy all optional results.

TEST TIP

The scuttlebutt is that if you just don't have a clue on a complex scenario question or if you're out of time, you should select answer A (meets all results) or D (meets none) because these are the most frequently correct answers. The recommended method, of course, is to know the material so that you never need to resort to this kind of superstitious decision.

For most questions, your first priority should be to note the required results. If the proposed solution does not satisfy the required result, you're done with the question and you can move on. Thus, there is no need to focus on the optional desired results unless the required result is satisfied.

There can be up to three optional desired results and each one must be evaluated independently. Usually, if an optional result is satisfied, specific words in the question contribute to the optional result. Use the practice exams to sharpen your skills at quickly identifying which optional results are satisfied by certain words in the question.

Another strategy that works for some people is to focus first on the question and results (both required and optional), writing down all related facts based on the question's wording. This strategy then evaluates the proposed solution, based on the previous question analysis. Because some people find the scenario questions to be ambiguously written and vague, this strategy can also lead to time wasted on unimportant or unnecessary analysis, especially if the proposed solution does not meet the required results.

Keep in mind that everyone takes an exam differently. Aside from intelligence, many different learning and understanding styles exist among adults. Some people find that their best strategy with scenario questions is to work backwards from the required results and later, if necessary, from the optional results. They break the question into its elements, find their own solutions, and then finally compare notes with the solution proposed by the exam.

For example, they might start from the required results, breaking down the case that created the final required result. Once they've built their own solution that meets the required result, they check their solution against the exam's proposed solution. By checking their conclusions against the exam's proposed solution and the givens offered in the question, they then decide which required and optional results are achieved. If they know the material, they can answer the scenario questions; they just do it in a way others would call backwards!

It's important for candidates to see the forest *and* the trees, and to know when to see each. In a question about a congested network, for instance, the candidate must decide whether the question is trying to go beyond the fact that FDDI is faster than Ethernet, or any knowledge about the installation and configuration details of FDDI. Candidates with extensive networking experience may be tempted to show off and choose the latter, when only the simple knowledge that FDDI is faster than Ethernet is required. Don't read information into the question that is not there!

EXAM INTERFACE QUIRKS—SYLVAN INTERFACE

The Sylvan exam interface has a peculiar quirk on long questions that can hurt you if you're not careful. This is particularly true if the testing center uses small monitors, so that more questions are longer than one screen. On these long questions there is an elevator or scrollbar on the right side of the screen, so you can use the mouse to move down to read the remainder of the question.

When you reach the bottom of the question but not the bottom of the screen, the left hand selection box on the outside bottom of the screen changes from *More* to *Next*. There is a built-in assumption that if you are not looking at the bottom of the screen when you select your answer, you've made a premature answer.

If you've moved back up the screen to reread the question, for example, with the very bottom of the screen *not visible* and you then check very near but not exactly on your answer, sometimes the box above your selection actually gets selected, rather than the box you intended to check. To correct for this quirk you should either be sure you are always looking at the very bottom of the screen before you select the answer, or you should back up from the next question by clicking the *Previous* question box to double-check your previous selection.

SELECT THE WRONG ANSWERS!

Okay, it sounds nuts, but the best advice is to begin the analysis of each question by selecting the answers that are clearly wrong. Every wrong answer eliminated gets you closer to the correct answer(s). Often two answers can quickly be eliminated, leaving you to focus your attention and time on the few remaining options.

By carefully structuring your time, you can answer more questions correctly during the allotted exam period. Eliminating wrong and distracting answers first helps narrow your attention to the most likely correct answers.

INDIRECT QUESTIONS

Microsoft exams are not straightforward. They often use questions that *indirectly* test your skill and knowledge without coming straight out and asking you about the facts they are testing. For example, there is no exam question that actually asks *Is the Windows NT 4.0 Emergency Repair Disk bootable?* and there is no question that says *The Windows NT 4.0 Emergency Repair Disk is not bootable: True or False?* But you better know that the *Emergency Repair Disk* (ERD) is *never* bootable. By knowing this, you can eliminate at least one wrong answer, and therefore come closer to the right answer, on one or more exams. *By the way, after you've once had an unfortunate experience that calls for actually using the Windows NT ERD, you'll never again have a doubt about whether you can boot to it— the ERD repair occurs considerably later, well after booting the computer.*

After you've taken a Microsoft exam or two, if you think you would be good at composing their style of indirect questioning that tests many facets and levels at the same time, check out this URL where you can get information about being a contract test writer for Microsoft: http://www.microsoft.com/Train_Cert/Mcp/examinfo/iwrite.htm.

Scheduling an Exam

When registering, be sure to specify the exam number. Also know the exact title of the exam, so that it's familiar when the test registrar reads it back to you.

The Microsoft MCSE exams are administered by or through VUE (Virtual University Enterprises, a division of National Computer Systems, Inc.) or Sylvan Prometric. Either Sylvan or VUE can provide MCSE testing. Both have access to your records of previous MCSE tests, and both vendors report your test results directly to Microsoft. Taking an examination through either vendor organization does not obligate you to use the same organization or testing center for any other examination.

VUE began testing for Microsoft in May, 1998 after requests for another vendor from the Microsoft professional community. They began by offering exams only in English and largely in North America. VUE anticipates significant growth during 1998 and 1999 with worldwide coverage available by June 1999.

It's a good idea to call your testing center the day before the exam to confirm your appointment. Anything could go wrong and you'll want to know *before* you get to the testing center.

SYLVAN PROMETRIC

To schedule yourself for an exam through Sylvan or for information about the Sylvan testing center nearest you, call 800-755-3926 (800-755-exam) or write to Sylvan at:

Sylvan Prometric
Certification Registration
2601 88th Street West
Bloomington, MN 55431
To register online:
Sylvan Prometric (Nav1)
www.sylvanpromteric.com

Sylvan also offers 16 short sample online exams called Assessment Tests that cover various Microsoft products. (Although Sylvan has offered online registration for several months, reports have continued that exam candidates are unable to use the online registration despite valiant attempts—good luck!)
Phone: 800-755-3926

VIRTUAL UNIVERSITY ENTERPRISES (VUE)

To schedule yourself for an exam through VUE or for information about the VUE testing center nearest you, call 888-837-8616 or visit VUE's Web site to register online 24 hours a day, 365 days a year:

Virtual University Enterprises (VUE)
To register online: www.vue.com
North America: 888-837-8616 (toll-free)
5001 W 80th Street Suite 401
Bloomington, MN 55437-1108

VUE is a new kid on the block, but never fear; they are seasoned test people and their promise to the industry has been new thinking in technology and service, and higher levels of candidate and testing center service. They have a *we try harder* attitude and back it up with higher standards for testing centers (800 × 600 video resolution on Windows 95 machines) and an agile, new 32-bit testing engine. VUE is in expansion mode—you should expect some growing pains, but also watch for some new thinking and professional amiability.

For instance, VUE immediately found a way to offer live online 24-hour, seven days a week exam scheduling and rescheduling of Microsoft exams for busy professionals. And VUE offers onsite exam scheduling and rescheduling *at testing centers*. These conveniences are tremendously valuable to individual candidates. Because VUE's operation is based on heavy Internet bandwidth, they are able to use secure Java-based system management and site administration software to handle all testing and services. Also, VUE delivers exams quickly to testing centers over the Internet, rather than by modem and telephone lines, as Sylvan does.

When You Arrive at the Testing Center

Arrive early. It can put you at ease to check in 30 to 60 minutes early. Relax a bit before you actually sit for the exam. Some exam centers won't complete your check-in until the last minute before your scheduled time, and others get you signed up and then tell you to *let them know* when you're ready to begin. Sometimes they'll even offer to let you begin *early*. Starting a little late is also sometimes tolerated if you want to review your notes one more time—be sure to ask first.

To check in, you'll be asked to provide proof of your identity. Two pieces of ID with your name and signature are required, one must have a photograph—a driver's license or passport and a credit card are adequate. There are testing center rules you'll be asked to read, sign, and date. Microsoft has also begun to require on all new exams that the candidate agree to a non-disclosure statement, discussed shortly.

Testing center staff then explain their procedures and show you to the testing computers. This is the time to ask any questions about the testing rules. Find out, for instance, if you'll be allowed to leave the exam room to visit the restroom (with the *clock still running* on your exam) if your physical comfort demands a break.

CARRY WATER ONLY

Some folks bring bottled water, vitamins, or medications into the exam room for their own comfort. You should consider what will make you most productive during the 90 minutes of your exam and prepare accordingly.

Of course, the downside to drinking soda, coffee, or water during or even before the exam occurs when you are nearing the end of the 90-minute exam and really need to visit the restroom.

WRITING MATERIAL IN THE EXAM ROOM

This is a touchy area. Testing centers are required to be very picky about cheat notes carried *into* or *out of* the exam. There is a story of a candidate who had an ordinary napkin wrapped around a can of soda in the exam room and carried it out for disposal at the end of the exam. The person was challenged about the napkin and would probably have been disqualified or worse had the napkin contained any writing.

Always ask for writing implements. Paper and pen are easier to use, but some testing centers do not allow them. Instead they issue marking pens and plasticized writing cards that are difficult to use. The marking pens commonly have a wide tip that makes writing difficult and they dry out very quickly between uses if they will write at all; you must remember to replace the cap or the pen will refuse to write the next time you try. Get the finest tipped pens available. The tips seem to widen with use, so newer pens are better. Ask the testing center to open a *new* package of pens and ask for two or three pens in case they go completely dry.

Also ask for another sheet or two of the 8" by 10" plasticized writing material. If you have a large network drawing in mind, for instance, use the back of the card; two inches of the card's front are already in use by Sylvan Prometric. Don't force yourself to try to use those awkward marking pens in a small space—start another side or another sheet!

TEST TIP

Don't waste your precious exam time writing down any memorized notes on the writing material. Write down any memorized notes *before the exam* during the time that could be used on the how-to-use-this-exam-software tutorial (discussed next). Some exams call for more memorization than others and some exams have a tremendous amount of minute detail. Use your time wisely by recording any easily forgotten formulae, rules of thumb, and mnemonics *before* you begin the exam *after* you enter the exam room.

The day before the exam, practice writing down all the notes you've decided will help you on your exam. Force yourself to write from memory only in order to prove you can remember it long enough to write it down in the exam room.

ONLINE TUTORIAL

An optional exam tutorial may be available before the MCSE exam. The tutorial is designed to show you how the computer-administered exam software works and to help you become familiar with how the exam will proceed *before the clock starts on your real exam.* Don't become confused by the presence of the tutorial. If the clock in the upper-right corner is ticking, you are taking the real exam, not the tutorial!

NERVOUS?

If you happen to be nervous before an exam, it might help reduce your anxiety to take some off-the-clock time with the optional tutorial to breathe deeply and calm yourself down and get into the right mood for passing the exam. Even if you've already seen the tutorial and know exactly how to run the exam software, the tutorial can be a safety valve to give you a little time to adjust your attitude. Controlling your own use of time before the exam can give you just the boost you need!

REQUIRED NON-DISCLOSURE AGREEMENT

Microsoft requires certification candidates to accept a non-disclosure agreement before taking certain exams. If you take an exam that was first released after February 1998, you'll be required to provide an affirmation that you accept the terms of a brief, formal non-disclosure agreement. This policy will eventually cover all MCSE exams. Microsoft says this policy will help maintain the integrity of the MCP program. The text of the agreement is provided in the sidebar and is also available at http://www.microsoft.com/mcp/articles/nda.htm.

NON-DISCLOSURE AGREEMENTS AND GENERAL TERMS OF USE FOR EXAMS DEVELOPED FOR THE MICROSOFT CERTIFIED PROFESSIONAL PROGRAM

This exam is Microsoft-confidential and is protected by trade secret law. It is made available to you, the examinee, solely for the purpose of becoming certified in the technical area referenced in the title of this exam. You are expressly prohibited from disclosing, publishing, reproducing, or transmitting this exam, in whole or in part, in any form or by any means, verbal or written, electronic or mechanical, for any purpose, without the prior expressed written permission of Microsoft Corporation.

Click the Yes button to symbolize your signature and to accept these terms. Click the No button if you do not accept these terms. You must click Yes to continue with the exam.

Mandatory Demographic Survey

Microsoft says they appreciate your participation in the mandatory demographic survey before each exam. For years the survey was optional; now it is mandatory. Microsoft estimates the survey takes most candidates less than five minutes. Of course, the survey time does not count against your clocked exam period.

To motivate you to furnish sincere and valid answers on the mandatory survey, Microsoft stresses that the survey results are vital to the program and useful for setting the passing score of each exam, validating new exam questions, and in developing training materials for MCSE candidates. Microsoft says, "By providing accurate and complete information on this survey, you will help Microsoft improve both the quality of MCP exams and the value of your certification."

The mandatory demographic survey collects information, keyed to your Social Security number, about your work experience, your work environment, the software tested by the exam, and information about your exam preparation methods. The survey has three components. One portion is common to all exams, another is keyed to the exam track, and the third portion is specific to that one exam. Carefully note the wording of any promises of confidentiality, data cross-matching, or disclosure of your personal information.

CHECK THE EXAM NUMBER AND EXAM TITLE

Although it is unlikely, there have been stories about the wrong test being loaded for an exam candidate. The first task of taking a Microsoft exam is to be sure you are beginning the exam *you intended to take*. By double-checking the exam number and exam title, you might save yourself and the testing center hours of difficulty if somehow the wrong exam showed up for you. So be sure you check the exam title before you begin the clock on the exam. Checking the exam title doesn't need to be part of your timed exam.

ADAPTIVE TESTING

In October 1998 Microsoft introduced a new examination methodology called *adaptive testing* for the TCP/IP exam. Rather than always presenting 58 questions, a shorter series of moderate to difficult questions are asked.

When a wrong answer is given, the candidate then receives one or more simpler questions probing their understanding of that context area. By answering 15 or 25 tough questions correctly, a candidate can pass the exam with a much smaller number of questions overall.

With adaptive testing, however, you may not mark a question to return to it later. You must complete each question as it is presented. You cannot go back to reconsider a previous question.

Further developments in adaptive testing are expected. As this study guide goes to press, the only information available from Microsoft is at this address:

```
http://www.microsoft.com/MCP/articles/tesinn.htm
```

SOURCES OF ADDITIONAL INFORMATION
Microsoft maintains a large staff to handle your questions about the MCSE certificate. Give them a call at 800-636-7544. If you have a CompuServe account, you can access the Microsoft area with the command GO MEC.

Microsoft Newsgroups
By pointing your Internet news-reading software to the NNTP news server at Microsoft, you can read ongoing news, questions, answers, and comments on dozens of topics close to Microsoft products. The Microsoft Public NNTP server is at msnews.microsoft.com. Two typical hierarchies for your attention are microsoft.public.windowsnt and microsoft.public.inetexplorer.

The Saluki E-mail Mailing List
Saluki is a very active majordomo Internet e-mail list. Some days have 50 to 100 messages about MCSE studies and related topics. To subscribe, send an e-mail message to:

```
majordomo@saluki.com
```

In the body of the message write:

```
subscribe mcse Yourfirstname Lastname
```

For example:

```
subscribe mcse Scott Armstrong
```

You can use an alias if you wish.
For further information about Saluki, write to Scott Armstrong at saluki@gate.net or Dean Klug at deano@gate.net.

The TCP/IP Exam

TCP/IP is not a core exam, but it is popular because it is the foundation for Microsoft's efforts to capitalize on the tremendous growth of the Internet. The exam is from the administrator's point of view and encompasses Windows NT Server, WINS, DNS and DCHP servers, Internet routing and TCP/IP Subnetting. TCP/IP is usually taken late in the exam sequence, and by definition the TCP/IP exam has a high degree of overlap with the Networking Essentials exam. TCP/IP is commonly taken after the Windows NT Server in the Enterprise exam or the Networking Essentials exam.

The TCP/IP exam is heavy on particular details of everyday support and troubleshooting for Windows TCP/IP networks, such as installing and configuring Microsoft TCP/IP Printing, DHCP Relay Agent, *Simple Network Management Protocol* (SNMP), and IP forwarding. The TCP/IP exam covers installing and configuring WINS, DNS and DCHP Servers, UNIX printers, routing, and handling IP address and name resolution. The exam also includes ample helpings of network monitoring, optimization, and troubleshooting with various Microsoft renditions of TCP/IP utilities. This is quite a plateful. The cure, of course, is to gain solid experience in administering Microsoft TCP/IP networks in preparation for the exam.

Exam Room Notes

For the TCP/IP exam, here are typical items to memorize and write down as soon as you enter the exam room, before the clock starts:

- Networked HP printer or Jet Direct—DLC protocol
- TCP/IP—IP, mask (gateway), automatic—DHCP
- Trap—intruder alert
- TTL—time to live, increase on slow links
- ARP—IP to MAC address
- HOSTS file, DNS—IP address to host name
- LMHOSTS file, WINS—IP address to NetBIOS name
- UNIX—HOSTS file, DNS
- LPD—create, LPR—send, LPQ—check
- Route [add] destination mask gateway metric, -f = clear, -p = persistent

- 0   1–126
- 10   128–191
- 110 192–223

Subnet Bits	-	2	3	4	5	6	7	8
Subnet Mask	default	192	224	240	248	252	254	255
MaximumSubnets								
Class A	126	2	6	14	30	62	126	254
Class B	16K	2	6	14	30	62	126	254
Class C	2m	2	6	14	30	62	-	-
Maximum Hosts/Subnet								
Class A	16.7m	4m	2m	1m	.5m	.25m	131,000	65,000
Class B	65.5K	16,382	8K	4K	2K	1K	510	254
Class C	254	62	30	14	6	2	-	-

- IPCONFIG/all
- PING early, PING often (TRACERT)
- NETSTAT -e Ethernet -s protocol -r routes, connections
- NBTSTAT -n NetBIOS name cache, -R purge and Reload

MARGIN ICON DECODER

Throughout the remainder of this study guide, you will find square icons marking both text and tables. These icons are keyed to the official Microsoft Preparation Guide. The icons are intended to allow you to concentrate your study in areas where feedback from practice exams may indicate a weakness.

 Planning

 Installation and Configuration

 Connectivity

Monitoring and Optimization

 Troubleshooting

CHAPTER 2

TCP/IP in a Nutshell

This chapter provides an architectural overview of TCP/IP. It deals with an introduction to the protocol suite and identifies the key attributes you are required to know for the test. Before you read another word, you need to understand some TCP lingo. In TCP/IP, we talk often about hosts. Any network device or computer capable of loading TCP/IP is considered a host, be it a router, a computer, a cash register, a soda dispenser, or a reader board, as long as they communicate using TCP/IP.

TIP

If you are not familiar with general networking and network architecture, you should first turn to the Networking Essentials study guide for an introduction. This TCP/IP study guide assumes you are already familiar with basic networking principles.

TCP/IP: A Brief History

TCP/IP stands for *Transmission Control Protocol/Internet Protocol*. TCP/IP has been used in business networking on LANs and legacy networks for many years. *Digital Equipment Corporation's* (DEC) DECNET is a good example of an Ethernet LAN that has been running TCP/IP services for a while. Novell NetWare also had TCP/IP capabilities long before Windows was endowed with its grace and power.

The TCP/IP set of protocols was initially developed by the U.S. *Department of Defense* (DOD) to link different kinds of computers across an ocean of disparate networks—the result of DOD and the armed forces historical tendering to companies, like DEC and IBM, that in turn sold proprietary technologies to the U.S. government. Once it was adopted by business, TCP/IP became the most popular suite of protocols to be deployed across Ethernet and X.25 networks.

Although it has become the de facto suite of networking protocols, the successor to TCP/IP, which will be based on the *Open Systems Interconnection* (OSI) architecture, a child of the *International Standards Organization* (ISO), is already being tested. For now, TCP/IP is suitable for the needs of almost all client/server computing.

The work carried out by the DOD was at first successful because it provided for the delivery of the basic networking services, such as file transfer (FTP), electronic mail (SMTP), and remote logon (TELNET), across a very large number of client and server systems.

Corporations that have adopted TCP/IP as their chief LAN protocol (and many did years ago) have found a host of new products and development tools to install on their LANs that can make people more productive. LAN managers and IT staff have, for example, found it far easier to set up a corporate Web site and give their users Web browsers than to maintain the old bulletin board systems that were so popular but hard to use in the late '80s and early '90s.

During the Cold War years and earlier, the TCP/IP architecture was designed to be robust enough to automatically recover from any node or phone line failure. This design allows the construction of very large networks with less central management.

TCP/IP is an open standards industrial strength suite of protocols providing the facility to fully route packets of data over multiple TCP/IP network segments. TCP/IP was not available to the early Windows operating systems. Today, however, Microsoft provides TCP/IP so that Windows computers can communicate on TCP/IP networks, such as the Internet.

There are a number of sound technical reasons to load TCP/IP on your network . . . and similar reasons why Microsoft requires you to have a sound knowledge of its implementation:

- TCP/IP is an open architecture/open standards protocol maintained in the public domain. A large group of companies and individuals from the far reaches of the planet contribute to its ongoing evolution. They do this through the auspices of the *Internet Engineering Task Force* (IETF). Contributions to new features are channeled through the *Requests for Comments* (RFC) process and are publicly available on the Internet.

- TCP/IP is a true client/server platform, and TCP/IP is also a cross-platform communication medium. This means that Windows computers can communicate with non-Windows computers such as UNIX computers, OS/2, and Apple Macintosh computers; mainframes and minicomputers; and devices such as printers, scanners, network access units (routers and gateways).

- TCP/IP has a rich set of connectivity protocols (the IP part). These include the *File Transfer Protocol* (FTP), the *Simple Mail Transport Protocol* (SMTP), and the *Terminal Access Protocol* (TELNET). FTP allows you to transfer files to another computer, SMTP is a protocol for transferring, storing, and forwarding email, and Telnet allows you to remotely log onto a terminal server-type computer, such as an IBM mainframe or UNIX server.

- Last on this list, but by no means the least important, TCP/IP is the means by which our computers connect to the Internet. It is the de facto protocol providing connectivity and networking over the world's ultra-heterogeneous network of networks and information repositories. A computer program or a computer incapable of connecting to or communicating with other computers on the Internet is like a soccer player on the field incapable of kicking the ball. Such computers might as well not be connected to anything but themselves.

If you want to study TCP/IP in depth several good books are available. My bible is the *Stevens* volumes *TCP/IP Illustrated* by W. Richard Stevens. However, you can also study the RFC papers. RFC stands for *Request for Comments*. These RFCs are the means by which the world's network engineers can contribute to the ongoing evolution of the Internet.

DON'T GET SIDE-TRACKED BY RFCS

You can access white papers and RFCs from the IETF via FTP and the WWW. However, accessing these papers to help you pass the Microsoft exams is a bad idea. They are filled with all manner of highly specialized TCP/IP engineering issues, many of which will serve only to confuse you and delay your certification. There are also many items in these papers that Microsoft will not test you on.

After obtaining your MCSE, go back and study the Internet RFCs, and perhaps get involved in the RFC process if you have a penchant for making history!

TCP/IP Architecture

TCP/IP is a layered architecture just like any other network architecture. Each layer carries responsibility for certain functions in the networking process. By now, you should be familiar with the OSI reference model of networking. Let's recap here, briefly, so that you can see that layers of the TCP/IP *wafer* correspond to the layers of the OSI Reference model. (Refer to Networking Essentials for a more detailed discussion of the OSI layers.) The seven layers of the OSI reference model are shown in Table 2.1.

Table 2.1 Activities and Responsibilities of the *Open Systems Interconnection* (OSI) Reference Model

Layer	Activities and Responsibilities
Application	Services and procedures for user applications, file transfers, and e-mail
Presentation	Provides data compression, encryption, final formatting
Session	Opens and closes network communication dialog, retransmits upon connection failure, synchronizes the flow of data, name lookup, and security functions
Transport	Provides error recognition and correction, assembly, disassembly, priority, sequencing, acknowledgment of receipt
Network	Routes logical addresses to physical addresses, provides packet resizing if needed, handles network congestion

Layer	Activities and Responsibilities
Data Link	Translates bits to frames or frames to bits, provides flow control, replaces lost or damaged frames, handles error recovery
Physical	Defines physical connection to network media, transfers bits across the link

Now notice that a typical TCP/IP model contains four layers as shown in Figure 2.1; and in Table 2.2 note how the four layers approximately map to the OSI reference model.

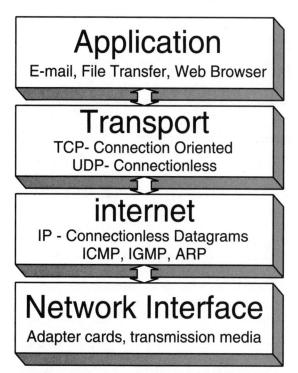

Figure 2.1   The four layers of the TCP/IP model or system, often referred to as the TCP/IP *stack*.

There is somewhat less agreement between experts on the exact depiction of the TCP/IP stack—some say there are three or four layers; others say five. The point here is that layered network operations require certain corresponding tasks and responsibilities on the *same* layer of two communicating computers. Table 2.2 shows a typical mapping of the mapping of the TCP/IP stack layers to the more agreed-upon OSI reference model.

Table 2.2   Four Layers of the TCP/IP Stack, Mapped to the OSI Reference Model Layers.

TCP/IP Stack	OSI Reference Model
Application	Application Presentation Session
Transport	Transport
internet	Network
Network Interface	Data Link Physical

Like the OSI Reference model you studied in Networking Essentials, each layer has a special duty or realm of accountability. Think of it as a department store, the Sears of networking, with a different department on each floor.

1. The *Network Interface* department caters to device drivers and their corresponding network hardware plugged into the bus of the computer. This layer is often referred to as the *link-layer* or the *network interface layer*. All activities centered around the hardware—*Network Interface Cards* (NIC), cables, media access units, and so forth—are handled by this layer.

2. Next floor up is the *Network* department. In TCP/IP, this layer is often referred to as the *internet layer*. (The *i* is lower-case because we are not referring to *the* Internet.) The internet layer is responsible for the routing of data packets. The collection of protocols that deal with routing packets is under the *Internet Protocol* (IP) area of accountability. These services are IP, *Internet Control Message Protocol* (ICMP), where we get the ping process, and the *Internet Group Management Protocol* (IGMP).

3. Third floor is the *Transport layer.* As the name implies, this layer makes sure data packets get from point X to point Y on the network. Two key protocols are at work in this layer, *Transmission Control Protocol* (TCP) and *User Datagram Protocol* (UDP). It is important to understand that they cater to two separate philosophies of data transmission. I like to think of these in terms of firearms shooting ammunition (data) at targets: TCP is the rifle-shot, good at shooting a single bullet at one target (one-to-one); UDP is the buck-shot, good for shooting many packets to many targets (many-to-many).

TCP is considered a reliable computer-to-computer communication method with acknowledgment and receipt mechanisms built into the protocol. It is a means of providing reliable data transfer. UDP, on the other hand, is broadcast protocol. It has no mechanisms to ensure or report reception of data on the other side of the connection.

The two protocols have their place in the TCP/IP application mix. However, how they are used or implemented by the application layer is more for the concern of software developers and generally not network engineers or MIS people.

4. The top floor is where we find TCP/IP applications, the *Application layer.* This layer deals with how applications communicate down the TCP/IP protocol stack and how to send and receive data. Some good examples of application layer processes include FTP programs, mail transfer agents, and Web browsers.

TIP

Concentrate on what you need to know about troubleshooting an application that doesn't seem to be communicating properly. Most of the time, a TCP/IP problem is related to the first three layers of the stack, rather than the application layer. If it truly is an application problem (in other words, if diagnostics indicate TCP/IP is *working*), there is not much more you can do with that application (unless, of course, you are the person who wrote the application code to begin with).

OK, so now you know that the TCP/IP stack is, like the OSI Reference model, a layered architecture, not unlike the many floors in a department store. But what takes place in a layer and where do the various protocols do their gifted work? Let's stick with the department store analogy and dig deeper.

For starters, each layer is able to pass data to the next layer, up or down. The packets are encased in information *envelopes.* Whatever one stack adds to the packet when it sends data to another computer, the corresponding stack removes and analyses. Like the department store, workers are able to send information upwards or downwards. Inside each department store you'll find staff doing their work, like the protocols at work in each layer. Figure 2.2 shows how the protocols are distributed though the layers of a typical TCP/IP model.

Six primary protocols are at work in the layers of the stack:

- *Transmission Control Protocol* (TCP)

- *User Datagram Protocol* (UDP)

- *Internet Protocol* (IP)

- *Internet Control Message Protocol* (ICMP)

- *Internet Group Management Protocol* (IGMP)

- *Address Resolution Protocol* (ARP)

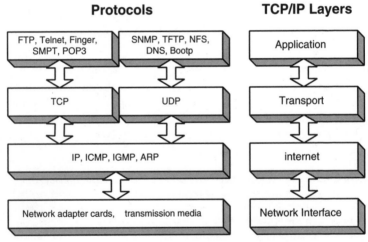

Figure 2.1   The distribution of the protocols through the layers of a typical TCP/IP model.

Understanding the *Transmission Control Protocol* (TCP)

Think now about a maritime exercise between two warships. Instead of using radio communications that can be heard by the enemy, the two warships need to come up alongside and establish a physical connection between the two. A cable is fired to the second ship and, once connected, the second ship sends back an acknowledgment. At this time, a communication session has been established.

TCP works in a similar fashion to the warships above. Two computers begin communications by first establishing a session between them. Until the session has been established, no data is transmitted. TCP is considered to be a reliable transmission mechanism because it is designed to confirm that the packets it sends are received on the other side. If packets are lost, the sending computer resends the data. This is achieved with *acknowledgments* (ACKs), the datacom equivalent of a return receipt request used when sending certified mail through the postal service.

Before transmission takes place, however, the application needs to know where to send the data, or which entrance, if you will, is to provide the doorway or portal to a *tunnel* connecting to the other side. TCP achieves this with the use of ports and sockets.

Ports

When a receiving application is waiting to know which type of data to receive, it needs to know which port to listen to. A port is a 16-bit number.

When two computers establish a session, they agree that data will be transmitted via a certain port assignment, or a port number. TCP can, in fact, now send and receive on any of 65,000 ports. However, several port assignments have been singled out as being the standard port assignment used by an application to gain the service of a protocol. FTP happens to be typically assigned port 21.

For example, unless an FTP application specifically sends data to port 13498, the default port number will be 21. The default port numbers are also known as the documented or assigned ports and by the *Internet Assigned Numbers Authority* (IANA) as *well-known* ports. Well-known ports range from 1 to 1023.

So you may think that you just need to know a collection of well-known ports to handle TCP/IP networking. On the contrary, in the real world, it is important to understand how to assign and work with ports because it is key to setting up firewalls and specialized TCP/IP software running on Windows NT server. (Network Address Translation is another area in which knowledge of port usage is a must.) Table 2.3 gives a short list of well-known ports that is more than enough for the exam.

Table 2.3
For the Exam, You Should Know a Few "Well-Known" Port
Numbers, Particularly FTP.

Port Number	Abbreviation	Description
7	Echo	Echo (PING) Service
17	QOTD	Quote of the Day
20	FTP-Data	File Transfer Protocol—Data
21	FTP	File Transfer Protocol—Control
23	TELNET	Telnet—Remote Login Service
25	SMTP	Simple Mail Transfer Protocol
37	TIME	Time Service
53	DNS	Domain Name System
67	Bootps	Bootstrap Protocol (DHCP) Server
68	Bootpc	Bootstrap Protocol (DHCP) Client
69	TFTP	Trivial File Transfer Protocol— WWW
70	GOPHER	Gopher—multiprotocol menu browser
79	Finger	Finger
80	HTTP	Hypertext Transfer Protocol
88	Kerberos	Kerberos Security Authentication
110	POP3	Post Office Protocol—Version 3
119	NNTP	Network News Transfer Protocol—USENET
161	SNMP	Simple Network Management Protocol
220	IMAP3	Interactive Mail Access Protocol—Version 3

Sockets

You will also come across the term sockets during your TCP/IP sojourn. Sockets are not something you will need to know to install and manage TCP/IP networks. Sockets belong in the software developer world. Sockets are essentially an Application programming interface, just as is the NETBIOS.

Sockets were popularized by the University of California at Berkeley. Born to the UNIX world, sockets are a means of obtaining a *handle* to a bi-directional network service. Obtaining the handle and reading and writing to the service is almost identical to obtaining a handle to a file that you can read and write to. The difference is that the socket you create is associated with the network and the transport mechanism, while the file is associated with the file system.

Once you have the socket, you can either bind it to a port on the local computer or, via TCP, you can connect it to a port on a remote computer (at least that's what developers do, not certified network engineers). Once a port has been created and used in TCP mode, it can *listen* for and accept connections. Any computer on your network can now connect to the port and send data to the computer hosting the port. Ports have queues that maintain the network connections. The client processes establish a maximum size for the queue when it needs to start listening to the ports.

By writing this support into applications, developers have thus given the servers and the clients the ability to listen to each other and correspond. Servers can now send packets of data to individual client computers and the clients can respond in kind with reciprocal data.

We won't go into further detail here because you will not be tested for software development issues. You can see, however, how a TCP connection using sockets and ports can trigger a corresponding application on a remote computer.

Now you see how Windows has not only borrowed from the UNIX world, its adoption and built-in support for TCP/IP sockets gives it a robust alternative to the proprietary and limited protocols of its past, such as mailslots and named pipes.

Transmission Under TCP

TCP is a reliable point-to-point communication process that can be used, like named pipes, to establish continuing bi-directional and real-time communications between clients and servers.

First the server creates the socket and binds it to a port on the local computer. Then the server enables the socket, puts it into listening mode, and waits to accept a connection. As soon as a connection is detected, data can be transferred between the server and the client. On the client side, the local (client) computer also creates a socket and establishes the necessary support to enable the server to connect to the socket and transmit data.

To explore this idea fully, let's turn our attention to the actual transmission process. TCP/IP networks can support three types of network packet structures. These are IP packets, TCP packets, and UDP packets.

IP packets are commonly known as raw data packets that can be directed at a computer or broadcast on the network. They do not use the port arrangement described above and you would not want to use raw packets for most computer setups.

UDP packets, similar to the OS/2 mailslot packets, can be *shot* to ports on various computers or broadcast on the network. All ports listening will detect the packets and accept the communication.

In the TCP packet mechanism, again similar to named pipe packets, the data are transmitted once point-to-point communications have been established between specific clients and servers. These packets can be aimed at specific computers on the network (to their ports) and these computers can respond in kind.

Let's zoom in on the TCP process. Say two computers have each loaded a TCP/IP stack. Both computers have enabled sockets and have established an ongoing communication session between them. The computers could be running software created by a single software vendor, or they could be products from different companies. In this example, we have two computers involved in a computer telephony application: an NT-based PBX (NT1) and an NT-based voice mail system (NT2).

When a call arrives from the outside world, it rings on a voice channel on NT1. NT1 harbors both switching cards and voice processing cards so it can provide both switching services and an automated attendant service. A client enters the extension number of a representative or agent and NT1 knows in an instant that the call cannot be transferred (because it is managing the extensions). The extension status indicates that the extension is busy and the PBX transfers the call instead to a voice messaging channel on NT2, a remote computer.

Then NT2 receives the redirected call on its channel, but it needs advance advice on the mailbox service to activate. It needs to know which mailbox greeting to play for the caller because it has hundreds of mailbox greetings but only four channels. By the time the channel goes off hook NT1 has already communicated this to NT2 via TCP. How did this happen?

What took place was the following: NT1, configured as IP address 198.1.6.1, requested a connection to the voice messaging server (NT2) at IP address 198.1.9.2. TCP sends a packet to IP with information (flags) to indicate that this is the initial phase of the communication. IP receives the information and undertakes an address resolution process to determine the location (the location of the physical network interface electronics of NT2). When IP gets this information, it transmits an IP datagram to NT2. At this point, NT1 has hailed NT2, and in human lingo, this would be the equivalent of "Yo, voice mail. You there?"

When NT2 (at 198.1.9.2) gets the datagram, it transmits an acknowledgment packet back to NT1 effectively saying "Yo, X. I got you." NT1 transmits a second packet to NT2 saying "Yo, voice mail, this is big X. Stand by." At this point in the communication, a point-to-point communication has been established between NT1 and NT2, our so-called session. Both computers are now ready to exchange data and more packets are transmitted. The communication will now resemble the following: *Yo, voice mail. That call you just answered on channel 4 is for mailbox 414.*

That's the process in a nutshell. Of course what we have discussed here is very basic indeed. Not only is the actual IP and TCP setup complex (there are several management issues), but the telephony environment also brings problems and pressures to bear on the entire process.

Transmission Under UDP

Many communication situations require sessions to be established between computers or for reception of data to be confirmed—TCP is used for those situations. Think of UDP as the opposite of TCP. UDP communications are not reliable. This means that a UDP sender has no way of knowing that a remote computer has received its packets. There is no complex and complicated hand-shaking mechanism in place.

Does UDP transmission have a place in the TCP/IP suite? You bet. I like to think of UDP as similar to television or radio broadcasting. The broadcasters do not really know if you are at home sitting in front of the television or radio watching or listening to their channels.

Nevertheless, they broadcast. Good examples in the TCP/IP world are the Internet news broadcasters that transmit audio and visuals all day long. If you happen to be using an application that knows how to display the data, it will present it for you every time a broadcast is transmitted.

The IP Address Space

Each network technology has its own convention for transmitting messages between two computers within the same network. On a LAN, messages are sent between computers by supplying the six-byte unique identifier (the *MAC* address). In an SNA network, every computer has Logical Units with their own network address. DECnet, AppleTalk, and Novell IPX all have a scheme for assigning numbers to each local network and to each workstation attached to the network.

On top of these local or vendor specific network addresses, TCP/IP assigns a unique 32-bit number to every device in the world hosting the TCP/IP stack. This *IP number* is a four-byte value that, by convention, is expressed by converting each byte into a decimal number (0 to 255) and separating the bytes with a period. For example, the UUNet server is 198.196.63.6.

Historically, to gain access to the public addresses, an organization would send e-mail to `hostmaster@INTERNIC.NET`, requesting assignment of a network number. For many years, until the mid-90s, it was still possible for almost anyone to get assignment of a number for a small *Class C* network in which the first three bytes identify the network and the last byte identifies the individual computer. Larger organizations received *Class B* networks where the first two bytes identify the network and the last two bytes identify each of up to 64,000 individual workstations.

The organizations then connect to the Internet through one of a dozen regional or hundreds of specialized network suppliers, the *Internet Service Providers* (ISPs). The network vendor is given the subscriber network number and adds it to the routing configuration in its own computers and those of the other major network suppliers.

There is no magical mathematical formula that translates the numbers 198.196.63.6 into *UUNet Technologies*. The computers that manage large regional networks or the central Internet routers, formerly managed under contract by the National Science Foundation, can only locate these networks by looking each network number up in a *Domain Name Service* (DNS) table. There are thousands of Class B networks, and over two million Class C networks, but computer memory costs are low, so the tables at first were not unreasonable.

Customers that connect to the Internet, even customers as large as IBM, do not need to maintain any information about other networks. They send all external data to the regional carrier to which they subscribe, and the regional carrier maintains the tables and does the appropriate routing.

Routing

The IP part of the protocol stack carries the responsibility for routing or directing datagrams from one network to another. If a particular computer or device is configured or set up as a router, it means that certain routing protocols are brought into play to ensure that packets not intended for the local segment are routed to a remote segment. We will deal with these protocols in later chapters.

WHAT IS A HOP?

Other than the bitter flavor in beer, what are hops? Each time that a datagram passes through an intermediate router, between the packet's node of origin and the packet's destination device, that routing transition is called a "hop." If a packet has not gone through a router, it has not incurred a hop. One hop occurs in each intermediate router. If a packet traverses three routers to reach its target computer, we say the destination is three hops away.

TIME-TO-LIVE

When working in routing issues, you will almost always be encountering a presentation of the *time-to-live* or *TTL* field (the *live* pronounced *liv* as in *liver*). The TTL field in the transmitted data packet is initialized by the originator of the packet and set at a certain value, usually 32 or 64. Then each time the datagram passes through a router, this value is decremented by one. When the value reaches 0, the datagram is discarded.

The idea behind the TTL field is that a packet or datagram must not be allowed to live forever. You can imagine the mess if *lost* datagrams were allowed to continue bouncing around the Internet forever trying to find their destination computer. This process thus allows the datagram to traverse a preset number of routers before it is zapped.

Internet Control Message Protocol

The *Internet Control Message Protocol* (ICMP) is considered part of the IP that controls and manages error messages and reporting. ICMP provides the *Ping* utility that every network systems engineer needs to use to diagnose network problems. Ping, allegedly a contraction of *packet internet groper*, is derived from the sonar operation of sending out sound waves to locate objects and determining how far away they are. The Ping is the bounced wave that comes back. Submariners use the echo (*ping*) of a sonar device to determine location and position of another vessel.

The first time you will use the ICMP is to test if the Windows TCP/IP stack is loaded and if the network hardware is working. It is by no means an exhaustive testing utility for all networking issues, and its main use is to prove out TCP/IP communications, connectivity, and especially routing, addressing, and subnetting.

ICMP messages come in two flavors: error messages and query responses. You see them when executing Ping. (In order to Ping something, you need an IP address or an IP hostname as the target.) Error messages include:

- Destination or host unreachable. This message tells you that a network problem is preventing the datagram from reaching its intended target. It usually means that the packet cannot be delivered or forwarded to the network address the host is residing on. You will get this message, for example, when trying to Ping a remote computer while not connected to the network. And if you get this message, first check to see if the network cable is plugged in. Other variations of this message are *network unreachable* or *gateway unreachable*.

- Timeout or time exceeded. This message is sent by a router or gateway when a packet is discarded on expiration of its TTL value.

- Redirect. The redirect message is sent by a router to the sender of an IP datagram to the effect that the packet should have been sent along a different route. This message occurs when you have more than one router in your network. Although you don't usually see this message, the router is actually telling the sender host to send to the alternate router by default the next time a packet transmission is attempted.

- Source quench. The source quench is sent by a receiving host to a source of datagrams because the receiver is receiving more information than it can deal with. Computers that receive source quench messages drop back transmission rates as soon as they receive the message, and then attempt to resume to their default rate of transmission thereafter.

The Internet Group Management Protocol

A host can become a member of an IGMP address group. All members of the group receive the same broadcast data. Hosts need only leave the IGMP group to stop receiving packets to that group. A good example of IGMP at work is an array of flight information data-boards in a modern airport. A single host sends data to the board group that represents international flights. These boards are all part of a single address group. Another group of boards represents domestic flight information.

ARP AND RARP

ARP is used by TCP/IP to resolve the physical address of a network interface device. *ARP* stands for *Address Resolution Protocol* and the first *R* in RARP stands for *Reverse*. At the physical layer, network interface devices are represented by a 48-bit Ethernet address. This address is also known as the MAC (*Media Access Control*) address.

Most of the time your software and processes will never need to deal with the MAC address. But what happens if you have more than one card in a computer (multi-homed) and you need to direct IP traffic to one or the other card in order to reach a network segment? Think you'll never need ARP? Just wait until you have to direct *illegal* address traffic to the Internet over one of three NIC cards in a multi-homed NT-based router.

You can see these wonders in the TCP/IP stack at work when running *ipconfig /all* from the command line under Windows NT, which is shown below. Both the IP address and the MAC address are displayed along with all IP settings bound to each interface device.

```
Windows NT IP Configuration
    Host Name . . . . . . . . . : ponlysrv.Emissary
    DNS Servers . . . . . . . . : 199.170.88.29
       199.170.88.10
    Node Type . . . . . . . . . : Hybrid
    NetBIOS Scope ID. . . . . . :
    IP Routing Enabled. . . . . : Yes
    WINS Proxy Enabled. . . . . : No
    NetBIOS Resolution Uses DNS : Yes
```

```
Ethernet adapter PNPWNT1:
        Description . . . . . . . . : Novell 2000 Adapter.
        Physical Address. . . . . . : 00-C0-6D-16-A2-1D
        DHCP Enabled. . . . . . . . : No
        IP Address. . . . . . . . . : 10.0.1.60
        Subnet Mask . . . . . . . . : 255.255.255.0
        Default Gateway . . . . . . :
        Primary WINS Server . . . . : 10.0.1.21
        Secondary WINS Server . . . : 10.0.1.60

Ethernet adapter NdisWan4:
        Description . . . . . . . . : NdisWan Adapter
        Physical Address. . . . . . : 00-00-00-00-00-00
        DHCP Enabled. . . . . . . . : No
        IP Address. . . . . . . . . : 0.0.0.0
        Subnet Mask . . . . . . . . : 0.0.0.0
        Default Gateway . . . . . . :
```

For Review

- TCP/IP is an open architecture/open standards protocol maintained in the public domain.

- TCP/IP is a layered architecture consisting of the Network Interface, internet, Transport and Application layers.

- TCP/IP contains two primary transmission protocols: TCP and UDP.

- Every Internet connected device hosting the TCP/IP stack is assigned a unique 32-bit number.

- The IP part of the protocol stack carries the responsibility for routing or directing datagrams from one network to another.

- The *Internet Control Message Protocol* (ICMP) is considered part of the IP that controls and manages error messages and reporting.

- A group of devices can be broadcast to *as a group* by the Internet Group Management Protocol.

- ARP is used by TCP/IP to resolve the physical address of a network interface device.

From Here

See Chapter 8 for information on installation and configuration of a DNS server and Chapter 7 describes how to use a HOSTS file.

CHAPTER 3

The IP Address

A 32-bit number is assigned to every network interface of every device communicating on a TCP/IP network. This number is known as an Internet address or an IP address.

IP addresses are much like telephone numbers in that they are assigned with almost complete ignorance of the physical network. This is similar to the *Public Switched Telephone Network* (PSTN). It does not matter whether the subscriber uses a cell phone, a digital station, or a POTS telephone (plain old telephone service) . . . if you dial the number you speak to the person or get a busy signal.

If a device has more than one network interface on one or more TCP/IP networks, the device will have more than one IP address. When we talk about a device with more that one network interface, we say that it is *multi-homed*. A Windows NT router with more than one NIC is a multi-homed computer.

If you want to make a network accessible to the public, then any IP addresses you expose must be unique to the entire Internet. The Internet authority for each country provides these addresses by assignment (usually through the auspices of an *Internet Service Provider* or ISP). In the United States, the organization with this chore is the *Internet Network Information Center*, better known as the InterNIC. Long ago, these duties were performed by the Internet Activity Board.

IP addresses are a collection of four decimal numbers separated by dots *(dot-decimal notation)*. For example, one of the Tekmatix DNS servers is located at IP address 209.215.182.5.

Take note that the dotted decimal notation is for human consumption. IP actually works in computers in binary notation. Decimal values are converted to binary and are then joined together by IP to form a 32-bit binary address. In the UNIX world, some people prefer to work with dotted hexadecimal, and some even use C-style hexadecimal. Don't worry about these last two methods turning up on the Microsoft TCP/IP exam, however.

Table 3.1 shows available IP addresses for five classes of Internet address.

Table 3.1 Internet IP addresses are classically divided into five classes.

Class	Beginning IP Address	Final IP Address
A	1.0.0.1	126.255.255.254
B	128.0.0.1	191.255.255.254
C	192.0.0.1	223.255.255.254
D	224.0.0.1	239.255.255.254
E	240.0.0.1	247.255.255.254

 So there are five different classes of addresses: A to E, and their the traditional class boundaries are shown here:

- Class A has the address range of 0.0.0.0 to 126.255.255.255.

- Class B has the address range of 128.0.0.0 to 191.255.255.255.

- Class C has the address range of 192.0.0.0 to 223.255.255.255.

- Class D has the address range of 224.0.0.0 to 239.255.255.255.

- Class E has the address range of 240.0.0.0 to 247.255.255.255.

NOTE

The address range of 127.0.0.0 to 127.255.255.255 is reserved for loopback testing on the local computer and is not a valid network address. The loopback address is discussed later in this chapter.

TEST TIP

For the exam, Microsoft is not concerned about Class D and Class E ranges. Most tested examples are from the Class B range and the Class C range. If you are offered an available answer in the Class D or E ranges, it probably is a wrong or distracter answer.

Because Class D and E networks are not relevant to the exam, little more will be said of them, and we will focus from here on primarily on Class A, Class B, and Class C networks.

The addresses within the above ranges consist of four 8-bit values we fondly refer to as the *octets*. Although the dotted IP address notation is easy to read, there are many times that you will need to convert from the decimal system to the binary system (subnetting is one reason discussed in the next chapter), but we will deal with that shortly. Let's now examine what the octets represent.

The IP address comes in two variable parts: the network ID (also referred to as the network number) and the host ID or number. For example, in the following Class C address, 208.212.170.142, the first three numbers (208.212.170) make up the network ID. The last number, 142, is the host ID. We can refer to the network as the 208.212.170.0 network, and sometimes the host may be referred to as host number 0.0.0.142.

In this Class C IP address, the first three octets represent the network identity or ID, and the final octet represents the host identity or ID. The division of IP addresses into network (left side) and host (right side) portions is a foundation concept that you must grasp in order to prepare for more complex divisions (subnetting) in the next chapter. This simple view of the network classes and four octets assumes that the default subnet mask is in use (see Table 3.2).

Now, because some people find it easier to think about IP addresses in binary, Table 3.3 gives you the binary equivalents for Class A through Class C.

Table 3.2 Each class has its own default subnet mask. Note the patterns in the decimal and binary numbers.

Address Class	Decimal Value of Subnet Mask	Binary Value of Subnet Mask
A	255.0.0.0	11111111.00000000.00000000.00000000
B	255.255.0.0	11111111.11111111.00000000.00000000
C	255.255.255.0	11111111.11111111.11111111.00000000

Table 3.3 Patterns here are more complex—visible only if you seek them. Note the patterns.

Address Class	Decimal Value	Binary Value
A		
First IP Address	1.0.0.1	00000001.00000000.00000000.00000001
Last IP Address	126.255.255.254	01111110.11111111.11111111.11111110
Default Mask	255.0.0.0	11111111.00000000.00000000.00000000
B		
First IP Address	128.0.0.1	10000000.00000000.00000000.00000001
Last IP Address	191.255.255.254	10111111.11111111.11111111.11111110
Default Mask	255.255.0.0	11111111.11111111.00000000.00000000
C		
First IP Address	192.0.0.1	11000000.00000000.00000000.00000001
Last IP Address	223.255.255.254	11011111.11111111.11111111.11111110
Default Mask	255.255.255.0	11111111.11111111.11111111.00000000

Remember that computers do the network routing voodoo that we're about to explain (in the next chapter or so) with binary numbers, so understanding how the binary IP addresses work will bring us closer to our beloved network computers. Computers are our friends, right?

Now fire up the Windows *scientific calculator*

```
Start | Programs | Accessories | Calculator | View | Scientific
```

and examine the first octet in the Class C address 208.208.208.208. If we convert the decimal octet of 208 to its binary equivalent, we get the value 11010000. Is that right? Let's check. We have from right to left the following:

```
128+64+0+16+0+0+0+0
```

And if we add 128 + 64 + 16 we do get 208. So this binary value is correct because it is an 8-bit number and adding the on bits (or the decimal value of the on or 1 bit) brings us to a value of 208.

Remember that there are four octets. So when you evaluate each of the four octets, you get a whole 32-bit IP address.

Confused?

If the calculations in last three paragraphs make no sense to you, here is a slightly longer explanation: Each place in an IP address octet has a value, explained more thoroughly in the next chapter when we discuss subnetting. For now, just take it for given that the binary place values for the octet 11111111 are as shown in Table 3.4.

Table 3.4 Each place in a binary octet has a defined value based on powers of 2.

Octet Place	1	1	1	1	1	1	1	1
DecimalValue	128	64	32	16	8	4	2	1

So, referring to Table 3.4, the decimal value of the binary octet 11111111 is 128 + 64 + 32 + 16 + 8 + 4 +2 + 1 = 255.

Similarly, the value of the octet 11010000 would look like the example shown in Table 3.5.

Table 3.5   To evaluate the octet, add the decimal values for each 1 in the octet.

Octet	1	1	0	1	0	0	0	0
Decimal Value	128	64	0	16	0	0	0	0

So the value of the binary octet 11010000 is 128 + 64 + 0 + 16 + 0 + 0 + 0 + 0 = 208. In the same way, the decimal value of the binary octet 00000000 is 0 + 0 + 0 + 0 + 0 + 0 + 0 + 0 = 0.

So what you should remember about this is that *any* decimal value between 0 and 255 can be represented using this system of 8-bit binary octets with the decimal place values as shown in Table 3.4. For example, Table 3.6 shows several more decimal values selected at random. Practice these conversions using Table 3.4 frontwards and backwards until you are sure you understand the principles behind them. Note that this system cannot represent decimal values greater than 255.

Table 3.6   Practice these examples for decimal to binary conversion. Some folks add the place values represented by 1s, and other folks subtract from 255 the place values represented by 0s. Find a method that works for you.

Decimal Value	Binary Octet
47	00101111
75	01001011
121	01111001
125	01111101
127	01111111

continues

Table 3.6 Continued

Decimal Value	Binary Octet
227	11100011
250	11111010

Also remember, four octets are in each IP address (IP addresses are also referred to as *dotted quads*). Each of the four octets can be evaluated using the place values shown in Table 3.4. When all four octets have been converted from binary to decimal, the IP address is in its *human-friendly* form. Computers like the binary flavor, of course. Table 3.7 shows both the decimal and binary versions of the IP address 208.208.208.208.

We will illustrate binary math more as you progress. Binary math is not difficult—before long you'll see that you can do it in your head. Step by step, we're building a conceptual foundation here. It is our goal that you not only pass the TCP/IP exam, but that you also have a sound understanding of the IP address concepts required to subnet a network in the real world.

Under IPv4, without subnetting, there are 126 Class A networks with as many as 16,777,214 hosts on each Class A network. Similarly, the Class B range provides 16,384 networks with as many as 65,534 hosts on each Class B network. The Class C address space provides 2,097,152 Class C networks, each containing up to 254 hosts.

Jumping ahead, it is possible (and often convenient or necessary) to subdivide a standard Class A, Class B, or Class C network using subnetting. In effect, subnetting is a method of reducing (sacrificing) the maximum number of hosts in order to define smaller networks (called subnets) *within* the larger Class A, Class B, or Class C network. All the subnets share the same subnet mask, so that the network's computers can still communicate, even though they're on different subnets (or segments).

The Internet authorities long ago assigned all the Class A and B networks, and whole Class C networks are no longer available. If a network will not directly connect to the Internet, any class of network can be used, and there are very sound reasons why you would choose one over another.

Table 3.7 To evaluate the whole IP address, each octet must be evaluated.

Class C	Decimal IP Address	Binary IP Address
IP Address	208.208.208.208	11010000.11010000.11010000.11010000
Default Mask	255.255.255.0	11111111.11111111.11111111.00000000

You could number your private network 10.1.1.1 because it's convenient and private, even if you're only using 10 hosts. No one on the Internet ever needs to know about it (and, as a Class A network, you have the ability to address in excess of 16 million hosts if your organization experiences explosive growth). A Class A or Class B network is often used in Network Address Translation because it is often convenient to address hosts in the low numbers. On the other hand, if you are tasked with networking every device in a new airport facility or replacing every terminal owned by a huge car manufacturer, then you may even run out of Class B addresses if you're trying to stick to one network segment and have lots of devices to address.

Is there a way that you can tell address classes apart? Yes. You can mostly just glance at the first octet to decide (and that will come with time and setting up many networks). However, I have set up dozens of IP networks, and many private addresses in the Class A and B ranges, and I still have to think for a second when determining the Class.

A first octet of 10 is easily identified as a Class A address. But what about 191? Is it a Class B or Class C address? The way to be sure is to go back to the little decimal conversion exercise we performed earlier and convert the first octet to its binary equivalent.

Remember that the octet is an 8-bit binary number. Take out your scientific calculator and convert the decimal value of the first octet to its binary equivalent. If the address starts with a 0 (from left to right), then your address is Class A. For example, 21 decimal = 10101 binary, according to the calculator. Now pad to the left with zeros until you have eight bits (for the decimal value 21, add three left zeros to the binary conversion result). The full 8-bit number is 00010101. What we have here is a Class A address because it starts with 0.

Now convert the number at the end of the Class A range and the beginning of the Class B range to see how the respective class' border numbers change classes—127 and 128. The calculator says the binary equivalent of decimal 127 is 1111111, but you have only seven binary bits here, so pad to the left with one zero to get 01111111. It still starts with zero, so you are technically still in Class A. Next decimal number up: The binary value of 128 is 10000000. This number starts with one and needs no padding. The decimal value 128 in the leftmost position is a Class B IP number because the second binary bit is a zero.

To summarize: If you convert decimal to binary and the first of the 8 bits (starting on the left, and often known as the most significant bit or MSB) is 0, then you are dealing with the Class A address space. If the first bit is on or 1 and the second is off or 0, then you are dealing with a Class B address. And if the first two bits are *1* or *on*, then you are dealing with Class C . . . and so it goes. Table 3.8 gives a summary. Please turn back to Table 3.3 and confirm for yourself that the binary values for each class shown conform to the rules shown in Table 3.8. It is important for your understanding of routing and subnetting that you become familiar with the binary representations of IP addresses.

Table 3.8 The Most Significant Bits are another way to recall and identify the three largest classes.

Class	Leftmost Binary Bits of First Octet
A	0
B	10
C	110

THE TEST CALCULATOR — USE IT OR DON'T

You may need to perform decimal to binary conversion of an IP address in the TCP/IP test, particularly related to subnetting. So make sure you know how to perform this conversion, the binary order of the first octets, and how they map to the three largest Class IDs.

Memorizing the conversions is best, but, for the few subnetting questions on the current exam, it may be acceptable to use the calculator available throughout the exam. Using the calculator was considered too wasteful of time in previous exams that heavily emphasized subnetting, so memorization was favored. Some exam pundits still recommend against use of the calculator—I think it's up to you and how you best handle the subnetting questions. Either memorize or *quickly* use the calculator.

Also, when you are an MCSE, make sure you have a scientific calculator and you know how to use it. The freebie one that ships with Windows is adequate and available during the exam. I personally prefer a hand-held calculator because switching between windows and dialogs onscreen can become irritating and time-consuming.

One last thought on this topic—testing centers may not ordinarily allow you to take a calculator into the exam room, so check in advance if you want to carry a calculator.

Understanding The Address Classes

The *Class A addresses* are used to address many devices in a single network. While public Class A addresses are all assigned to the like of IBM and early-adopter universities, Class A addresses are used every day in private *intranets*. Many international airports use Class A addresses to address their myriad hosts on a single closed TCP/IP network.

In a Class A address, as illustrated in Table 3.3, the first 8 bits of the address *quad* are reserved for the network ID. This means that you can only have up to 126 networks in the Class A range (0.0.0.0 is meaningless because it represents the actual network to IP). The rest of the octets to the right, that is, the remaining three octets, make up a host ID. In this case, the host is addressed as a 24-bit number represented as the three dotted decimal numbers. The 24-bit number can translate into a possible 16,777,214 addresses (or $2^{24}-2$). If we address a host with IP address 126.208.123.156, it means that on network ID 126.0.0.0, the host address is 0.208.123.156.

Do not forget that the rightmost three decimal numbers making up the host ID can be set from 0 to 255, but 0 and 255 represent the network and broadcast numbers respectively. The rightmost host numbers actually used in host IP addresses, therefore, are 1 to 254, as shown back in Table 3.3.

When setting TCP/IP addresses under Microsoft Networking, you are prevented from assigning an address consisting of all zeros (0.0.0.0) or anything in the Class D and E ranges. There are good reasons for this, as you will soon see in the next section.

There are certainly a lot of *Class B networks* on the Internet, 16,384 or 2^{14} to be precise. Class A only has 126 networks. It is likely clear to you now that you can use both the first and second octets to make up a Class B network ID portion of the IP address. As mentioned, the public Class B network IDs are all assigned (many went to Ma Bell and her brood). But, again, Class B addresses are also used every day in private TCP/IP networks.

In a Class B address, and as illustrated in Table 3.3, the first 16 bits of the binary address, or the first half of the decimal *quad*, are reserved for the network ID. With 16 bits to work with and the limitation from Table 3.8 that the first binary octet must begin with 10 (meaning that the first decimal value must be within the range of 128 to 191), 16,384 networks can be defined. The rest of the octets, that is, the remaining two octets, make up a host ID.

A standard Class B host computer is addressed as a 16-bit number represented as the rightmost two dotted decimal numbers. Those rightmost 16-bits can translate into a possible 65,534 addresses (or

$2^{16}-2$). So, for example, assuming the default subnet mask, if we address a host with an IP address of 180.208.123.156, that means the computer is on Class B network ID 180.208.0.0, and the computer's host ID is 0.0.123.156.

Class C networks are everywhere on the Internet. There are 2,097,152 Class C networks available to be precise. While Class C networks abound, the InterNIC has no more to assign for public use. Who would have thought the Internet would become as popular as french fries? When I first used it a decade ago, it was the most cryptic, unfriendly, and sterile public utility around.

Many ISPs who hold Class C networks are chopping them up and assigning *bits* and *pieces* to their customers as subnets or segments between routers. It is not uncommon for an ISP to ask you to justify the need for an entire Class C by listing the number of hosts you will need to address. Today, the largest network you are likely to get as a small business is 62 hosts, or about one-quarter of a full Class C network.

Soon any new Internet customer organization will be assigned one public *gateway*, a few public hosts, such as mail server, name server, and web server (which can all reside on one host computer if traffic is light) and the organization will be required to translate the rest of its hosts into a private network of the customer's choosing with software.

Once you are assigned a *piece* of a Class C, you will see by looking at the first three binary octets, or the first 24-bit grouping, that it is entirely possible that another organization is using the same network ID. In a standard Class C address (without subnetting), the first three octets are the network ID, while the remaining octet can be used to number up to 254 hosts.

Class D networks are used for multicasting and the *Class E addresses* are reserved for future use.

In review, for the exam and as shown in Table 3.9, you should know that Class A provides the largest number of IP hosts per network (about 16 million), that Class B provides over 16 thousand networks of over 65 thousand hosts per network, and that Class C provides over two million networks, and that Class C networks may have up to 254 hosts per network.

Table 3.9 The trade-off, or the dynamic tension, in network design always attempts to balance the number of network segments needed with the number of network hosts that must be addressed on each network.

	Range of First Decimal Value	Number of Networks	Maximum Number of Hosts
Class A	1 to 126	126	16,777,214
Class B	128 to 191	16,384	65,534
Class C	192 to 223	2,097,152	254

When planning a TCP/IP network, each network segment (or subnet) will need its own network ID (or subnetwork ID). Each physical or administrative unit may even require its own network ID. If a large private network requires less than 126 network segments (allowing lots of room, of course, for future growth), then they can be set up as a group of Class A networks. If you estimate, with future growth, that a large private network will require more than 126 and less than 16,000 network segments, then it may be created as a group of Class B networks. Become familiar with the limitations and values shown in Table 3.9.

Likewise, when planning a TCP/IP network, each host computer and each router interface will require its own unique host ID—its own IP address. Each network printer must also have its own IP address, if it is directly connected to the network, rather than connected to a computer on the network. Any TCP/IP-capable network device that requires its own IP address (be it a computer, a router interface, a printer, a WAN link, or *whatever*) must be counted when estimating the maximum number of hosts that a network must accommodate. Routers, by definition, have a network interface on two or more network segments, so each router typically has *at least two host IP addresses*—one for each network ID that the router is directly connected to.

So, for example, if a network plan, after leaving room for future growth, calls for over 254 host IDs, then the network can't be set up as a Class C network, because too few host IDs are available. If over 65 thousand host IDs are needed, Class B is too small. You get the idea.

The exam will expect you to balance the desired maximum number of hosts per segment required in a planned network with the number of network segments (or subnets) required, so it is essential that you understand the principle just presented. And in real life, you won't want to change your network's subnet mask twice if only one change is necessary—get it right the first time.

Working with Addresses

No matter whether you are assigning public network addresses or private ones, there are a few rules you must follow in the assigning process. The following guidelines present options, limitations, and some diagnostic capabilities.

Because IP addresses are hierarchically arranged (network on the left, host number on the right), routers can know that *all computers* connected to the 208.208.0.0 can be communicated with through a single gateway (router) that serves the 208.208.0.0 network. This kind of information efficiency is crucial to the explosive growth of the Internet.

The size of the routing tables at the Internet backbone must be controlled to accommodate continued growth. Table 3.10 provides an initial set of special or reserved IP addresses to begin your understanding of routing rules and to deepen your understanding of IP addresses. You will see these addresses in routing tables (in decimal format) soon enough, so begin to become conversant with them.

Table 3.10   These IP addresses have special meanings.

IP Address	Meaning
0.0.0.0	*Default route* in RIP routing.
Network 127 Class A 01111111.x.x.y or Class A 127.x.x.y	Reserved for TCP/IP loopback (self) testing. Does not cause network traffic.
Host Address ID of all 1s Class A 0.11111111.11111111.11111111 Class B 0.0.11111111.11111111 Class C 0.0.0.11111111 or Class A 0.255.255.255 Class B 0.0.255.255 Class C 0.0.0.255	*All hosts on this network* The network portion of the IP address determines the network on which *all hosts* are targeted.
11111111.11111111.11111111.11111111 or 255.255.255.255	*Broadcast to all hosts on this network* or *all 1 is broadcast.*

LOOPBACK ADDRESS

As you will see in the chapters to come, devices that support TCP/IP also support a *LOOPBACK ADDRESS* or *INTERFACE*. The loopback address is the network ID of 127, at the top of the Class A range and below the Class B range. The standard loopback address can be any host ID having this form (127.x.x.y); the address typically used is 127.0.0.1. In the formula, the value of x can range from 0 to 255. However, the value of y is more limited; y can only range from 1 to 254. It may help to think of this last octet as a host ID, so that all 1s and all 0s are not allowed.

Transmitting to the loopback address immediately returns each packet to the host. In other words, all that is happening is that you are able to transmit a packet to the so-called *localhost*. If the packet is returned normally, then the TCP/IP stack is working on the local-host computer and TCP/IP is bound to the device. A packet addressed to 127.0.0.1 is never sent out on the network; it can only be returned to the local device.

Note that the IP address that is assigned to a host can also function as an alternate loopback address for diagnostics.

 We can now test the loopback by running *ping* 127.0.0.1 from the command prompt. A successful ping to the loopback is shown next, indicating TCP/IP has been installed and configured correctly on this host.

```
Pinging 127.0.0.1 with 32 bytes of data:

Reply from 127.0.0.1: bytes=32 time<10ms TTL=128
Reply from 127.0.0.1: bytes=32 time<10ms TTL=128
Reply from 127.0.0.1: bytes=32 time<10ms TTL=128
Reply from 127.0.0.1: bytes=32 time<10ms TTL=128
```

If the host does not respond to the command ping 127.0.0.1, *either TCP/IP or the network card has not been installed correctly on that host.*

When we ping the localhost's unique IP address, notice that the results are almost identical.

```
Pinging 10.0.1.60 with 32 bytes of data:

Reply from 10.0.1.60: bytes=32 time<10ms TTL=128
Reply from 10.0.1.60: bytes=32 time<10ms TTL=128
Reply from 10.0.1.60: bytes=32 time<10ms TTL=128
Reply from 10.0.1.60: bytes=32 time<10ms TTL=128
```

Zero-based Host or Network IDs Not Allowed

For the Microsoft TCP/IP examination, recall that you cannot assign zero as a network ID or as the last octet in a host ID because the network is represented by the rightmost decimal zero and you cannot have a zero-based host (the binary value of zero is zero). For example, it is nonsensical to assign 10.1.2.0 as a host IP address—it is a network ID. Likewise, it is nonsensical to assign a network ID of 0, so the IP address 0.208.254.129 is not allowed. Zeros *are allowed in the middle two octets, of course. So it is perfectly reasonable to assign 10.0.1.6 as an address and even 208.212.0.1.*

TIP
You can test the validity of an IP address in the dialogs to set up TCP/IP addresses. The invalid addresses are rejected by the software and cannot be assigned to an interface.

To end this chapter, look at Figure 3.1 to see if what you have learned above makes sense. The diagram represents two networks sharing the Class C address space of network 209.214.220.0. The network has been assigned to two organizations—each organization is given a group of host computer addresses. Each organization can use up to 62 host addresses on its network segment. The first organization can use host addresses from 0.0.0.65 to 0.0.0.127, and the second from uses 0.0.0.129 to 0.0.0.191.

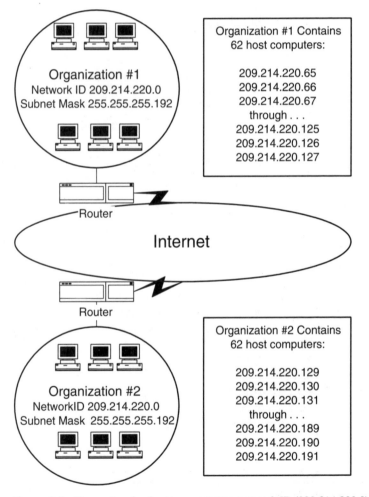

Figure 3.1 Two networks sharing a common network ID (209.214.220.0) and Subnet mask (255.255.255.192).

For Review

- A 32-bit number is assigned to the network interface of every device communicating on a TCP/IP network.

- The 32-bit number is made up of four groups of 8-bit numbers known as octets and separated using dot notation (208.212.170.142).

- A Class A address means that the network ID or number is the first octet in the address; A Class B address means the network ID is the first two octets, and so on. The remaining octets are respectively assigned to host interface cards.

- Focus on Class A, Class B, and Class C.

- Class A addresses have the address range of 0.0.0.1 to 126.254.254.254;

- Class B have the address range of 128.0.0.1 to 191.254.254.254;

- Class C have the address range of 192.0.0.1 to 223.254.254.254;

- Class A: 126 networks, maximum of 16,777,214 hosts on each.

- Class B: 16,384 networks, maximum of 65,534 hosts on each.

- Class C: 2,097,152 networks, maximum of 254 hosts on each.

- The address 127.0.0.1 address is assigned the loopback address, which can be used to test if TCP/IP is working correctly.

- More than one organization can be assigned the same network ID—only the respective hosts in each organization are unique.

From Here

We learned in this chapter that it is possible to chop up a network into small networks, but we haven't yet covered how to do it. These pieces of networks are known as subnets. The next chapter explores subnetting in more detail.

CHAPTER 4

Subnets and Subnetting

This chapter covers many topics, including the following:

- Concepts of Subnetting
- Advantages of Subnetting
- Binary Math Refresher
- IP Address Classes
- What is a Subnet Mask?
- Host IDs and Network IDs
- *ANDing*
- Borrowing Bits to Make Subnets
- New Subnetted Host IP Addresses
- Subnetting Examples

Subnet Planning

To successfully subnet a network, there are five steps in chronological order:

- Step 1: Do a needs analysis.
- Step 2: Select the optimal new subnet mask.

- Step 3: Calculate the new subnetwork IDs.

- Step 4: List the resulting host IDs for each new subnetwork.

- Step 5. Implement the subnet plan by changing all the settings on all the devices.

After we build a conceptual foundation for subnetting, we will return to this planning process and flesh it out in a section called Steps to Subnet Success, later in this chapter.

Concepts of Subnetting

At first glance, subnetting does not appear difficult because the concept is rather simple. Yet somewhere between the concept and the application, many people encounter an obstacle. This chapter will help you avoid that.

Subnetting is actually nothing more than taking a number and breaking it into smaller parts. To relate it to a real-world analogy, subnetting would be like taking a large family residence and turning it into a four-unit rental property.

NOTE

Also keep in mind that this first explanation is purely conceptual and not for practice. All of the technicalities will be explained soon. In the interim, read the following and focus on the concepts.

If the house we are about to remodel has the address 150 Elm Street, the four new apartments in the building could be labeled, for instance:

```
150 Elm Street, #1
150 Elm Street, #2
150 Elm Street, #3
150 Elm Street, #4
```

Subnetting a network ID is done much the same way.

Here's another example from the world of computers. For purposes of this explanation, let's assume the IP address we are working with is 150.100.0.1. This IP address is assigned to a single computer. A computer's IP address lets other computers on the Internet find it. So, the IP address works like the apartment building addresses described above.

In this example, shown in Figure 4.1, all three computers share the network ID of `150.100.0.0`. In this small network, a single computer acts as a router, or *gateway,* for the other computers. In doing this, the Internet is still accessible to all computers on the network.

Network ID   150.100.0.0
Subnet Mask 255.255.0.0

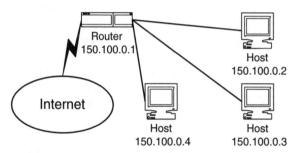

Figure 4.1   Several computers can share a single network ID number.

If you imagine the three host computers in the example are instead whole networks of computers, that's how subnetting works —two, three, or more networks have a network ID which they all share. They all can be addressed by the routers on the Internet. There is a lot more to explain, and this short introduction gives you a foundation for details coming later in the chapter.

In subnetting, like the apartment building on Elm Street, the whole network is broken into units (subnets) that allow the parts to still be part of the network. Figure 4.2 shows what the network could look like when the subnetting is done.

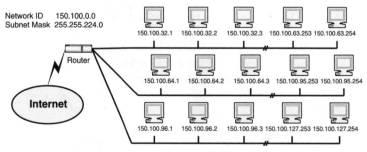

Figure 4.2   Several subnets can share a network ID number by using a subnet mask.

RFC 950 requires that all TCP/IP host interfaces support subnetting. This means it is feasible and desirable to organize TCP/IP networks into small segments known as subnets.

One of the main reasons for subnetting is because the large Class A and Class B divisions described in Chapter 3 are often tedious to work with as large blocks. Because the 126 Class A networks are theoretically some of the largest networks in the world, it would be surprising if these were not significantly subnetted. The Internet is also running out of IP addresses (under the old class system), and thus many ISPs are subnetting as a means of conserving valuable IP address resources and making *additional* IP addresses available for customers.

Like the example shown in Figure 4.1, when you drive down Elm Street, you see the apartment building, not the four individual apartments. Similarly, when a computer on the Internet looks for the IP address 150.100.0.3, it sees the network labeled 150.100.0.0, which is where the data is sent. Once the data arrives at a router that considers network 150.100.0.0 a local network, that router is responsible for sending the data to 150.100.0.3.

You (or at least your router or gateway) cannot view a computer's IP address just in terms of its network ID and host ID. You also must view it in terms of a default mask or *subnet mask*. In essence, a computer cannot be accessed or perform on the network without the inclusion of a subnet mask in the overall IP routing picture. To communicate with each other, all computers on the same network (having the same network ID) must use the *same* subnet mask. Otherwise, they will think they are on different networks and will try to communicate through routers, rather than directly through the network itself.

In the previous chapter, we did not explain completely the concept of the subnet mask. Let's pick up that task again. We need some means of identifying each subnet. Subnets are not simply addressed as subnet 1, 2, or 3, and so forth. A subnet must be addressed by telling a router (and the IP protocol) to which network a packet must be sent (routed). The subnet mask can also be used, as on the exam, to define how many IP addresses a subnet or segment of network can use. In many respects, the subnet mask is also merely a filter for the IP.

TIP
Understanding network IDs is crucial to understanding how to set up a DNS to resolve host IDs (see Chapters 7 and 8).

If you own a Class A network, your network number assigned by InterNIC will be the first octet. If your organization owns a Class C network, your assigned network ID will be the first three octets, or the first 24 bits, as in the case of network 208.212.170.0, which belongs to UUNet. (Class A and Class B networks are chopped up into many small networks, and there is no specific requirement as to how they are subnetted. By the end of the chapter, you will see all the options available on the exam.)

Advantages of Subnetting

One of the reasons to subnet was already mentioned at the beginning of this chapter, which is because enormous, non-subnetted networks can be exhausting to administer. Small organizations often can get by with a single network, because a single network segment can meet the needs of hundreds of users. When the organization is larger or already has several or many network segments in operation, however, a single, *unbounded* network is often no longer feasible. So the first reason to subnet is to create smaller, more discrete network identities for physically separate subnetworks that are part of the larger IP network.

Organizations also deliberately subnet their networks to connect geographically disparate, smaller networks into a larger network. WAN links and routers connect the many smaller parts into a larger whole. As a direct result, as you might expect, router manufacturers and distributors are big on subnetting. You may be too, after considering these attractive advantages:

Advantages of Subnetting

1. *Reduces network traffic.* By placing routers between parts of the network, subnetting can reduce at-large network traffic. Local high-traffic areas are isolated from other areas, so everyone does not experience slow-downs or a worse situation. Only traffic leaving a subnet moves out onto the network at large, by way of the routers.

2. Offers *Better Network Performance.* By reducing network traffic, subnetting can make overall network performance more manageable and easier to enhance if resources are available. The whole network can become more efficient.

3. Promotes *Modular Network Management*. Troubleshooting and other network management duties are simplified if the network is divided into discrete, semi-isolated subnet segments.

4. *Facilitates WAN Connections*. When a network is large and re- quires expensive WAN links to unite it, subnetting provides a logical and coherent way to bring the whole together. WAN links will readily become bottlenecks unless useless local traffic is kept off the WAN links. Subnetting does the trick.

5. *Obscures the network's structural details to outsiders*. Placing a gate- way router and/or a firewall between your network and the Internet, combined with a subnetted network structure and a non-default subnet mask, makes your network less visible to out-' siders. Subnetting alone is not an adequate security measure; however, subnetting can be a part of a plan to increase the pri- vacy and security of a network.

So buy routers, become familiar with subnetting and start reaping the benefits. If none of the above convinces you that you must learn to subnet, how about this: At least until the advent of adaptive test- ing, three to 10 subnetting questions would be on a TCP/IP exam. Are you ready to pass the exam, missing *only* those questions?

The most common subnetting questions require selecting the appropriate subnet mask for a given organization, to identify which subnet a particular host is on or to identify and/or correct a bad subnet mask. To do these things quickly, you will need to study and practice with the material in this chapter.

Do I Need an IP Address? Where Do I Get One?

If you intend to access the Internet, whether from a single com- puter or on a network, you will need an IP address (at least tem- porarily). Even large organizations with numerous network segments can access the Internet through one IP address. A real router, or a computer configured as a router, is assigned one of the main IP addresses and becomes a *gateway* for the remainder of the network.

Ultimately, IP addresses come from InterNIC, the top organiza- tion that dispenses IP addresses and domains. InterNIC participates with other organizations in joint management of the Internet and helps regulate routing data and everything else on the Internet. You can visit InterNIC online at www.internic.com. IP addresses, however, are scarce commodities. In most cases, you will obtain an IP address from an *Internet Service Provider* (ISP), such as PrimeHost on America Online, Illuminati Online or Netcom, as shown in Table 4.1.

Table 4.1 Use this table to find an ISP that can supply IP addresses.

Internet Service Provider	WWW Address	IP Address
PSI.NET	www.psi.net	38.15.254.104
AOL.COM	www.primehost.com	152.163.210.52
UUNET.NET	www.uunet.net	199.170.0.30
IO.COM	www.io.com	199.170.88.11
MCI.NET	www.mci.net	204.70.133.140
ANS.NET	www.ans.net	204.151.55.184
AGIS.NET	www.agis.net	204.157.203.4
NETCOM.COM	www.netcom.com	206.217.29.10
DIGEX.NET	www.digex.net	207.87.16.114
BBN.COM	www.bbn.com	207.121.185.180
SPRINT.NET	www.sprint.net	208.27.196.10

If you are building an INTRANET, a network of computers that is never seen by the Internet, you can use any old IP addresses you want. Just be sure you choose a class with enough devices available per network. You can even use the official IP address for Microsoft, Coca-Cola or Xerox, or you can make up IP addresses. As long as you do not connect to the Internet, you can do any thing you want with your IP addresses. The rules of subnet masks may still apply, but as for classes and the rest, go for it.

Binary Math Refresher

For those who did not easily understand binary mathematics in Chapter 3, and for those who have not yet taken the time to practice binary-to-decimal conversions until you can do conversions with your eyes closed, this section marks our steps as we go along so we can find our way back. If you already have binary-to-decimal conversions built into your head, skip ahead now to *IP Address Classes*. If you later find the binary concepts are getting away from you, come back here to get clear on it again.

Binary Operations Are the Same as Base 10

Do you remember how you learned to multiply in grade school?

$0 \times 0 = 0$ $2 \times 1 = 2$ $5 \times 1 = 5$ $8 \times 1 = 8$

$0 \times 1 = 0$ $3 \times 1 = 3$ $6 \times 1 = 6$ $9 \times 1 = 9$

$1 \times 1 = 1$ $4 \times 1 = 4$ $7 \times 1 = 7$

Do you also remember learning addition?

$0 + 0 = 0$ $1 + 1 = 2$ $5 + 1 = 6$

 $2 + 1 = 3$ $6 + 1 = 7$

$0 + 1 = 1$ $3 + 1 = 4$ $7 + 1 = 8$

 $4 + 1 = 5$ $8 + 1 = 9$

You may not have realized it at the time, but while you were learning addition and multiplication in *Base 10*, you were also learning math in binary, *or Base 2*, because the same rules apply.

If you go back and remove all the Base 10 information that does not apply, you have the following: multiplication and addition in binary. Notice the rules are the same in binary. If you multiply anything by zero, you get zero. If you multiply 1×1, you get one. The same kind of correspondence happens in addition and subtraction.

$0 \times 0 = 0$ $0 \times 1 = 0$ $1 \times 1 = 1$

$0 + 0 = 0$ $0 + 1 = 1$

Carrying the Results

Now, let's take this one step farther.

In Base 10, we count using the 10 numbers 0, 1, 2, 3, 4, 5, 6, 7, 8 and 9. When the numbers are combined to create larger numbers, such as 9 + 1 = 10 or 19 + 2 = 21, we *carry* the results. Carrying the results means we use the higher place values to represent larger numbers.

Here is an example:

$$
\begin{array}{r}
9 \\
+\quad 1 \\
\hline
10
\end{array}
$$

In this example, the numbers are added and the one is carried.

In Base 10, numbers have places, so a number such as 1,000 is dissected like this:

Thousands	Hundreds	Tens	Ones
1	0	0	0

Each column represents a value. When a number is placed in a column, the value of the column is multiplied by the number. So, 1,000 equals a thousand units of something, and 222 equals 222 units of something.

Binary, or Base 2, is identical to Base 10 in the way numbers are represented by placement in columns. In binary, the columns are given their place values based on powers of two, just as Base 10 place values are based on powers of 10.

The only thing that changes is the value of the columns and the numbers that are used. The following table, Table 4.2, represents the values of the binary or Base 2 columns and how they would correlate to Base 10. This may not make sense immediately; however, you should recognize the Base 2 values in sequence. The Base 2 values are the same ones we mentioned that you should memorize in Chapter 3.

Table 4.2 Use this table as a comparison between Base 10 and Base 2 place values.

Base 10 - This is the value of each place in Base 10.							
10,000,000	1,000,000	100,000	10,000	1,000	100	10	1
Base 2 - This is the value of Base 2 places.							
128	64	32	16	8	4	2	1

Base 10 Place Values

A number such as 29,342,056 looks like this in Base 10:

10,000,000	1,000,000	100,000	10,000	1,000	100	10	1
2	9	3	4	2	0	5	6

In this example, each number in a column represents a value. Because there is a 2 in the 10,000,000 column, there are two times 10 million, or 20 million. In Base 10, therefore, the numbers would add up like this:

Column	Number	Actual value
10,000,000	2	20,000,000
1,000,000	9	9,000,000
100,000	3	300,000
10,000	4	40,000
1,000	2	2,000
100	0	0
10	5	50
1	6	6
		29,342,056

Naturally, when you look at a number, your mind does not go through all of this to multiply or add-because you have learned to think in Base 10. In understanding how our number system works, seeing how the principles apply to regular numbers we use every day is a crucial link to understanding other numbering systems, such as binary.

Binary Place Values

Now let's see how all of this applies to binary, or Base 2. Remember, Base 10 uses the numbers zero through nine.

Base 2 uses only the numbers zero and one. Remember, only zeroes and ones are allowed.

Let's say we are working with this number in Base 2: 11000011. Here is how it would look broken down into its appropriate place values:

Octet	1	1	0	0	0	0	1	1
Value	128	64	32	16	8	4	2	1

Now let's apply the same method we just used for calculating the values of this number in Base 10. So, the decimal value of 11000011 is 128 + 64 + 2 + 1, or put in another, possibly more familiar way:

Column	Number	Actual value
128	1	128
64	1	64
32	0	0
16	0	0
8	0	0
4	0	0
2	1	2
1	1	1
		195

Just as you added up the value of the columns in Base 10, you also add up the columns in Base 2. The binary number 11000011 has a decimal value of 195.

Now, assume each place in a Base 2 number is occupied, or 11111111.

Table 4.3   Each place in a binary octet has a defined value based on powers of two.

Octet	1	1	1	1	1	1	1	1
Value	128	64	32	16	8	4	2	1

Using the method above, add up the values of each column, or

```
128 + 64 + 32 + 16 + 8 + 4 + 2 + 1 = 255
```

The bits on the left side of the octet are called *higher order* bits, because they have higher place values. Bits on the right side are called *lower order* bits, because they have lower place values.

In the simplest explanation, subnet masks denote how many higher order bits are dedicated to the network ID and how many lower order bits are dedicated to the host IDs.

 Remember this fact: A binary octet of all ones, or 11111111, equals 255. By the end of the chapter, you will probably also want to memorize 254, 252, 248, 240, 224, 192, and 128—they form an easy-to-visualize pattern in binary, as shown in Table 4.4:

Table 4.4   These decimal values will appear throughout subnetting and this chapter.

Decimal Value	Binary Value
128	10000000
192	11000000
224	11100000
240	11110000
248	11111000
252	11111100
254	11111110
255	11111111

Binary Subtraction

One more illustration of binary mathematics will finish our refresher preparation. Binary subtraction is much the same as Base 10 subtraction. The hardest concept about regular Base 10 subtraction, as you may recall from second grade, is borrowing from the next larger column to fill values in the lower-valued columns. The same is true of binary math. We will not need binary subtraction until the end of the subnetting process, so do not be surprised if you have forgotten how it works by the time we have come around to binary subtraction again.

Remembering that in binary we may only use zeroes and ones, here are three binary subtraction examples. The first example, Table 4.5, is easy to comprehend because it looks familiar. Is the second example, Table 4.6, easy for you to visualize? This is how binary *borrowing from the next larger column* works.

Binary subtraction borrows from larger columns to the left, just like Base 10 subtraction.

Now, here's one last tougher example, Table 4.7, of binary subtraction, for those of you who *really* want to understand it. Look at the binary values in particular, to be sure you understand the pattern. Borrowing from the next larger column, to subtract, works about the same as in Base 10, correct?

That's the most complicated binary math we will need to explain subnetting. What a relief, right? This discussion of binary math has attempted to build the foundation for subnetting that you will need as you proceed through this chapter. It may leave you with unanswered questions now; however, the point is to understand the math elements. Full integration into subnetting will come soon.

At this point, it is a good idea to review what you have read so far until it is clear. Perhaps it would be a good idea to go back and practice the conversion examples in Table 3-6. If you are getting fuzzy, put the book down and do something else for a while or read something different. Then come back when you are ready to proceed with subnetting.

Table 4.5 Subtracting the second 32-bit address from the first 32-bit address yields the 32-bit address shown in the third row. It appears logical in both decimal and binary, right?

Subtraction	Decimal Value	Binary Value
	156.255.255.255	10011100.11111111.11111111.11111111
Minus 1	1	00000000.00000000.00000000.00000001
Result	156.255.255.254	10011100.11111111.11111111.11111110

Table 4.6 Subtracting the second 32-bit address from the first 32-bit address yields the 32-bit address shown in the third row. We borrowed from one leftward column.

Subtraction	Decimal Value	Binary Value
	156.255.255.254	10011100.11111111.11111111.11111110
Minus 1	1	00000000.00000000.00000000.00000001
Result	156.255.255.253	10011100.11111111.11111111.11111101

Table 4.7 This binary subtraction requires borrowing from the 13th column from the right.

Subtraction	Decimal Value	Binary Value
	223.247.48.0	11011111.11110111.00110000.00000000
Minus 1	1	00000000.00000000.00000000.00000001
Result	223.247.47.255	11011111.11110111.00101111.11111111

One More Time Through Binary to Decimal Conversion

Again, if you have already got binary to decimal conversion smooth as silk from Chapter 3, great. Skip forward to *IP Address Classes*.

Remember the example of an IP address we used in the beginning of this chapter? It was 150.100.0.1. A bit is the smallest unit of a binary IP address, because a bit can have the value of either one or zero. In the address 150.100.0.1, the binary notation is:

Table 4.8 This chapter displays all calculations in both decimal and binary.

Decimal Value	Binary Value
150.100.0.1	10010110.01100100.00000000.00000001

In TCP/IP IP addressing, we will use 32-bit binary addressing. That means we will use four of the 8-bit binary address groups instead of one. Each 8-bit binary address is called an *octet,* which by no coincidence means a group of eight. Each IP address is composed of four octets.

So back to our example. We must convert the IP address 150.100.0.1 and put it into binary address slots. In effect, we will work in reverse by figuring out how each octet translates to its corresponding 8-bit binary address.

In other words, if we are working with 150, which binary slots add up to 150?

Table 4.9 An 8-bit binary number is evaluated by its place values to convert it to decimal.

Octet	1	0	0	1	0	1	1	0
Value	128	64	32	16	8	4	2	1

The answer is $128 + 16 + 4 + 2 = 150$. This binary method can represent any decimal number from zero to 255 with a single binary octet, because eight bits of binary are needed to write those numbers. If we had nine bits to work with, we could write more numbers, but we do not have nine bits.

The same process is then repeated for each of the remaining octets until all are translated:

Table 4.10   Four 8-bit binary addresses become a 32-bit binary address.

Decimal Value	Binary Value
150.100.0.1	10010110.01100100.00000000.00000001

So How Does All of This Apply to TCP/IP Subnetting?

You must be able to quickly and easily think in binary numbers to dispatch the subnetting questions on the TCP/IP exam, so that you can proceed to the other questions and obtain a passing score. At least until the advent of adaptive testing, the subnetting portion of the exam required simple binary math, reliance on pre-calculated, memorized tables or magical rituals not covered here.

The recommended procedure is to be so familiar with subnetting that you can easily analyze and rectify an incorrect subnet mask, locate the proper subnet for a particular host IP number and assign a satisfactory subnet mask that provides the requisite number of host addresses and subnetworks.

The most basic elements of the subnetting process are the IP address classes, so we now progress to a review of the important features of IP addresses.

IP Address Classes

By now you are familiar with the appearance of an IP address. Consisting of four octets, it is a series of Base 10 numbers that represent a binary address. Here is the IP address we have been using as an example: 150.100.0.1.

Historically, IP addresses have been distinguished by their class. This is certainly what the exam expects. The class of the IP address is determined by the *first* octet. IP addresses always use at least the first octet as a network ID. As the numeric value of an IP address increases, it changes the class and determines how many octets are used for network IDs and how many are used for host IDs (see Table 4.11).

Table 4.11 The IP address classes are the key to understanding TCP/IP subnetting.

Class	Subnet Mask	Range for address range values (n) in first octet	Possible Networks Available	Range for Host values (h)	Possible Hosts Available	Network IP
Class A (n.h.h.h)	255.0.0.0	1 - 126	126 using one octet (n)	0.0.1 through 255.255.254	16,777,214	001.0.0.1 through 126.255.255.254
Class B (n.n.h.h)	255.255.0.0	128 - 191	16,384 using two octets (n.n)	0.1 through 255.254	65,534	128.0.0.1 through 191.255.255.254
Class C (n.n.n.h)	255.255.255.0	192 - 223	2,097,152 using three octets (n.n.n)	1 through 254	254	192.0.0.1 through 223.255.255.254

Read on for an explanation about what each of these class identifications mean.

What Is a Subnet Mask?

A subnet mask is a filter. The subnet mask cuts down dramatically on the time it takes to resolve an IP address.

Theoretically, there might be another way data could find the IP address by searching every host on a network and/or subnet. But what if you were administering the network at Microsoft, and you were not using subnet masks? (Of course, you must use subnet masks, but for sake of example, assume you do not.) Without a subnet mask, the computer would not be able to distinguish between local and remote hosts.

Every time you, or a user from anywhere in the world, select a hyperlink to a Microsoft Web page, it tells a computer to search for an IP address and bring back data from the computer using that IP address. The search string of data you send would then travel via the telephone lines and Internet links to Microsoft and begin its search for the remote Web server IP address.

Without subnet masking, *each* computer at Microsoft, for instance, might have to be contacted until a match is found. You might luck out and get a quick match early in the process. But what if Microsoft has 500,000 computers? You might as well go make dinner and hopefully, when you get back, you or one of the other 50 million users around the world might make contact.

Obviously, this is an exaggeration. By applying a subnet mask, however, the path to the computer with your target IP address only travels along a minimal number of routers and computers-instead of 500,000. With a subnet mask, each router along the way says, "No, the IP address you are looking for is not here," or "Yes, that IP address is on this subnet. Come on in, because the computer you want is on one of my subnets."

Default subnet masks for the standard IP address classes are shown in Table 4.12.

Table 4.12 Each class has its own default subnet mask. Note the patterns in the decimal and binary numbers.

Address Class	Decimal Value of Subnet Mask	Binary Value of Subnet Mask
A	255.0.0.0	11111111.00000000.00000000.00000000
B	255.255.0.0	11111111.11111111.00000000.00000000
C	255.255.255.0	11111111.11111111.11111111.00000000

 The default subnet mask is applied when there is no subnetting. It is required simply because there must be some subnet value to apply to the IP addresses on that network.

Understanding the Difference Between a Host ID and a Network ID

The previous section on IP Address Classes explained how IP addresses are constructed. Assuming the default subnet mask in each class, a portion of the IP address is reserved for the network ID and a portion of the IP address is reserved for the host computer ID.

You must commit to memory this rule:

You cannot alter the network ID portion of an IP address.

The network ID portion is represented by *n*. Only the host ID can be configured by subnetting. IP addresses, in terms of network and host IDs, are expressed in the following ways, using *n* for network and *h* for host:

Class A = n.h.h.h
Class B = n.n.h.h
Class C = n.n.n.h

Therefore, if you have a Class A IP address, only the last three octets can be potentially used for subnetting, and you must leave two or more bits on the right-hand side for host IDs.

Here is an example of a Class A IP address: 75.2.2.254. The host portion can be modified for subnetting. The Network ID is fixed and cannot be modified.

Table 4.13   For the TCP/IP exam, learn to see the network ID and host ID in every IP address.

IP Address	Network Portion	Host Portion	Network ID	Host ID
75.2.2.254	75.	2.2.254	75.0.0.0	2.2.254

Here is an example of a Class B IP address, using our example of 150.100.0.4. The host ID portion can be modified for subnetting. The Network ID is fixed and cannot be modified.

Table 4.14   Every IP address has both a network ID and a host ID.

IP Address	Network Portion	Host Portion	Network ID	Host ID
150.100.0.4	150.100	0.4	150.100.0.0	0.4

Remember, the number of bits in the network portion and host portion change based on the IP class-A, B, or C.

And finally, here is an example using a Class C IP address: 200.100.100.1. The host ID can be modified for subnetting. The network ID is fixed and cannot be modified.

Table 4.15   Network IDs end in zero to leave bits for the network hosts.

IP Address	Network Portion	Host Portion	Network ID	Host ID
200.100.100.1	200.100.100	.1	200.100.100.0	.1

ANDing (Local Traffic or Not Local Traffic)

TCP/IP subnetting applies a fancy name to binary multiplication called *ANDing*. It is generally done vertically as opposed to horizontal multiplication,

$$0 \times 0 = 0 \qquad 0 \times 1 = 0 \qquad 1 \times 1 = 1$$

but the rules are the same.

As it is used in TCP/IP, the subnet mask distinguishes between addresses that are on the *same network* and addresses on another network. ANDing helps accomplish this process.

Applying the subnet mask occurs when a client computer, on a subnet that is running TCP/IP, is started. In essence, the IP address tells the computer or device who it is, and the ANDing process tells the computer using TCP/IP which network it occupies.

Table 4.16 demonstrates ANDing with the Class C default subnet mask and the IP address 200.100.100.1. To *and* these two 32-bit binary rows, multiply each bit in the top row by the corresponding bit in the second row, as shown in Table 4.16.

 We already have mentioned that the subnet mask acts like a filter. Now we will demonstrate how to apply a mask to an IP address. *When you assign an IP address, you must also assign a subnet mask.*

When there is no subnetting on a network, the *default subnet mask* is automatically assigned. In binary form, the default Class B subnet mask for our example of IP address 150.100.0.1 looks like Table 4.17.

When a subnet mask is applied to an IP address, the ANDing process is used. Remember, this is nothing more than binary multiplication of each corresponding bit (see Table 4.18).

Notice when the default subnet mask is ANDed with a regular Class B IP address, everything is converted to zeroes except the first two octets, which returns the value of the network ID of 150.100.0.0. The default subnet mask, designed for a Class B IP address, defines the *network portion of the IP address*. The subnet mask allows a network device to discover what network it is part of, or the network to which it is *local* (see Table 4.18).

Let's say that again, in a different way. Upon initialization, because the IP address is 150.100.0.1 and the subnet mask is 255.255.0.0, a TCP/IP-savvy device knows two things:

- It is part of a regular Class B network, with no subnetting-because the *default* Class B subnet mask is used with an address in the Class B range.

- The local device is 150.100.0.1, and the local network is 150.100.0.0.

Table 4.16 Remember, the binary rules are 0 x 0 = 0, 0 x 1 = 0 and 1 x 1 = 1.

ANDing	Decimal Value	Binary Value
Default Mask	255.255.255.0	11111111.11111111.11111111.00000000
AND	200.100.100.1	11001000.01100100.01100100.00000001
Result	200.100.100.0	11001000.01100100.01100100.00000000

Table 4.17 If no subnet mask is supplied, the default subnet mask is implied.

Decimal Value	Binary Value
IP Address	150.100.0.1	10010110.01100100.00000000.00000001
Default Mask	255.255.0.0	11111111.11111111.00000000.00000000

Table 4.18 ANDing reveals the network ID.

ANDing	Decimal Value	Binary Value
Default Mask	255.255.0.0	11111111.11111111.00000000.00000000
AND	150.100.0.1	10010110.01100100.00000000.00000001
Result	150.100.0.0	10010110.01100100.00000000.00000000

ANDing the IP address with its subnet mask exposes the network portion of the IP address. If the network portion of the IP address is not a local network, routers (and other network computers and devices) know to send the data elsewhere, usually to a default gateway or another router.

So What Happens when a Network Is Subnetted and the *Default* Subnet Mask Is Not Used?

Instead of the default subnet mask, a subnet mask is selected *specifically for use on that network*. When TCP/IP initializes, the specially created subnet mask and the IP address are ANDed and cached in memory on the local computer, becoming a *network identifier* (network ID) for that device.

 When a router receives data destined for an IP address, the requested IP address is ANDed with the network's subnet mask and the result is compared to the router's cached network ID. If they match, the router knows it is the local router of the IP address sought. If not, the router sends the data to another network (router), where the same process is repeated until a match is found.

Before moving on, let's take a few moments to apply a different IP address to the local cache from the ANDing in Table 4.18 to see if they match. This will allow us to see how the local cache determines whether the router should send data to a local network, host, or to another router.

This method is used to determine whether an IP address is local or remote. Let's say the incoming data is for IP address 200.100.100.101, with a default subnet mask of 255.255.255.0. Remember, we are comparing a device's network ID that represents the cached results obtained in Table 4.18. If the device with IP address 150.100.0.1 and subnet mask 255.255.0.0 (on network 150.100.0.0) receives incoming data for 200.100.100.101, it does not recognize the target network ID as a match and does not see the packet addressed to the local computer or local network.

Table 4.19 This packet is destined for network ID 200.100.100.0.

ANDing	Decimal Value	Binary Value
Default Mask	255.255.255.0	11111111.11111111.11111111.00000000
AND	200.100.100.101	11001000.01100100.01100100.01100101
Result	200.100.100.0	11001000.01100100.01100100.00000000

Table 4.20 If a packet is not for a local network, a router sends the packet to another router.

Local Test	Decimal Value	Binary Value
Cached Network ID	150.100.0.0	10010110.01100100.00000000.00000000
Target Network ID	200.100.100.0	11001000.01100100.01100100.00000000
Result	No Match	No Match

If this were the local network, the results would match. This time, however, they do not, meaning the target IP address is somewhere else, on a different network.

Notice the difference between the first octets in both examples. TCP/IP knows the local network is 150.100.0.0 because the cached results, its unique *network identifier*, were created when TCP/IP initialized. In this instance of ANDing, the previously cached results must match the current results for the IP address to be local.

The bits for 200.100.100.101 return an ANDing result of 11001000. 01100100.01100100.00000000 , compared to 10010110.01100100.00000000. 00000000 for 150.100.0.0. The different results tell TCP/IP that the local network does not contain 200.100.100.101—so this packet must be sent on to another router.

With the information that the target IP address does not match the local network ID, packets are moved on toward another router to perform the same ANDing process, until the network portions of the ANDing results are identical.

A subnet of 255.255.255.255 is considered a *broadcast* IP address, because in binary it is composed of all ones, 11111111. 11111111.11111111.11111111. ANDing all ones to an IP address returns the same value (same IP address) as the result of the ANDing. ANDing all zeroes to an IP address gives a result of all zeroes.

So, you should now see that subnet masks are necessary partners with IP addresses. Without a subnet mask, IP addresses are ambiguous and meaningless. With a subnet mask, an IP address is precise and powerfully meaningful.

Borrowing Bits to Make Subnets

The term *bit* is important to understanding subnetting. Remember, IP addresses are 32-bit binary numbers. With IP addresses, we have only 32 bits to work with to describe all aspects of the network and host computer, so that messages can find one computer in the forest of other computers.

During the next section, we introduce the idea of borrowing bits from the host portion of an IP address to create a subnet mask.

How are you doing so far? The next section brings all of this full-circle. You are almost done with understanding subnetting. If you need a break, however, this is a good place to take one.

Determining the Number of Hosts and Networks

This formula, 2^n-2 = *number of hosts*, is used as a shortcut to help you determine the number of hosts or networks you need. The n is the number of borrowed bits needed to subnet (enumerate) the network.

Memorize this formula. You will need to refer to it often.

```
2ⁿ - 2 = number of hosts
2ⁿ - 2 = number of networks
```

Let's practice by taking an example: $2^2-2 = 2$

When a number is raised, such as 2^2 in this example, it is called an *exponent*. For 2^2 it means multiply 2×2. If this were 2^3, it would mean to multiply $2 \times 2 \times 2$, which equals 8.

What is really going on here is that we are making sure we have enough bits to write all the numbers required to describe the network and each of the computers on the network. If we ran out of bits, we would be limiting ourselves to fewer host IDs or fewer networks than are really needed-so we plan in advance to have enough bits to write all the binary numbers necessary, using only the subnet and host portions of the 32-bit binary numbers we call IP addresses.

Now, here is what it means using a real-world example, similar to something you might see on the TCP/IP exam:

Given: You are the system administrator for a medium-size network. Recently, you added Internet access and created a Web site, using the IP address of 150.100.0.1. After a proper needs analysis and consultation with your colleagues, the decision is made to subnet the network using the single network ID: 150.100.0.0.

Proposed Solution: Subnet the network. After planning for growth, you will require a minimum of 20 subnets and a maximum of 30. You may encounter a scenario somewhat like this on the test. So let's find the solution now, step-by-step.

First, after reading the problem and proposed solution, we must determine what is really being asked. The real question is how to subnet a network with at least 20 subnets. So we apply the formula:

```
2ⁿ - 2 = 20
```

We insert the value 20 here because we know we must have *at least* 20 subnetworks. Now we need a rough and ready solution for the value of *n*.

The next step is a rapid process of elimination, which you will surely memorize soon, shown in Table 4.21.

Table 4.21 Memorizing the powers of two up through 10 or 15 makes this step easier.

Power of 2	Multiplication	Product	2	= Hosts Available (Comment)
2	2 x 2 =	4	-2	= 2
3	2 x 2 x 2 =	8	-2	= 6
4	2 x 2 x 2 x 2 =	16	-2	= 14 *(no good, less than 20 hosts.)*
5	2 x 2 x 2 x 2 x 2 =	32	-2	= 30 *(too many, but enough—just right)*
6	2 x 2 x 2 x 2 x 2 x 2 =	64	-2	= 62 *(way more hosts than required)*

So we see $2^5 - 2 = 30$ is the best fit because we need 30 or fewer subnets. We also see 2^4 only gives us 16 subnets, which is too few. And 2^6 yields triple the requirement.

Next, we take the default subnet mask for the Class B IP address we are subnetting, shown in Table 4.22.

And we start *borrowing* host bits from the left edge of the host portion of the address to define our new subnets. Remember, the ones in a subnet mask define the network portion of IP addresses when they are ANDed with the IP address, and zeroes mask out the host portion of the IP address so only the network is seen. We are creating new subnetwork IDs out of former host bits, by placing ones in the subnet mask where there were zeroes before. *Following the network ID portion, which cannot be changed,* start changing zeroes to ones from the left of the first (left) octet in the *host* portion of the subnet mask, as in Table 4.23.

Table 4.22 All binary subnet representations must begin from the default subnet mask.

Class B	Decimal Value	Binary Value
Default Mask	255.255.000.000	11111111.11111111.00000000.00000000

Table 4.23 Note the patterns in the number of bits used and the decimal and binary values.

Class B Masks	Decimal Value	Binary Value
Default Mask	255.255.000.0	11111111.11111111.00000000.00000000
1 Bit New Mask	255.255.128.0	11111111.11111111.10000000.00000000
2 Bit New Mask	255.255.192.0	11111111.11111111.11000000.00000000
3 Bit New Mask	255.255.224.0	11111111.11111111.11100000.00000000
4 Bit New Mask	255.255.240.0	11111111.11111111.11110000.00000000
5 Bit New Mask	255.255.248.0	11111111.11111111.11111000.00000000
6 Bit New Mask	255.255.252.0	11111111.11111111.11111100.00000000
7 Bit New Mask	255.255.254.0	11111111.11111111.11111110.00000000
8 Bit New Mask	255.255.255.0	11111111.11111111.11111111.00000000

Notice that the third octet of the new binary subnet masks looks a little like Table 4.4.

Table 4.24 This is a useful table to memorize.

Decimal Value	Binary Value	Borrowed Bits
128	10000000	1
192	11000000	2
224	11100000	3
240	11110000	4
248	11111000	5
252	11111100	6
254	11111110	7
255	11111111	8

For additional network IDs (subnetwork IDs), borrow bits from left to right, filling in ones where there were zeroes, adding zeroes to the remainder of the host portion of the 32 bits to create a new, subnetted network mask.

In creating network IDs, bits are borrowed from the first host octet. Start with the first bit on the left of the first host octet. Notice when you create subnetwork IDs, the borrowed bits are filled in with ones, expanding the network (and subnetwork) portion while the remainder of the host portion remains masked with zeroes.

Remember, the network portion cannot be changed. Also remember when you are borrowing bits, *the octet you begin borrowing from* depends upon the Class ID of the subnet mask with which you begin.

Notice in the example (Table 4.23) that after the bits are borrowed, the remaining bits of the octet are filled in with zeroes to create a new, subnetted network mask.

Table 4.25 Borrow bits according to the Class ID of the subnet mask. In this example, begin borrowing with the *italic octet*, starting with the first bit in italics and working left to right.

	Default Subnet Mask	Binary Address with initial octet to borrow host bits from to create subnets from in italic
Class A	255.0.0.0	11111111.*00000000.00000000.00000000*
Class B	255.255.0.0	11111111.11111111.*00000000.00000000*
Class C	255.255.255.0	11111111.11111111.11111111.*00000000*

After borrowing the bits and converting the binary address to decimal, you have a new subnet mask. So let's calculate that decimal value:

In Table 4.26, we first evaluate the revised third octet in the new subnet mask.

Table 4.26 The sum of the place values for this octet is 128+64+32+16+8 = 248.

Octet	1	1	1	1	1	0	0	0
Value	128	64	32	16	8	4	2	1

With five borrowed host bits for subnetting, the remainder of the octet is zeroes, for masking the remaining host bits.

Table 4.27 After we have borrowed five host bits from the Class B subnet mask, there are still 11 host bits remaining.

Decimal Value	Binary Value
255.255.248.0	1111111.11111111.11111000.00000000

We borrowed bits from available host IDs. Next we must calculate the decimal value of the new subnet mask by adding *that portion of the octet that was borrowed,* which is 128, 64, 32, 16 and 8.

$$128$$

$$64$$

$$32$$

$$16$$

$$\underline{+\ 8}$$

$$248$$

So, the new subnet mask is `255.255.248.0`.

Before continuing, take a good look at what happened to this subnet mask. Remember, we are working with a Class B default subnet mask of `255.255.0.0`, and we are now subnetting with one octet of previous host bits-now subnet bits. When we create subnetwork IDs *using only one host octet* of a Class B network, the third octet is modified for subnetwork IDs and the fourth octet remains masked for host IDs, as shown in Table 4.28.

Although it is not on the TCP/IP exam, it is also entirely possible to keep right on subnetting into the fourth octet. You must reserve at least two bits for hosts, but if you want to subnet eight bits from the third octet and six more bits from the fourth octet, it is possible, as shown in Table 4.29.

With 14 bits of subnet masking, there are $2^{14} = 16{,}384$ subnetworks available from this Class B network, with *only* two host computer IP addresses available on each subnet. The reason we can only have two IP addresses on each subnet is because there are only two bits left to enumerate the host IDs. With only two bits, only two hosts can be identified:

```
00   Invalid host address
01   Host #1
10   Host #2
11   Invalid host address
```

Table 4.28 Class B third octet subnets, shown with their bit cost or value.

Default Mask	255.255.0.0	11111111.11111111.00000000.00000000
I Bit New Mask	255.255.128.0	11111111.11111111.10000000.00000000
2 Bit New Mask	255.255.192.0	11111111.11111111.11000000.00000000
3 Bit New Mask	255.255.224.0	11111111.11111111.11100000.00000000
4 Bit New Mask	255.255.240.0	11111111.11111111.11110000.00000000
5 Bit New Mask	255.255.248.0	11111111.11111111.11111000.00000000
6 Bit New Mask	255.255.252.0	11111111.11111111.11111100.00000000
7 Bit New Mask	255.255.254.0	11111111.11111111.11111110.00000000
8 Bit New Mask	255.255.255.0	11111111.11111111.11111111.00000000

Table 4.29 These extended Class B subnet masks are not in some of the other subnetting tables.

9-Bit New Mask	255.255.255.128	11111111.11111111.11111111.10000000
10-Bit New Mask	255.255.255.192	11111111.11111111.11111111.11000000
11-Bit New Mask	255.255.255.224	11111111.11111111.11111111.11100000
12-Bit New Mask	255.255.255.240	11111111.11111111.11111111.11110000
13-Bit New Mask	255.255.255.248	11111111.11111111.11111111.11111000
14-Bit New Mask	255.255.255.252	11111111.11111111.11111111.11111100

So, Where Do I Get My New Host IP Addresses?

That is what this is all about, right? We were subnetting network 150.100.0.0. All we got out of it so far, however, is a new 5-bit subnet mask of 255.255.248.0. Well, not quite.

Now, let's figure out what you get for all of your work and how you apply it in the real world. First, we will perform an intermediary step, and then we will calculate the new subnetted host IDs for our 150.100.0.0 network. The intermediary step is to find the subnet IDs for the new subnetted network. Knowing the subnet IDs is not useful itself, but knowing the subnet IDs does get us close to knowing the actual subnet host IDs available on the network. So let's figure the subnet IDs.

You should now focus on the five bits that were borrowed at the beginning of the first host octet, as shown in Table 4.30.

Table 4.30 Five host bits were borrowed to create space for enumeration of subnets.

Decimal Value	Binary Value
255.255.248.0	1111111.11111111.11111000.00000000

After determining the number of bits to borrow, return to the *subnet mask* to complete the task of divvying up the actual network IP addresses on the subnets. Use the remaining host bits that were not used in the subnet mask to enumerate the host IDs available.

What is really going on here? If you are still having trouble understanding the concept of subnetting, then think of it as dividing the IP class address ranges even further into mini-classes. In essence, that is exactly what you are doing. You are creating a custom mini-class IP address range that only a specific network will use.

What subnetting really does is create another level of description between the network portion of the IP number and the host portion of the number. Here is an example:

Table 4.31   Subnet IDs are created from borrowed (or sacrificed) host bits.

Network ID	Subnet ID	Host ID
150.100.0.0	0.0.248.	0.0.1

So let's go back to that subnet mask and those five borrowed host bits:

Table 4.32   Five host bits were borrowed to create the subnets.

Decimal Value	Binary Value
255.255.248.0	1111111.11111111.11111000.00000000

Take the first host octet out and manually create all of the possible 5-bit subnet ID combinations you can imagine, with those five borrowed bits on the network side of the octet, as shown in Table 4.33.

So, after we throw out two invalid networks (the all zeroes and all ones combinations), it is clear that the new subnetwork space created by a 5-bit subnet mask can be used to write at most 30 different subnet IDs.

Now, to find the subnet IDs we have all been waiting for, we put each of these combinations back into the octet and *translate the whole octet* to decimal numbers using our binary translator, as shown in Tables 4.34, 4.35, 4.36 and 4.37.

You see what is happening-the octet's value is increasing by eight each time we re-calculate with the next binary combination of five bits. The change in value from one subnet to the next is exactly eight each time. This consistent, incremental change value is also called a *delta*, because it represents the successive change from one subnet ID value to the next.

Obviously, it could take a long time to figure out all of the possible combinations of zeroes and ones, especially if you borrow more than five bits. There is an easier way to enumerate the new subnet IDs, however. Notice how each of the combinations above increase in increments by eight. Now, look again at the subnet mask of 255.255.248.0 as shown in Table 4.38.

Table 4.33 Write down all the possible combinations of the borrowed bits. With six or more borrowed bits, use the shortcut explained next.

							All Possible Binary Combinations of five bits	
Binary Value	Decimal Value	Binary Value	Decimal Value	Binary Value	Decimal Value	Binary Value	Decimal Value	
00000	0	01000	8	10000	16	11000	24	
00001	1	01001	9	10001	17	11001	25	
00010	2	01010	10	10010	18	11010	26	
00011	3	01011	11	10011	19	11011	27	
00100	4	01100	12	10100	20	11100	28	
00101	5	01101	13	10101	21	11101	29	
00110	6	01110	14	10110	22	11110	30	
00111	7	01111	15	10111	23	11111	31	

Table 4.34   The sum of the place values for this octet is 8 = 8.

Octet	0	0	0	0	1	0	0	0
Value	128	64	32	16	8	4	2	1

Table 4.35   The sum of the place values for this octet is 16 = 16.

Octet	0	0	0	1	0	0	0	0
Value	128	64	32	16	8	4	2	1

Table 4.36   The sum of the place values for this octet is 16+8 = 24.

Octet	0	0	0	1	1	0	0	0
Value	128	64	32	16	8	4	2	1

Table 4.37   The sum of the place values for this octet is 32 = 32.

Octet	0	0	1	0	0	0	0	0
Value	128	64	32	16	8	4	2	1

Table 4.38   Focus on the lowest-order (last) borrowed bit. Observe the decimal value of that bit.

Decimal Value	Binary Value
255.255.248.0	11111111.11111111.11111000.00000000

Notice the last bit borrowed for the new subnet mask is in the 8 slot of the third binary octet. The increment value we just observed is eight, and the place value of the lowest-order bit in the subnet IDs is also eight. This is the key to a quick rule of thumb for knowing how much to increment new subnet IDs. After creating a new subnet mask, look at the *last bit* used in the subnet mask, before the zeroes. The place value of this bit is always the first subnet's ID and the incremental delta between subnet IDs. This shortcut will save you the time of combining all those ones and zeroes.

Enumerate the Subnet IDs

Essentially, just start counting from the first increment value (*not zero*). In this case, begin with eight. The available subnet IDs are 8, 16, 24, 32, 40 and so on, up to the 30th subnet ID of 240. These subnet IDs may be written as follows:

Available Subnet IDs

0.0.8.

0.0.16.

0.0.24.

0.0.32.

0.0.40., and so on.

Now, let's do it for real.

Here are the new IP addresses on each of 30 subnets after borrowing five bits from 255.255.0.0, the default subnet mask of network 150.100.0.0. Remember that addresses of all zeroes and all ones are reserved.

Start with the network ID you are subnetting: 150.100.0.0. Table 4.39 shows all the subnet IDs.

Notice that the subnetwork IDs become obscured, because within this subnet the third octet does not remain the same. For example, on network 150.100.0.0, the subnetwork 0.0.8 contains not just IP numbers like 150.100.8.245 that are obviously part of subnetwork 0.0.8., but also IP numbers such as 150.100.12.12 and 150.100.14.170. Within a single subnet, the host bits in the higher-order octet (in this case the third octet) increment each time the fourth octet reaches 255, so the host IDs must be displayed in two octets, such as 8.237 or 32.195. The host bits in the higher-order octet are changing to increase the decimal number in the third octet. The subnet ID is not changing within the subnet.

Table 4.39 Network 150.100.0.0 has 30 subnets with a subnet mask of 255.255.248.0.

Subnet host IDs for network 150.100.0.0 *subnetted with five bits of host IDs for a subnet mask of* 255.255.248.0, *or* 11111111.11111111.11111000.00000000

Decimal Address—First IP Address to Last IP Address	Binary Address—First IP Address to Last IP Address
150.100.8.1 to 150.100.15.254	10010110.01100100.00001000.00000001 to 10010110.01100100.00001111.11111110
150.100.16.1 to 150.100.23.254	10010110.01100100.00010000.00000001 to 10010110.01100100.00010111.11111110
150.100.24.1 to 150.100.31.254	10010110.01100100.00011000.00000001 to 10010110.01100100.00011111.11111110
150.100.32.1 to 150.100.39.254	10010110.01100100.00100000.00000001 to 10010110.01100100.00100111.11111110
150.100.40.1 to 150.100.47.254	10010110.01100100.00101000.00000001 to 10010110.01100100.00101111.11111110
150.100.48.1 to 150.100.55.254	10010110.01100100.00110000.00000001 to 10010110.01100100.00110111.11111110
150.100.56.1 to 150.100.63.254	10010110.01100100.00111000.00000001 to 10010110.01100100.00111111.11111110
150.100.64.1 to 150.100.71.254	10010110.01100100.01000000.00000001 to 10010110.01100100.01000111.11111110
150.100.72.1 to 150.100.79.254	10010110.01100100.01001000.00000001 to 10010110.01100100.01001111.11111110
150.100.80.1 to 150.100.87.254	10010110.01100100.01010000.00000001 to 10010110.01100100.01010111.11111110
150.100.88.1 to 150.100.95.254	10010110.01100100.01011000.00000001 to 10010110.01100100.01011111.11111110

Decimal Address—First IP Address to Last IP Address	Binary Address—First IP Address to Last IP Address
150.100.96.1 to 150.100.103.254	10010110.01100100.01100000.00000001 to 10010110.01100100.01100111.11111110
150.100.104.1 to 150.100.111.254	10010110.01100100.01101000.00000001 to 10010110.01100100.01101111.11111110
150.100.112.1 to 150.100.119.254	10010110.01100100.01110000.00000001 to 10010110.01100100.01110111.11111110
150.100.120.1 to 150.100.127.254	10010110.01100100.01111000.00000001 to 10010110.01100100.01111111.11111110
150.100.128.1 to 150.100.135.254	10010110.01100100.10000000.00000001 to 10010110.01100100.10000111.11111110
150.100.136.1 to 150.100.143.254	10010110.01100100.10001000.00000001 to 10010110.01100100.10001111.11111110
150.100.144.1 to 150.100.151.254	10010110.01100100.10010000.00000001 to 10010110.01100100.10010111.11111110
150.100.152.1 to 150.100.159.254	10010110.01100100.10011000.00000001 to 10010110.01100100.10011111.11111110
150.100.160.1 to 150.100.167.254	10010110.01100100.10100000.00000001 to 10010110.01100100.10100111.11111110
150.100.168.1 to 150.100.175.254	10010110.01100100.10101000.00000001 to 10010110.01100100.10101111.11111110
150.100.176.1 to 150.100.183.254	10010110.01100100.10110000.00000001 to 10010110.01100100.10110111.11111110
150.100.184.1 to 150.100.191.254	10010110.01100100.10111000.00000001 to 10010110.01100100.10111111.11111110
150.100.192.1 to 150.100.199.254	10010110.01100100.11000000.00000001 to 10010110.01100100.11000111.11111110

continues

Table 4.39 Continued

Subnet host IDs for network 150.100.0.0 *subnetted with five bits of host IDs for a subnet mask of* 255.255.248.0, *or* 11111111.11111111.11111000.00000000

Decimal Address—First IP Address to Last IP Address	Binary Address—First IP Address to Last IP Address
150.100.200.1 to 150.100.207.254	10010110.01100100.11001000.00000001 to 10010110.01100100.11001111.11111110
150.100.208.1 to 150.100.215.254	10010110.01100100.11010000.00000001 to 10010110.01100100.11010111.11111110
150.100.216.1 to 150.100.223.254	10010110.01100100.11011000.00000001 to 10010110.01100100.11011111.11111110
150.100.224.1 to 150.100.231.254	10010110.01100100.11100000.00001111 to 10010110.01100100.11100111.11111110
150.100.232.1 to 150.100.239.254	10010110.01100100.11101000.00000001 to 10010110.01100100.11101111.11111110
150.100.240.1 to 150.100.247.254	10010110.01100100.11110000.00000001 to 10010110.01100100.11110111.11111110

Table 4.40 All ones or all zeroes in the host portion of a binary IP address indicate an invalid host ID.

	Decimal Value	Binary Value
Invalid Host	150.100.0.0	10010110.01100100.00000000.00000000
Invalid Host	150.100.247.255	10010110.01100100.11110111.11111111

Of course, the decimal numbers 150.100.0.0 and 150.100.248.255 cannot be used as host IDs, because they represent all ones or zeroes in the host portion of the address when written in binary form, as shown in Table 4.40.

The address with all zeroes in the host portion is this subnet's ID and means *only this network*. The address with all ones in the host portion is the broadcast address for this subnet. Losing these two IP addresses is why the formula $2^n - 2 = hosts$ subtracts two. Every subnet must have a subnet ID of its own and a broadcast address, also. In this subnetting example, just 30 subnets are created, not 32.

For those of you who remember your binary addition and subtraction from earlier in this chapter, a shortcut method is also available for finding the actual host IDs on each subnet. The first host on each subnet is one more than the all-zeroes subnetwork ID number. The last host on each subnet is one less than the all-ones broadcast address for that subnet. And the all-ones broadcast address is one less than the next subnetwork ID number. Because most people are not ready to perform binary subtraction on a daily basis, use this shortcut only if you stay sharp on your binary math rules-or if you use the Windows calculator in scientific view.

As mentioned, when a TCP/IP device is started, TCP/IP ANDs the subnet mask with the IP address to obtain the network ID and caches both the IP address and the local network ID. The result of the ANDing is established as the *local network*.

In this example, we pick one of the newly created subnet IDs to test whether the new subnet mask actually tells TCP/IP that an IP address on a subnet is local. Table 4.41 shows the ANDing of a host IP address with the new subnet mask to create the new *subnetted* network ID. Table 4.42 shows that the network portion of the new network ID still matches the old pre-subnetting network ID.

Notice the network portions of the results are identical, indicating that the target IP address, on a subnet of the original network, is still on the local network. The third octet differs, indicating a *subnet* of the local network contains the target IP address.

Table 4.41 This packet is destined for network ID `150.100.0.0`, subnet `0.0.8`.

ANDing	Decimal Value	Binary Value
Subnet Mask	255.255.248.0	11111111.11111111.11111000.00000000
AND	150.100.8.217	10010110.01100100.00001000.11011001
Result	150.100.8.0	10010110.01100100.00001000.00000000

Table 4.42 This packet is destined for a local network that contains a subnet. The `8.` subnet contains the target host.

Local Test	Decimal Value	Binary Value
Cached Network ID	150.100.0.0	10010110.01100100.00000000.00000000
Target Network ID	150.100.8.0	10010110.01100100.00001000.00000000
Result	Networks Match	Networks Match

The Subnet Mask in Action

To demonstrate how packets find their way to a destination host, let's assume a packet has arrived at the router like a lost tourist at Miami International Airport, looking for a way to get somewhere inside the United States. The packet arrives at the router with a Class B destination IP address of 148.126.16.50 and a subnet mask of 255.255.255.0. The packet has arrived at the right Class B network 148.126.0.0 but is looking for subnet 0.0.16., host 0.0.0.50.

Table 4.43 The Class B network 148.126.0.0 is subnetted with the 8-bit subnet mask 255.255.255.0.

IP Address	Network ID	Subnet ID	Host ID
148.126.16.50	148.126.0.0	0.0.16.	0.0.0.50

Of course, the router must know that subnet .16. exists, and this information is stored in its routing tables (see Chapter 5 for more on routing). In this case, subnet 0.0.16. can be reached by accessing a known router, behind which the host interface numbered 0.0.0.50 can be reached.

Now we must deal with the subnet mask. To make life a little easier, let's assume a subnet mask of 255.255.255.0 has been added to the routing tables of the gateway for network 148.126.0.0. (When you set up a computer to dial-up an ISP, 255.255.255.0 is usually the default Class C subnet mask you enter for Microsoft TCP/IP Networking.) In this case, the mask of 255.255.255.0 on a Class B (148.126.0.0) network tells the router it is on a Class B network, where 8-bits of host IDs have been reserved for the subnet IDs (allowing 254 subnets) and eight bits are available to be used for the host IDs (allowing 254 hosts).

Now a new packet arrives with the destination address 148.126.10.50. Notice the subnet ID is different from the earlier packet.

Table 4.44 Each subnet has its own subnet ID.

IP Address	Network ID	Subnet ID	Host ID
148.126.10.50	148.126.0.0	0.0.10.	0.0.0.50

IP routing makes the necessary decision and routes accordingly. The subnet mask of 255.255.255.0 tells IP routing that the octets numbered 255 are the network and subnetwork parts of the address, and the zero in the mask represents the host IDs. From the IP address and subnet mask, IP also knows that a maximum of 254 subnetworks (of up to 254 IP devices on each subnetwork) are available on network 148.126.0.0.

Steps to Subnet Success

In order to successfully subnet a network, there are five steps, in chronological order:

- Step 1: Do a needs analysis.
- Step 2: Select the optimal new subnet mask.
- Step 3: Calculate the new subnetwork IDs.
- Step 4: List the resulting host IDs for each new subnetwork.
- Step 5: Implement the subnet plan by changing all the settings on all the devices.

Step 1: Needs Analysis Highlights.

1.a. How many computer hosts will be required on the most populated segment?

1.b. How many subnets (segments) will the network contain?

With the address classes and their network IDs in hand, determine how many networks you need after subnetting and how many hosts you need on each network. This needs analysis, or synthesis, is an essential part of the subnetting exercise.

Once a particular network with all its supporting processes, such as DNS, e-mail, routers, firewalls and more, is in operation, you don't want to make major changes lightly. The threat of major network disruption can prevent both users and management from achieving their highest states of happiness.

Assess the business needs, goals and objectives, expansion plans and so on, of the organization. The two most important aspects of the needs analysis are finding out how many different subnets are needed and what the maximum number of hosts required on any one subnet will be. Whatever you need now, triple or quadruple it. If you have a Class B address space to play with, then triple it again.

Here is an example: As the Network Administrator of a social security division in your state, you find the payment-processing center currently employs 10 people. The state is growing, however, and the total workforce in payment-processing will soon exceed 30 warm bodies, probably within two years. You should plan to be able to address *not fewer than* 100 hosts over the lifetime of the payment-processing center. So, to leave room for unknown future growth, planning for the ability to address 254 hosts should be your goal. Also, you won't want to create a mini-net (subnet) that will leave you with the ability to address, say, only 62 hosts.

There is nothing worse than building an infrastructure to suit today's requirement, only to trash it a year down the road with a lot of pain and heartache. If you find the network ends up with far more host numbers than needed, you can always subnet the subnet.

Study the enterprise business plan, meet with the leaders and division heads and assure yourself and the IT/MIS department the result will suffice for many years (of course you need to take technology changes into account as well).

NETWORK PLANNING GUIDELINES

Find out where the users are located and how many are in each location. Investigate, baseline and monitor how much network traffic is generated at each location.

- Count *every* device that requires an IP address:
  - Workstations
  - Servers
  - Each router interface
  - Network printers (with their own NICs)
  - WAN links
- Place a backup domain controller on each subnet.
- Consider multi-homing servers that serve more than one subnet.
- Put similar users together on a single subnet and let them share data and resources. In other words, locate users on the same subnet with servers and other resources they need.

After you know the desired maximum number of hosts per segment, if there are two or more optional subnet masks that satisfy the required number of hosts, then use the subnet mask that provides the greatest number of subnets with an adequate number of hosts.

As you should recall from your Networking Essentials study, some common network designs (such as 10BaseT) are limited to slightly more than 1,000 hosts per segment—so huge segments of many thousands of hosts are not necessarily desirable, even if they are theoretically possible. And, as Heywood and Scrimger point out in their discussion of subnetting in *Networking with Microsoft TCP/IP*, you would not want to end up with segments of 2,046 hosts anyway, because there would be too much traffic on the segment. So allow for more segments, rather than fewer segments with more hosts per subnet.

Once you know what the maximum number of hosts required on any one subnet is and how many different subnets are needed, you are ready to move on to Step Two.

Step 2: Create a Subnet Mask.

Now, select the correct subnet mask to affect the subnetting scheme. Let's first look at a Class C address, because ISPs are chopping these up every day—and you may likely be dealing with a subnetted Class C on any given day of the week. Table 4.45 reminds us of some basic characteristics of Class C networks.

Let's use Class C network ID 209.214.220.0. Without subnetting, this Class C network can support up to 254 hosts like any other Class C network. By subnetting, we chop it up so a router can be placed between the subnet segments and route packets to more than one network (possibly serving two new customers who need only 62 hosts or fewer). So, let's try some subnetting options to see what happens.

As discussed earlier, the default subnet mask for a Class C address is 255.255.255.0. Converted to binary, this results in 11111111.11111111.11111111.00000000. The one bits here represent the network ID octets 209.214.220. So what the mask is telling you is that the zero representation on the final host ID octet means the full range of addresses can be used.

Table 4.45 Class C networks all begin with the most significant binary bits of 110 and use no more than the final (one) octet for host addressing.

Class C	Decimal IP Address Human Friendly Dotted Quad	Binary Equivalent of IP Address
First IP Address	192.000.000.001	11000000.00000000.00000000.00000001
Last IP Address	223.255.255.254	11011111.11111111.11111111.11111110
Default Mask	255.255.255.000	11111111.11111111.11111111.00000000

By subnetting, we now must tell IP we want to split the network. The new mask will dictate the new maximum number of hosts that can be addressed on each resulting subnetwork, how to route to it with the subnetwork ID and exactly how many subnetworks may use that same network ID. To do this, we need to borrow bits from the fourth host octet. Borrowing host bits to create subnets, as mentioned in Chapter 3, has the effect of shrinking the available number of hosts on the network.

Adding all ones to the octet results in a broadcast address that may not be used to enumerate a host. When we borrow only two bits from the host portion, however, we are left with a new network mask of 255.255.255.192, or 11111111.11111111.11111111.11000000 (remembering our binary math, that is 128 + 64 = 192).

Well, two bits are not much to work with. We have only two bits to write the subnet IDs for our new network, and there are not many subnets you can write with only two bits. Two bits can be combined in only four ways, and two of those are invalid:

11 Invalid

01 Subnet #1

10 Subnet #2

00 Invalid

To determine the maximum number of subnets that result, we will perform a calculation of the bits available to describe the subnet. The formula for the calculation is two raised to the power of the number of host bits used to subnet, minus two, or, in this case $2^2-2 = 2$. On a calculator, the function to use often appears as an x^y button. It means x raised to its yth power.

In the example above, we borrowed two bits from the host ID. Thus, we can now calculate the value as follows: ($2^2-2 = 2$). This calculation gives us only two subnets.

So, from a single-address space (network 209.214.220.0) serving 254 hosts, we now have two new networks each masked as 255.255.255.192.

To further illustrate subnetting, let's work next with a Class B address: We have determined from our needs analysis that we must create a group of networks each capable of addressing 254 hosts. The Class B address space we have is 150.10.0.0. To review, the network ID is 150.10.0.0, and IP knows where to send packets addressed to network 150.10.0.0. The original, default network mask is 255.255.0.0. The default mask tells us the last two octets can be used as the host address. Recall that this can give us a total of 65,534 potential computer hosts on one network.

If we convert the entire binary address to decimal, we get the new value of the subnet mask. Again, we ignore one and zero, but notice we can keep stealing away from the third octet until all the bits are used and we have the value of 255 in the third octet: 255.255.255.0. If we steal all eight bits, we will find ourselves at the default Class C subnet mask, which provides a maximum of 254 hosts.

But how many subnetworks does that leave us? We started with one network and kept subnetting until we arrived at 254, borrowing all eight bits from the third octet. When we raise two to the eighth power, 2^8-2 = subnetworks, we arrive at the number of subnetworks IP can recognize. In this case, there are 254 subnetworks available. The 254 subnetted network IDs will now start at 150.10.1. and increment by one, all the way to 150.10.254.; representing, essentially, all new *Class C* addresses available because we have created a new subnet mask.

If we needed more hosts on each of the new subnets—say 2,046 IP addresses are required on each subnet—we would have stopped borrowing at bit five. If we raise two to the fifth power, 2^5-2 = 30, we discover 30 new networks.

To determine the new network IDs, we just increment each subnet from the first increment by the decimal value of the last subnet (one) bit of the subnet mask, or lowest-order subnet bit. For example, if we used the fifth bit, whose decimal value is eight, as we did in Table 4.39, the first subnet would be 0.0.8. and each subnet thereafter is an increment of eight more. When we name the new subnets, the first value in the third octet is eight, the second subnet is 16, the third is 24 and the fourth is 32 and so on, until we reach the broadcast address for the last subnet.

To make life a little easier, we have included three tables detailing Class A, B, and C subnetting.

You could also take the number of borrowed bits and calculate all the possible networks by trying various binary combinations of one and zero (but never all zeroes or all ones); however, this is tedious when dealing with three or four bits and almost impossible with more than five bits.

TIP
Take some time to fully understand and practice using the x^y function on your scientific calculator. You will get subnetting questions in the exam, and if you fuss around with ones and zeroes, you will lose valuable time.

Table 4.46
Use this table to subnet Class A networks by borrowing two or more bits from the second binary octet.

Class A Subnets

Bits Borrowed	Maximum Subnets Available	Maximum Hosts per Subnet	Subnet Mask
0	None	16,777,214	255.0.0.0
1	NA	NA	NA
2	2	4,194,302	255.192.0.0
3	6	2,097,150	255.224.0.0
4	14	1,048,574	255.240.0.0
5	30	524,286	255.248.0.0
6	62	262,142	255.252.0.0
7	126	131,070	255.254.0.0
8	254	66,534	255.255.0.0

Table 4.47
Use this table to subnet Class B networks by borrowing two or more bits from the third binary octet.

Class B

Bits Borrowed	Maximum Subnets Available	Maximum Hosts per Subnet	Subnet Mask
0	None	65,534	255.255.0.0

Bits Borrowed	Maximum Subnets Available	Maximum Hosts per Subnet	Subnet Mask
1	NA	NA	NA
2	2	16,382	255.255.192.0
3	6	8,190	255.255.224.0
4	14	4,094	255.255.240.0
5	30	2,046	255.255.248.0
6	62	1,022	255.255.252.0
7	126	510	255.255.254.0
8	254	254	255.255.255.0

Table 4.48
Class C subnets for two to six borrowed bits in the fourth binary octet.

Class C			
Bits Borrowed	Maximum Subnets Available	Maximum Hosts per Subnet	Subnet Mask
0	None	254	255.255.255.0
1	NA	NA	NA
2	2	62	255.255.255.192
3	6	30	255.255.255.224
4	14	14	255.255.255.240
5	30	6	255.255.255.248
6	62	2	255.255.255.252
7	NA	NA	NA
8	NA	NA	NA

TIP

For the Microsoft exam subnetting questions, knowing these subnetting tables and how to use them is sufficient to answer the subnetting questions—if you understand the subnetting concepts and have practical experience applying them.

Step 3: Calculate the new subnetwork IDs.

Make sure you have enough binary bits to write all the subnet and host numbers required to describe the network and each of the network interface cards on the network. Plan to have enough bits to write all the binary numbers necessary.

Whether you use the lowest order subnet ID bit's decimal value or you write out all the binary combinations available with the borrowed bits, either way you start the *subnet ID numbers* at the first increment *above* the previous, non-subnetted network ID, not at zero.

Step 4: List the resulting host IDs for each new subnetwork.

Each device using TCP/IP must have a unique IP address, so you must assign new subnetted IP addresses to all workstations, all router interfaces, all WAN connections, all network printers (connected directly to the network) and every other device using TCP/IP.

Step 5: Implement the Subnet Plan.

After the routers are set up and configured between all the network segments and the plan has been tested and checked by all the powers-that-be, eventually the new subnetting plan may be implemented. What can you expect to go wrong? Everything. Plan for everything that you can think of in advance.

All the old IP addresses will instantly become obsolete or wrong, and any hardware or software that was manually configured with the old IP addresses may or will begin to malfunction. Devices that obtain their IP addresses through a DHCP server will be easier to handle—however, the DHCP servers themselves must be reconfigured to use the new subnetting scheme at the same time as the scheme is implemented on the routers and other network devices.

Bringing it All Together—Practice

Now that you have invested all this time in understanding the process of subnetting, you may be shaking your head and saying to yourself, "Are they kidding? I can't do this kind of stuff on a 90-minute test."

Well, guess what? We are not kidding. The Microsoft TCP/IP test has required thousands of MCSE candidates before you to understand this stuff, but not from beginning-to-end, as this chapter has demonstrated. What you have reviewed in the last 30 or so pages is *crucial* as the foundation for what has been required for three to 10 questions on the test, at least until the advent of adaptive testing.

The MCSE exams may ask you questions that take answers from the subnetting process. You must know the subnetting process well enough and have enough experience or practice to quickly understand where in the subnet process the question comes from and what you are being asked, and then decide on an appropriate answer.

So carefully read these examples, and use the questions that are asked as guidelines for how you should approach answering questions on the TCP/IP exam.

Before you begin the test, if you do not have it memorized yet, draw the powers of two on the scratch paper in reverse order for use in conversion from binary to decimal values:

Table 4.49 Use these decimal place values to evaluate binary numbers—to convert them to decimal numbers or to convert decimal number to binary numbers.

128	64	32	16	8	4	2	1

You may also want to memorize and/or write this next table down:

Table 4.50   These decimal values have also been called the TCP/IP high-bit sums.

Decimal Value	Binary Value	Borrowed Bits
128	10000000	1
192	11000000	2
224	11100000	3
240	11110000	4
248	11111000	5
252	11111100	6
254	11111110	7
255	11111111	8

Also, memorize the Class A, B, and C tables for subnets—Tables 4.46, 4.47, and 4.48, to save time on several questions. This preparation will allow you to spend more time on other questions.

Subnetting Examples

These examples are intended to give you one more way to prove to yourself that you have the subnetting part of the exam figured out. These examples, like this whole chapter, are written in complete detail so that no hidden assumptions are made and there are no magic tables. If you already understand everything about subnetting, try answering these without consulting our answer. After you have written your own answer, then check your answer against ours. Good luck.

If you find any errors here, or for that matter anywhere else in this book or in this series of study guides, please write to <TCPIP@Emissary.Net>. I am grateful for your feedback.

Example #1

Given: You must find the total number of subnet *network IDs* for an IP address of 190.16.28.2. The subnet mask is 255.255.252.0.

When you see *total number of subnet network IDs* in a question, find the answer by asking yourself the following questions:

Question 1a. What is the binary equivalent of the subnet mask? Use either the Base 2 place values or memorized values to evaluate this:

Table 4.51 This is a 6-bit subnet mask for a Class B network.

Decimal Value	Binary Value
255.255.252.0	11111111.11111111.11111100.00000000

Step 1b. What portion is the network ID, and what portion is the host ID?

Remember 190.16.28.2 is a Class B IP address, which means:

Table 4.52 The third octet of this Class B address indicates the subnet ID.

IP Address	Network ID	Subnet ID	Host ID
190.16.28.2	190.16.0.0	0.0.28.	0.0.0.2

Step 1c. How many bits are being used in the host ID portion of the address to create the subnet mask?

Table 4.53 Six host bits were borrowed to create the subnet IDs on network 190.16.0.0.

	Decimal Value	Binary Value
Subnet Mask	255.255.252.0	11111111.11111111.11111100.00000000

The answer to Step 1c is six bits.

Step 1d. Place the answer to Step 1c in the formula $2^n - 2 = x$, which would be

$2^6 - 2 = 62$

So, there are 62 subnetwork IDs made available by borrowing six bits.

CAUTION

There is some controversy on this subject. Although the formula for finding hosts is definitely

2^n-2 = hosts

the formula for how many networks, according to some experts, is 2^n = x. Networking hardware and software purchased recently is likely to allow subnetwork ID numbers of all zeroes, so that there is no need to subtract the all-zeroes from the number of subnets available. The use of all-zeroes networks is by no means popular or widespread, however.

If you encounter an exam question that splits hairs in this area, you should protest to Microsoft during the post-exam comment period. One thing is certain: For networks numbered at the extremes (all zeroes and/or all ones), it is essential that *all* devices and all software on the network can address these unconventional network ID numbers.

Hosts are never addressed with the broadcast address of all ones in the entire host portion of the IP address. Hosts may be numbered, however, with *one full octet of all zeroes*, if the host portion of the IP address extends into another octet and something other than all zeroes is in the host bits in another octet.

This means that decimal host IDs of 0.0.3.0 and 0.0.1.0 are perfectly legitimate, *if* the host portion of the IP address extends into the previous, higher-order octet(s).

Now let's apply the same steps to another example:

Example #2

Given: You must find the total number of subnet *network IDs* for the IP address of 224.150.16.181. The subnet mask is 255.255.255.192.

When you see *total number of subnet network IDs* in a question, find the answer by asking the following questions:

Step 2a. What is the binary equivalent of the subnet mask?
Use either the Base 2 place values or the memorized table to
determine this:

Table 4.54 This is a subnetted Class C subnet mask.

Decimal Value	Binary Value
255.255.255.192	11111111.11111111.11111111.11000000

Step 2b. What portion is the network ID, and what portion is the
host ID?
Remember 224.150.16.181 is a Class C IP address, which means:

Table 4.55 This host is on subnet 0.0.0.128. of network 224.150.16.0.

IP Address	Network ID	Subnet ID	Host ID
224.150.16.181	224.150.16.0	0.0.0.128.	0.0.0.181

Step 2c. How many bits are being used in the host portion to
create the subnet IDs?

Table 4.56 Two host bits are borrowed to create subnet IDs for network 224.150.0.0.

	Decimal Value	Binary Value
Subnet Mask	255.255.255.192	11111111.11111111.11111111.11000000

The answer to Step 2c is two.
Step 2d. Place the answer to Step 2c in the formula $2^n - 2 = x$,
which would be:

$2^2 - 2 = 2$

The answer is two subnetwork IDs are available. See the caution for another interpretation and further details.

Example #3

The same questions can be applied when you are asked to find the *total number of Host IDs available in a subnet*. This example will use the same IP address and subnet mask as in Example #1.

Remember, this time you are calculating the number of available hosts on a network, not available subnetworks.

Given: Find the total number of subnet *host IDs* for a network containing the IP address 190.16.28.2. The subnet mask is 255.255.252.0.

When you see *total number of subnet host IDs* in a question, find the answer by asking the following questions:

Step 3a. What is the binary equivalent of the subnet mask?

Use either the Base 2 place values or the memorized table to determine this:

Table 4.57   This is a Class B network subnetted with six borrowed host bits.

Decimal Value	Binary Value
255.255.252.0	11111111.11111111.11111100.00000000

Step 3b. What portion is the network ID, and what portion is the host ID?

Remember, 190.16.28.2 is a Class B IP address, which means:

Table 4.58   This host is on subnet 0.0.28. of network 190.16.0.0.

IP Address	Network ID	Subnet ID	Host ID
190.16.28.2	190.16.0.0	0.0.28.	0.0.0.2

Step 3c. How many bits are being used in the host portion for the host IDs?

Table 4.59   Six host bits are borrowed to create subnet IDs for network 190.16.0.0, leaving only 10 host bits available to enumerate host IDs.

	Decimal Value	Binary Value
Subnet Mask	255.255.252.0	11111111.11111111.11111100.00000000

The answer to Step 3c is 10.

Step 3d. Place the answer to Step 3c in the formula 2^n-2 = hosts, which would be:

$$2^{10}-2 = 1022$$

So, 1,022 host IDs are available on each subnet of network 190.16.0.0, given the defined circumstances.

Example #4

Now let's find the available host IDs using the data we used earlier in Example #2. Remember, we are finding the available hosts, not subnet network IDs this time.

Given: Find the total number of subnet *host IDs* for a network containing the IP address 224.150.16.181. The subnet mask is 255.255.255.192.

When you see *total number of Host IDs* in a question, find the answer by asking the following questions:

Step 4a. What is the binary equivalent of the subnet mask?

Use either the Base 2 place values or the memorized table to determine this:

Table 4.60   This is a Class C network subnetted with two borrowed host bits.

Decimal Value	Binary Value
255.255.255.192	11111111.11111111.11111111.11000000

Step 4b. What portion is the network ID, and what portion is the host ID?

Remember, 224.150.16.181 is a Class C IP address, which means:

Table 4.61 This host is on the second and last subnet of the network 224.150.16.0.

IP Address	Network ID	Subnet ID	Host ID
224.150.16.181	224.150.16.0	0.0.0.128.	0.0.0.181

Step 4c. How many bits are being used for host IDs?

Table 4.62 Two host bits are borrowed to create subnet IDs for network 224.150.16.0, leaving only six bits to enumerate all the host IDs.

	Decimal Value	Binary Value
Subnet Mask	255.255.255.192	11111111.11111111.11111111.11000000

The answer to Step 4c is six.

Step 4d. Place the answer to Step 4c in the formula $2^n-2 =$ hosts, which would be:

$$2^6-2 = 62$$

The answer is 62 host IDs are available on each subnet of network 224.150.16.0, given the defined circumstances.

Example #5

Create an appropriate subnet mask.

Given: You need at least 37 subnetwork IDs on your network. The IP address of the PDC is currently 175.22.60.5. This network uses the default subnet mask for Class B IP addresses: 255.255.0.0. What is the correct subnet mask for the required subnetwork IDs?

Whenever you have a question that asks you, *What is the correct subnet mask for this many required subnetwork IDs?*, ask the following questions:

Step 5a. Using the formula $2^n-2 = x$:

```
2ⁿ-2 = 37
```

Run through the calculations, discovering $2^5-2 = 30$, *while* $2^6-2 = 62$. Thirty is too few, and although 62 has more than required, 62 is the correct answer because nothing less would satisfy the requirement of *at least* 37 subnets.

Step 5b. How many bits do I need to borrow to write 62 subnet IDs?

```
2⁶-2 = 62
```

The answer to Step 5b is six. The number two must be raised to the sixth power to identify all the subnets needed.

Step 5c. What is the binary equivalent of the subnet address?

Use either the Base 2 place value table or the memorized table to determine this:

Table 4.63 This is the default subnet mask for Class B networks.

Decimal Value	Binary Value
255.255.0.0	11111111.11111111.00000000.00000000

Step 5d. What portion is the network ID, and what portion is the host ID?

Remember, 175.22.60.5 is a Class B IP address, which means:

Table 4.64 The 175.22.0.0 network is not currently subnetted.

IP Address	Network ID	Subnet ID	Host ID
175.22.60.5	175.22.0.0	none	0.0.60.5

Step 5e. Borrow the required six bits from the host ID portion.

Table 4.65 Always begin to borrow bits from the left in the host portion of a subnet mask.

	Decimal Value	Binary Value
Subnet Mask	255.255.?.0	11111111.11111111.11111100.00000000

Step 5e requires us to borrow six bits from the host portion of the default Class B subnet mask.

Step 5f. Convert the binary number created in Step 5e to a decimal representation.

Table 4.66 The 175.22.0.0 network's new subnet mask is 255.255.252.0, allowing 62 subnets and up to 1,022 hosts on each subnet.

	Decimal Value	Binary Value
Subnet Mask	255.255.252.0	11111111.11111111.11111100.00000000

The new subnet mask will be 255.255.252.0.

Example #6

Let's apply the same technique to an example where we need 37 host IDs per subnet.

Given: You need 37 host IDs per subnet on your network. The DHCP server in the network has an IP address of 175.22.60.5 and uses the default subnet mask for this Class B IP address: 255.255.0.0. What is the correct subnet mask if no more than 50 hosts are required on each subnet?

Whenever you have a question that asks you, *What is the correct subnet mask for X many required host IDs per subnet?*, ask the following questions:

Step 6a. Using the formula 2^n-2 = hosts
$2^n-2 = 50$ hosts required
Run through the calculations, discovering $2^5-2 = 30$, and $2^6-2 = 62$. Thirty is too few, and although 62 is too many, 62 is the correct answer because nothing less would satisfy the requirement of no more than 50 hosts per subnet.
Step 6b. How many bits do I need?

$$2^6-2 = 62$$

From the formula, we see that two was raised to the sixth power, so we know that to enumerate all the subnetted host IDs we will need six binary bits.
Step 6c. What is the binary equivalent of the subnet address?
Use either the Base 2 place value table or the memorized table to determine this:

Table 4.67 This is the default subnet mask for Class B networks.

Decimal Value	Binary Value
255.255.0.0	11111111.11111111.00000000.00000000

Step 6d. What is the network ID portion, and what is the host ID portion?
Remember, 172.22.60.5 is a Class B IP address, which means:

Table 4.68 The 175.22.0.0 network is not currently subnetted.

IP Address	Network ID	Subnet ID	Host ID
175.22.60.5	175.22.0.0	none	0.0.60.5

Step 6e. A Class B network has only 16 bits of network address—the remaining 16 bits are for the hosts, or subnets and hosts. Out of the 16 bits (two octets) of host bits available, we know from Step 6b that only six bits of host IDs are required to describe the 50-host maximum each subnetwork will have. Borrow the remaining 10 bits for subnets, leaving only six bits for the host IDs.

Table 4.69 Always begin to borrow bits from the left in the host portion of a subnet mask.

	Decimal Value	Binary Value
Subnet Mask	255.255.?.0	11111111.11111111.11111111.11000000

Step 6e requires us to borrow 10 bits from the host portion of the default Class B subnet mask.

Step 6f. Convert the binary address in Step 6e to decimal representation.

Table 4.70 The 175.22.0.0 network's new subnet mask is 255.255.255.192.

	Decimal Value	Binary Value
Subnet Mask	255.255.255.192	11111111.11111111.11111111.11000000

The new subnet mask will be 255.255.255.192. This provides more than 1,000 subnets with at most 62 hosts per subnet, which is more than the given 50 host per subnet requirement.

Example #7

Finally, if you are asked to find the exact number of hosts available on a subnet, consider the following as an example of questions to ask yourself:

Given: Your new router has an IP address of 190.100.32.1 with a subnet mask of 255.255.224.0. How many hosts are possible on each subnet of the network?

Whenever you see the question *How many hosts are there on each subnet?*, ask the following questions:

Step 7a. What is the binary equivalent of the subnet mask?

Table 4.71 This is a subnetted Class B network's 3-bit subnet mask.

	Decimal Value	Binary Value
Subnet Mask	255.255.224.0	11111111.11111111.11100000.00000000

Step 7b. What is the network ID portion, and what is the host ID portion?

Remember, 190.100.32.1 is a Class B IP address, which means:

Table 4.72 The 190.100.0.0 network has already been subnetted.

IP Address	Network ID	Subnet ID	Host ID
190.100.32.1	190.100.0.0	0.0.32.	0.0.0.1

Step 7c. How many host bits remain after the subnet bits have been borrowed?

Table 4.71 There are 13 host bits remaining after borrowing three bits for the subnet IDs.

	Decimal Value	Binary Value
Subnet Mask	255.255.224.0	11111111.11111111.11100000.00000000

Step 7d. How many host IDs can be written with the 13 bits remaining?

(Use the formula $2^{13}-2 = hosts$)

$2^{13}-2 = 8,190$ host IDs are available on each of six subnets of network 190.100.0.0.

This last example also can be answered quite easily from Table 4.47. For the exam, many people memorize Tables 4.46 , 4.47, 4.48 and 4.50. They claim they can answer several questions quickly, directly from the tables, so that more time is available for them to concentrate on more taxing questions.

It is, on the other hand, probably better for your networking career if you become so familiar with TCP/IP that you can easily figure the subnets with or without the pre-calculated tables. Knowing how to re-create the tables—because you know TCP/IP subnetting inside-out, is therefore the ideal situation. That level of knowledge will place you far ahead of the pack—you will know *why* the tables say what they do, rather than just memorizing what the tables say.

IF YOU HAVE ALL OF THESE SKILLS, YOU ARE READY FOR THE SUBNETTING QUESTIONS ON THE EXAM:

1. Find the total number of subnetwork IDs available in a given situation.
2. Find the total number of host IDs available in a given situation.
3. Choose a subnet mask that will:
   3a. Provide the required number of hosts per network.
   3b. Provide the required number of subnet networks.
4. Find the exact host numbers available on a given subnet.
5. Find the subnet network ID from a given IP address and subnet mask.
6. Find the subnet mask from a given IP address and network ID.

For Review

- Subnetting allows you to create subnets of a network assigned by InterNIC.

- Subnetting is an effective means of managing IP networks.

- For a network of computers to communicate effectively, all devices on the network must use the same subnet mask.

- Subnet masks are part and parcel of the IP information that a Windows-based host needs to participate on a TCP/IP network.

- In a binary subnet mask, the ones represent the network or subnet IDs, and the zeroes represent the host IDs.

- Subnetting is affected by reducing the number of bits available to the host and adding those bits to the network (subnet) portion of the IP address. This results in reducing the total number of hosts available on the network and to each new subnet.

- A subnet mask determines the maximum number of hosts available on any one subnet (segment) and how many (sub)networks may share the same network ID.

- Many ISPs are subnetting their Class C networks to help conserve IP addresses (and sell more routers for Bay Networks and Cisco).

From Here

We learned in this chapter that a network can be divided into small networks, which reduces the number of hosts originally available. Packets are then directed to the correct network subnet using a router. The next chapter explores routing in more detail.

CHAPTER 5

Routing

Routing is likely the one subject that can make or break your quest to become proficient in TCP/IP networking. In years of TCP/IP work, the advanced stuff for me always hangs on routing.

Unless you fully understand routing and can set up routers and gateways to move IP packets from network to network, no extraordinary knowledge of other TCP/IP functions will be of any use to you in the network world. You will be like a basketball player who can run but cannot put the ball in the net.

NOTE
Many network engineers use the terms *router* and *gateway* interchangeably; however, the current preferred usage is router.

Routing can be best-defined as the functions or processes within TCP/IP that allow you to choose a shortest and fastest route between two networks. But routing also depends on routing hardware and software before it can be implemented. We discuss these systems before we tackle implementation.

Routers come in two primary forms: embedded systems, such as the standard Cisco 2500 series, or a multi-homed computer (which has more than one network interface card). Before the advent of

Windows NT, many network administrators used a UNIX host to route IP. Both operating systems today ship their products with routing software, and all you need to do to turn a computer into a router is configure it as a multi-homed device. You can have as many network cards as the computer bus will allow, with each one being a gateway to a separate network.

If you are planning a multi-homed computer-router, the first piece of advice you need is not to *dumb down* on the processor and hardware. With today's prices falling like swooping falcons, there is no need to go for anything less than a 266 MHz computer with at least 64MB of RAM. Routing is processor- and memory-intensive, and on a busy network that receives two tons of e-mail a day, you will need all the resources you can get.

Many firewall software solutions are installed on routers. A firewall is a packet filtering process. And, because many firewalls today include network address translation, the firewall software and the OS are about all you want to have running on such a computer.

A Windows NT computer does not come out of the box ready to route. You will need to set up several properties, IP addresses and such under the networking options in Windows NT before you are ready to route.

In the real world, you will also need to set up an embedded router. The most popular of these systems to route packets from the Internet to your LAN, or between any private IP networks, are the Cisco 1000 and 2500 series.

Again, if you are setting up a firewall on a Windows NT router to filter packets to-and-from the Internet, you will be routing on both the Windows NT computer and on the embedded router. Figure 5.1 illustrates the typical hardware involving a Windows NT router, which is connected to a standard router.

At the end of this chapter, we will also show how to make a *cross-over* cable that connects a Windows NT router to a Cisco router. This is about as essential to routing as a routing table. You cannot just take a ride to your local computer store and buy one, either. A cross-over cable is one of the most important pieces of hardware required for connecting gateways to routers.

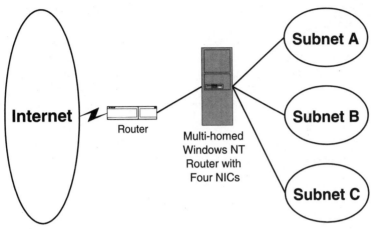

Figure 5.1 A Windows NT multi-homed computer connected to a standard router.

So What Is Routing?

As we mentioned earlier, routing is the process that determines the best way to transmit data between two networks

A router relays the IP datagrams between the TCP/IP stacks of two computers residing on separate networks. There are several factors that routing processes consider:

A router must know what routes are available, which it finds out from routing tables—both statically added or received via automatic publication from other routers (dynamic updates).

A router must be able to determine the shortest path between the two networks indicated in the routing tables; hence, *route metrics*.

A router may manipulate datagram formats to suit the supporting network technology. For example, a router may need to take IP datagrams and encapsulate them in SNA *envelopes,* allowing the information to be transmitted over an SNA network connected to a mainframe. Conversely, a router may need to open a SNA envelope and extract the encapsulated IP data for transmission over an IP network.

A router may also support and join different types of network technologies, such as Ethernet and Token Ring.

Routers also must support the fragmentation of packets, even though fragmentation is costly in resources. While fragmentation technology is beyond the scope of this book, it is important to understand that you may have to transmit data back-and-forth between, for instance, a 16 Mbps Token Ring network and a 4 Mbps Token Ring network.

Routers Versus Bridges

While bridges may appear cheaper and easier to implement (see the Network Essentials study guide), several reasons exist as to why a router offers substantial advantages in transmitting data between multiple network segments:

- Has the capability to choose the best route to a remote host
- Can route to networks of unlike technologies
- Has fault tolerance
- Debugs

Equipped with the ability to work with the new routing protocols of TCP/IP, routers are able to determine the best route to a remote host. Routers are also built to cater to the multitude of unlike technologies that exist in the world's internetworks.

Routers also have built-in fault tolerance. It is far more difficult to transmit bad data across a router than across a bridge. Granted, modern bridges are better-equipped to handle dirty packets. Routers, however, understand IP and prevent specific software failures. Bridges usually assume everything is working properly. Routers are more complex to set up, because they recognize so much more about the networks around them.

Routers also come equipped with error reporting ability (such as ICPM or Ping). They can also be used to debug some network problems and record error conditions. The Cisco router's monitor utility that reports on ICMP packets is a good example.

How Routers Use IP Addresses

Routers read network IDs or network numbers to decide how to transmit a packet to a network. A router must therefore have an IP address and a subnetwork mask that corresponds with each network to which it is routing. In other words, for every network a router is connected to, the router must be assigned a valid IP address and subnet mask that corresponds with each network. Figure 5.2 illustrates a router configured for two networks: a Class C network segment and a Class B network.

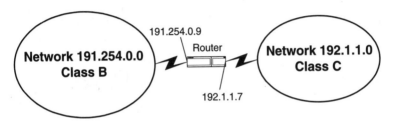

Figure 5.2   Routers have one IP address on each network they serve.

Where routers are not directly connected to a local network for which a datagram is intended, they relay the datagrams on to other routers in a better local position to transmit directly to the intended host.

When a router determines that a packet is destined to a host on the network it is directly connected with, or can be reached at a remote network (via a router), it calls the *Address Resolution Protocol* (ARP). ARP resolves the IP address of the interface device to its *Media Access Control* (MAC) address. IP is a 32-bit address, and the MAC address, from a device on a network such as an Ethernet LAN or a Token Ring network, is a 48-bit address, as illustrated in Figure 5.3.

When an IP packet is sent to a remote device, it is not really the IP address that is being routed to, but rather the MAC address as a frame transmission. Device drivers of network interfaces never use the IP address as provided in the datagram. The IP address is purely used to move information at the IP layer. See Table 5.1.

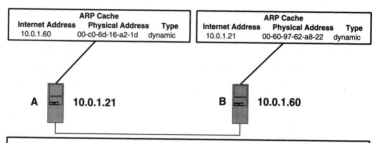

Figure 5.3 ARP resolves local IP addresses into MAC addresses.

Table 5.1 Route table entries look like Greek to most people.

Network Address	Net mask	Gateway Address	Interface	Metric
10.0.1.0	255.255.0.0	10.0.1.21	10.0.1.21	1
10.0.1.21	255.255.255.255	127.0.0.1	127.0.0.1	1
10.255.255.255	255.255.255.255	10.0.1.21	10.0.1.21	1
127.0.0.0	255.0.0.0	127.0.0.1	127.0.0.1	1
224.0.0.0	224.0.0.0	10.0.1.21	10.0.1.21	1
255.255.255.255	255.255.255.255	10.0.1.21	10.0.1.21	1

- The first line is a network route for the network 10.0.1.0. The local interface is specified as the path to this network.

- The second line is a host route for the local host. By specifying the loopback address, a datagram bound for the local host is handled internally.

- The third line is the subnet broadcast address (specifying the local network interface).

- The fourth line is the loopback address, 127.0.0.0.
- The fifth line is the IP multicast address.
- The sixth line is the limited broadcast address.

How Routers Use Routing Information

Every router or routing computer, when booted up, loads a routing table into its memory. Routing tables usually contain information representing the connections (through remote computers) that can be used to send information to a remote network. The tables are built by the operating system every time the computer boots. Under Windows NT, static routes that require persistence are saved to the registry and are loaded at run time into the routing table.

Routing tables are much like directions you need when you drive around looking for a destination. You have the address of the remote location, but you still need to determine your path.

If a packet arrives at a router and the router determines it is not for a network to which it is attached, the router sends the packet on to the next router for action. This forwarding, or relaying, activity is known as a *hop*. To get back to our driving analogy, when we get lost we drive into the nearest gas station, or we fire up the new global positioning system to determine if we are on the right track. Routers take similar action. They consult the information or data at hand in the route table and look for shortcuts or reliable directions.

If a router determines that the data is taking too long to reach its destination or is going around in circles, the router will return the packet to the sender with information that *too many hops* were required to deliver the packet. In this case, the routers determined that the packets would take too long to find their destination, if at all.

Routers also can be forced to send data along a fixed route. This is known as a static route. The static route cannot be changed unless the administrator deletes it. The path from A to C is through B.

It is easy to assign a static route. You simply tell the router, by adding an entry in the routing table, that in order to get a packet to *Network A* you need to send it to the *X* gateway.

Adding static routes to a routing table is not the norm for general routing through the Internet. It is not commonplace, either, to set up static routes through a collection of large networks. You will use static route entries frequently, however, when working with network address translation, or when you implicitly need to route a packet from one network to another.

For example, if you need to tell a router that packets from a private Class A address (or an illegal network) should be routed to the Internet via a legal gateway address, you would use a static route to tell the router that the way out of the closed network is through X or Y connection. You would need network address translation services, however, such as a proxy server, because those illegal addresses are not routable on the Internet. The IP addresses in the headers must be changed (translated) before the external network can accept them.

The most sensible way of routing packets is with TCP/IP routing protocols. These protocols update routing tables periodically and dynamically. They keep the routers updated with best path information. They are akin to the navigator in a motor car rally, constantly reading maps and updating the driver with best way information. We will deal with dynamic routing later in this chapter.

The information exchanged between routers is limited to what each router knows about a route, the road, the condition and the time it takes to reach the destination. Routing information is sent out on a regular basis, and the route information changes as new information comes in and when situations or conditions change.

Before we examine the routing protocols, however, become comfortable first with the layout of a route table.

```
C:\>route print
```

```
Active Routes:
```

Network Address	Net mask	Gateway Address	Interface	Metric
10.0.1.0	255.255.0.0	10.0.1.21	10.0.1.21	1
10.0.1.21	255.255.255.255	127.0.0.1	127.0.0.1	1
10.255.255.255	255.255.255.255	10.0.1.21	10.0.1.21	1
127.0.0.0	255.0.0.0	127.0.0.1	127.0.0.1	1
224.0.0.0	224.0.0.0	10.0.1.03	10.0.1.21	1
255.255.255.255	255.255.255.255	10.0.1.21	10.0.1.21	1

Route Tables

Route tables are to TCP/IP what thermometers are to doctors. Without the ability to read a patient's temperature, the diagnosis may be inaccurate-and without route tables, there can be no transmission or communication. Route tables *drive* the Internet.

Packets on a TCP/IP network are routed on a hop-by-hop basis. IP is not omniscient as far as where everything is on the Internet; it only knows that it can send information onto a next-hop router that leads somewhere. The next-hop router may not be the final destination, and if it is not, the next router will take the information and forward it along the path to its final destination.

A router undertakes several processes when it receives a packet. This activity is known in IP as the *routing mechanism.* Note: Routing mechanism is different from *routing policy,* which is the automatic or manual management of routing and decisions as to what is listed in a routing table.

1. The router will search the routing table for an IP address that matches the *destination address* of the packet. If the *destination address* entry is found, the router will forward the packet onto the next-hop router or directly to the interface if the network condition flag (metric) indicates it can. This operation always takes first priority.

2. If an IP address is absent from the routing table, the router will search the table for an entry that matches the *destination network ID.* If an entry matching the *destination network ID* is found, the router will forward the packet in the same fashion as #1. Said another way, the *destination network ID* is the transmission target in the absence of a destination IP address.

3. If none of the previous methods dispatch the data toward its destination, the router will search for a routing table entry listed as the default gateway. The information then is sent to the default gateway, and the gateway router then deals with the information as the gateway sees fit.

4. If the router comes up with none of the previous options, it will return that packet as undeliverable. If the packet comes back from the routing host, IP will report to the upper IP layers that the destination address is unreachable (either by a *host unreachable* or a *network unreachable* error). If for some reason the network crashes by the time the TCP/IP stack is loaded, the route table may be mostly empty, causing this sort of error.

Of course, there is still more work to perform before a packet is sent on to its destination interface. But let's continue with routing before we bite off more than we can chew.

The code above is an example of a route table on Windows NT. It can be viewed by typing the command *route print* at the command line (we will deal with route commands later and in Chapter 14). Notice that the table contains five columns: from right to left we have the *Network Address, Net mask, Gateway Address, Interface* and *Metric* columns.

Network Address: While this column displays full IP addresses, it is actually a record of all networks of which the router is aware. Also stored here are the networks on which default gateways, subnets and the broadcast, loopback and multicast addresses reside.

Net Mask: This entry provides the subnet mask for a known network.

Gateway Address: The gateway address is like the trap door or transom to which packets should be sent to reach the correct network. There is no way a router will know how to route a packet to a destination without knowing the gateway address. A good example is trying to exit a huge parking lot without knowing where the exit is—if there is no exit sign to point the way. Think of the Gateway Address as the parking lot exit sign for TCP/IP packets not intended for local hosts.

Interface: This entry represents the IP address of the interface device, usually a network interface card, which provides the connection to the network. The interface section also contains the loopback address. In the case of multi-homed computers, the IP addresses of all NICs are listed here, representing interfaces to more than one network.

Metric: Metrics are flags that provide hops and overhead information about a route. The metric column is known as the *Flags* column in UNIX systems. Most of the time the metric is one, which means that the router is advised that the network it is sending to is only one hop away.

You may also come across the following flags in the metric or flag columns in many routers:

U: The route is up.

G: The route leads to a gateway (meaning a router).

H: The route leads to a host. In other words, the route leads to a device that has an IP address.

D: The route was entered by a redirect.

M: The route was modified by a redirect.

In cases where the H flag is absent, the host IP address will be zero, meaning that the destination address is a network ID.

TIP

Microsoft tests the differences between dynamic and static routing. Carefully read this section and the next two to make sure you know the differences.

Dynamic Routing

We discovered earlier that it is possible to enter a static or fixed route into a route table. With the Internet being as big as it is, we can thank the engineers who invented dynamic routing protocols that automatically update routing tables everywhere, constantly apprising each other about networks to which they do not have direct connections.

Two of these dynamic routing protocols are RIP and OSPF. RIP stands for *Routing Information Protocol* and OSPF stands for *Open Shortest Path First.* Here we will deal mainly with RIP, because it is implicitly supported in Windows NT, while OSPF can be further explored in volumes such as the W. Richard Stevens collection on TCP/IP, *TCP/IP Illustrated.*

RIP is, however, not as hardy a protocol for large networks as OSPF. RIP uses a limited measure of performance with regard to condition of a route (the metric or hop count). RIP also limits its propagation of hop information to the number 15, and RIP also cannot support variable length subnet masks.

RIP is also known to be a network hog, because it uses Ethernet broadcast mechanisms for route table updating. RIP broadcasts are received by all processors on a LAN, even by hosts not concerned with routing. In many cases, a slow network can be attributed to RIP, so unless you explicitly need it, turn it off. You usually do not need RIP behind a router.

RIP

RIP is simple and easy to install and manage, which is why it is popular. RIP is one of the oldest broadcasting protocols. It relays information every 30 seconds onto the network for other routers to capture by broadcasting (UDP) through Port 520.

RIP broadcasts are known as advertisements, or *adverts*. So RIP broadcasting of route information is known as route advertising. When routers hear the advertisement, they listen and add the new network addresses found in the advertisement to their route tables. In turn, other RIP routers include their new information in their advertisements, and all the routes in the network are updated in turn.

While RIP is limited, a major advantage of the protocol is that it *can* store information about the number of hops between networks. This is known as *distance vector* routing.

As mentioned earlier, RIP will not keep track of a destination requiring more than 15 hops to reach. When RIP gets a second advertisement providing a shorter route (fewer hops) to travel, the router will prefer that path. The hop-count limit of 15 also prevents the possibility of a packet that keeps traveling, never to find its destination. Such an event would result in a *network unreachable* error, which would prompt the network administrator to seek possible configuration errors on network routers.

RIP routers that receive information providing better path information than current entries will automatically update their tables with the new information. In turn, they distribute this information to other RIP routers.

Static Routing

As discussed, a static router is not able to receive *adverts* from the dynamic routing protocols. Would you ever want to set up a static route table? Yes. Especially if you are connecting a LAN to the Internet via an ISP.

Most LANs today are connected to the Internet with a single router. This router may or may not be connected to a multi-homed Windows NT computer. Whatever the architecture, your router will probably need to connect to another router hosted by your ISP. Most of the time, the ISP's router is capable of dynamically updating your router. Or it will handle all broader routing requirements, routing only to-and-from your router as needed.

Your router must relay all its communications destined for the Internet to the upstream router to take care of the routing. Even if you enable dynamic routing on your router, your gateway or fire wall will not have much use for dynamic routing. Instead, static routes are essential when deploying a gateway or firewall. Of course, you will need to know how to add a static route to a computer or router, no matter whether it is connected to a gateway or to a hub.

Why would you use static routing on a Windows NT gateway, firewalled or not? Most LANs today are set up on private IP addressing schemes. Your gateway, assuming it is a multi-homed computer, contains two or more network cards. One is configured with an IP address of the legal routable address provided by your ISP. We call this NIC, the Internet NIC or public-side NIC.

The public-side NIC is configured with the legal IP address, its default or subnetted net mask and its default gateway, which is the IP address of the Ethernet port on your router. Your router is connected through serial ports to a CSU/DSU, and these serial ports also have IP addresses. The CSU/DSU connects to the channel bank equipment of your telephone company or service provider that provides the circuit to the ISP's equipment.

The second NIC in your gateway is configured with an illegal IP address; for example, a `10.0.0.0.` network. This NIC is also configured with a default or subnetted net mask. The illegal-side NIC is not configured with a default gateway, however, because the public-side NIC on the same computer provides the public gateway, or *exit*, to the Internet.

Now let's try to send information or communicate with the Internet. You might immediately identify a problem if one of your users calls to say he cannot download mail or surf the Web.

This is where you play submariner and shell out to the DOS command prompt screen to transmit a ping (ICMP) to the interface cards. The first action you would take, after hardware troubleshooting, would be to ping the private NIC. If you get a reply that the IP address was successfully pinged, your next action would be to try and ping the gateway and public-side NIC (see Chapter 14 for additional troubleshooting details).

This might result in a ping *timeout*, which tells you that NIC was not reachable from your internal network. If you ping the public card from the gateway computer, you will have success because the packet is not going out onto the network and is bouncing back on the local host. If you did not get a reply, then you would have several items to look for. Here are a few:

- The public-side NIC is not set up (a driver is not installed, etc.).
- TCP/IP has not been bound to the public-side NIC.
- The public NIC, connector or cable is broken.

TIP
You can use IPConfig /all to determine which physical (MAC) address is assigned to the public IP and vice versa (also see Chapter 14).

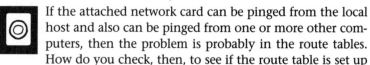

If the attached network card can be pinged from the local host and also can be pinged from one or more other computers, then the problem is probably in the route tables.

How do you check, then, to see if the route table is set up with correct entries? There are two Windows NT commands that investigate route tables: *netstat* and *route print*. Netstat is supported in Windows NT, and *netstat* is a UNIX inheritance. Route commands are more readily supported in Windows NT. Netstat is discussed in Chapter 14.

TIP
Microsoft tests knowledge of the *netstat, route* and *ipconfig* commands. They are discussed in more detail in Chapter 14.

Run *route print* from the DOS command line. You notice that the table has no information that can assist Windows NT to route packets from the private network to the public network. To set things straight, you must add a static route to the route table on the gateway.

The *route* command has a number of switch options you can use to build or manage a route table's static entries.

The first of these switches to use is the *Add* command. To add a route to the IP address 10.1.1.9 which sits behind the gateway with IP address 209.215.182.6 to the route table, simply type:

```
route add -p 10.1.1.9 255.0.0.0 209.215.182.6
```

TIP
You may be asked questions about adding a static route as described here. The -p specifies that the new route being added should be persistent and should survive a system reboot.

The syntax for the route add command is:

```
route add -p [destination] [netmask] [gateway]
```

What have we done? First, we added the -p switch to indicate that we want the entry to be persistent, and we want it to be present in the table the next time the computer boots. The -p preserves the entry in the registry.

The first IP address in the command represents the network and interface ID where the packet is destined (in this case, to a Class A *10* network). The second 32-bit IP number is the net mask of the destination network, and the third IP address is the IP of the interface card you intend to route TCP/IP packets through (the gateway).

Here is a typical exam question: Update the routing table so that packets from Computer A can be routed to Computer D. Figure 5.4 indicates that a computer (A) on a private network 10.1.1.0 needs to send packets to another computer (D) on private network 10.1.2.0. There are two gateway computers in this picture, just to confuse issues, and a router that takes the two private networks to the Internet.

The two gateway computers are B and C. Both B and C are multi-homed, supporting the two private networks 10.1.1.0 and 10.1.2.0.

To route packets to-and-from both private networks, you would add these routes:

```
Route Add 10.1.2.0 255.0.0.0 209.215.182.5
to Computer B: and

Route Add 10.1.1.0 255.0.0.0 209.215.182.6
to Computer C;
```

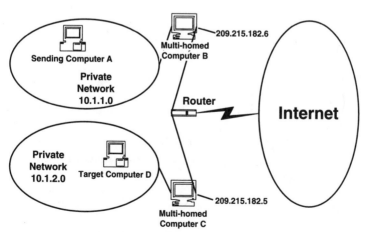

Figure 5.4 When routing packets, be sure to add the route for the right interface.

You could test the route table using the *ping* command again; however, this is a perfect time to introduce the *tracert* command.

Tracert

 A Microsoft version of Tracert is included in the TCP/IP command suite on Windows NT. Tracert is a contraction of the words *trace* and *route*, and that is exactly what it does. It traces the route a diagnostic packet takes as it makes its way across the network to a destination address. We discuss Tracert in more detail in Chapter 14.

To run Tracert, for example, shell out to the DOS command prompt again and type *tracert* 206.15.64.10. The following output is what I received:

```
Tracing route to well.com [206.15.64.10] over a maximum of 30 hops:
  1    130 ms    171 ms    120 ms  as4.wc-aus.io.com [206.224.86.4]
  2    121 ms    120 ms    140 ms  aus-gw-F0-0.illuminati.net [199.170.88.1]
  3    802 ms    320 ms    140 ms  WCC-GW.amap.waller.net [208.24.32.193]
  4    120 ms    150 ms    210 ms  aus1-core2-h1-1-0.atlas.digex.net [206.181.161.89]
  5    150 ms    130 ms    171 ms  dfw2-core2-pt4-0-0.atlas.digex.net [165.117.52.34]
  6   '200 ms    181 ms    180 ms  lax1-core1-s8-0-0.atlas.digex.net [165.117.50.25]
  7    311 ms    180 ms    180 ms  sjc4-core2-pt5-0-0.atlas.digex.net [165.117.53.74]
  8    190 ms    190 ms    191 ms  sjc4-core1-fa5-1-0.atlas.digex.net [165.117.244.1]
  9    611 ms    571 ms    561 ms  sjc2-core1-pos1-0-0.atlas.digex.net
[165.117.56.82]
 10    510 ms    571 ms    681 ms  198.32.184.34
 11    170 ms    180 ms    170 ms  fw1.bdr.hooked.net [206.80.17.12]
 12    180 ms    190 ms    201 ms  well.com [206.15.64.10]
Trace complete.
```

The packet reached its destination address. We learn, too, from the returned information how many hops the packet takes to get to its destination. We also can identify router IP addresses and host names, which tell us about the networks through which we are routing.

As the packet passes through the various routers, we can pinpoint the router into the final hop and finally at the target computer we are trying to locate. This is why it is sometimes difficult for SPAMMERS on the Internet to hide. We can sometimes trace an offending junk e-mail back to the mail server that sent it and then resolve the IP address or mail server name to the organization that allowed it to be used for disgusting SPAM.

Tracert is useful for more than just discovering information about a destination computer. It allows us to detect which routers and gateways are not functioning along the route. A hop that responds with an asterisk (*) indicates that an intermediate router (not the destination) is not relaying the packet.

Tracert also returns the time it takes for a packet to get through a router, or hop. This measurement is in milliseconds. If the time is long for a particular router, it may mean that the router is busy and needs upgrading.

These diagnostic tools are helpful in discovering network problems, as we discuss later. For example, Web surfers may complain that your Web sites are slow or that e-mail sent to you gets returned undelivered. You might use Tracert to discover that the ISP's router upstream from you is not routing your packets correctly. Sometimes one of the big ISPs, such as UUnet, brings down a key router, and major portions of the Internet grind to a halt. It is better to first do a tracert before you spend the next 10 hours replacing all your NICs and reinstalling Windows NT. Too many inexperienced network administrators spin their wheels because they always suspect it is something at home causing the problem. If they remember to use Tracert, they are less likely to suffer ignominy.

How to Build an NT-based Router

This chapter would not be complete without discussing how to build a Windows NT-based router.

TIP

You likely will be asked how to make a Windows NT server into a router. Review RIP and the differences between static and dynamic routing, and note that IP forwarding for multi-homed computers is enabled from

```
Start | Settings | Control Panel | Network | Protocols | TCP/IP
Properties | Routing
```

If you are installing a computer-based firewall, such as Checkpoint Software's Firewall 1, this next exercise is essential reading.

First, a Windows NT-based router contains more than one *Network Interface Card* (NIC). The term for such a computer is multi-homed.

Prepare your computer (with at least the latest Pentium system with no fewer than 64 Mbytes of RAM and agile hard disks), then set it up as a stand-alone or member server. You can also make the computer a back-up domain controller, but there is no need for it to do domain work.

For each network you are routing to, you will need a separate interface card. If three networks are connected to the router, then add three network cards to the computer. I typically use 3Com's 10/100 cards, model 3C905, which have always performed well.

To set up these cards, access Network in the Control Panel of Windows NT and select the Adapters tab and the Add button. Then select the driver for the cards from the NIC list dialog box. Next, select the *have disk...* option and supply drivers that are shipped with the card.

After the cards are installed, they will be listed in numerical order in the Adapters drop-down list. Move now to the Protocol tab and select TCP/IP service. Click on Properties to configure IP on one NIC at a time. Configure each card in this manner. After the cards are configured with the correct gateway and subnet information, they can receive information from the networks to which they are attached. You can test this by pinging each card from the local host, but not before Windows NT asks you to reboot. Refuse until all cards have been configured.

 Your computer is still not a router. You will need to switch to the routing tab under TCP/IP properties and check the *Enable IP Forwarding* option. You have now set up a static router, or gateway.

TIP
More than 60 people advised me that the Microsoft TCP/IP exam covers IP Forwarding and RIP options. There is little chance that you can avoid questions related to IP Forwarding and RIP.

Last, if you need to set up the Windows NT routing computer as a dynamic router, you must install RIP, as discussed earlier.

Now you can reboot the computer.

BUILDING A CROSS-OVER CABLE

This will unlikely be a MCSE exam question, and you will wonder why not when it comes your turn to connect your Windows NT-based gateway to a Cisco or similar router.

To connect a public-side NIC to the Cisco, you will need to build a cross-over cable. This is not the same as a roll-over cable that maps RJ45 pinouts with DB9 pinouts. A cross-over cable will allow the NIC to talk to the Ethernet interface on the router, which is the next IP address upstream from your public-side NIC on the Windows NT computer. Without this cable, you are not going anywhere in a hurry.

Crazy as it seems, you only need four of the eight wires connected to the RJ45 plugs. If you have a network patch cable, chop off the RJ45 plugs and expose about an inch of the wires. It would be better to use a length of Cat 5 cable (which usually comes with four twisted pairs) and cut back the non-solid colors from the pairs. In other words, chop off the blue-white, green-white, orange-white and brown-white-they are hard to see through the plastic of the RJ45.

The wires do not need to be connected according to any color code, and you use the colors only to guide you in making the cable. The following pin connections must occur: Connect pin one (the far left pin in the plug, when the flat side-lever facing down is facing you) to pin three on the other plug (also counting from the left). Then connect pin two on the one plug to pin six on the other plug. Next, you should connect pin three to pin one and pin six to pin two.

When you make a cross-over cable to connect a Windows NT multi-homed computer and a standard 2500 series Cisco router, the network cable is split into four pairs and connected to the pins indicated.

The following is my color code for connecting a cross-over cable.

1. Blue Wire: Pin one to Pin three.

2. Orange Wire: Pin two to Pin six.

3. Green Wire: Pin three to Pin one.

4. Brown Wire: Pin six to Pin two.

If you get a link light on either the NIC or the Ethernet port on the router, you are in business. If not, then the cable has been badly crimped or the wires are not assigned to the correct pins.

For Review

- Routing is best defined as the functions or processes within TCP/IP that allow you to choose a shortest and fastest route between two networks.

- Routers read network IDs or network numbers and then look for matching route information to decide how to transmit a packet to a network.

- Routers use route tables to discover how to best route the packet to the remote network or host.

- Route tables can be updated by a dynamic protocol such as RIP. They also can be manually managed with static route information using the route command.

- Two commands can be used to view the route table:
  ```
  Netstat
  Route print
  ```

- The syntax for the route add command is
  ```
  route add -p [destination] [netmask] [gateway]
  ```

- Tracert traces the route a diagnostic packet takes as it makes its way across the network to a destination address.

- To set up the computer as a router, check the Enable IP Forwarding option on the Routing tab in TCP/IP Properties.

From Here

We learned in this chapter how TCP/IP routes information from network-to-network. The next chapter begins our sojourn into the address- and name-resolving mechanisms of TCP/IP, and Microsoft will test you heavily here. So get ready to take notes.

CHAPTER 6

IP Address Resolution

B efore communication can occur on a network, a host must know the hardware address of other hosts with which it intends to communicate. Therefore, IP addresses must be resolved to a hard-coded MAC (media access control) address found on each network interface card (NIC).

As discussed in Chapter 2, TCP/IP in a Nutshell, TCP/IP uses the *Address Resolution Protocol* (ARP) to resolve an IP software address to the physical hardware address of a network interface device. Detailed information on ARP can be found in RFC 826 and in Chapter 5.

Host name and NetBIOS name resolution (discussed in Chapter 7, Host Name Resolution, and Chapter 9, NetBIOS Name Resolution), cannot occur until IP addresses have been resolved to MAC addresses.

Media Access Control (MAC) Address

Remember in the OSI reference model that the Data Link Layer consists of two sublayers, the Media Access Control Sublayer and the Logical Link Control Sublayer. A computer's MAC address is a hard-coded, unique, 48-bit address found on the computer's NIC card. Because the address is hard-coded, it never changes. The user can change the NetBIOS name and even the IP address if desired, but the MAC address remains constant unless the computer is given a new NIC card.

ARP

ARP performs IP address resolution by mapping a host's IP address to the MAC, or physical, address of its network adapter card.

The first step ARP takes in resolving an IP address is checking the ARP cache, which is discussed later in this chapter. If the desired IP address is not in the cache and the destination IP address is local, an ARP request containing the destination IP address is broadcast. The destination host, upon hearing its own IP address ARPed, will return an ARP reply containing its MAC address and the ARP cache will be updated.

Because the IP address and MAC address of the source computer are included in the ARP request generated by the source computer, the destination host can also add the IP address and MAC address of the source computer to its ARP cache.

The process just described is illustrated in Figure 6.1.

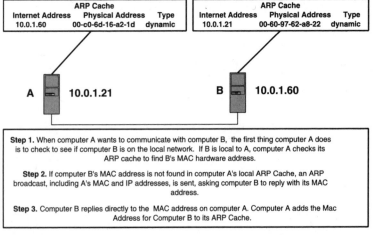

Figure 6.1 ARP resolves IP addresses to network adapter card MAC addresses.

If the destination IP address is remote rather than local, the ARP request will contain the default gateway of the source computer instead of the IP address of the destination host. A router is needed to forward data to the destination host's network.

The ARP Cache

An ARP Cache is located on each computer that runs TCP/IP. The cache is a list of recently resolved IP address-to-MAC address mappings. The IP address and the MAC address are stored as one paired entry in the ARP Cache. These entries can be dynamic or static (manually entered).

The IP-to-MAC address mapping of the local host computer is also included in the cache.

To view the ARP Cache, type *arp -a* at a command prompt.

ARP.EXE

By typing *arp /?* at a command prompt, you can see a list of switches available to use with the ARP command. ARP can also be used to view and modify the entries in the ARP Cache.

Troubleshooting Address Resolution Problems

Address resolution problems are often tracked to incorrect subnet masks.

As mentioned earlier in this chapter, if ARP determines the destination address is local, ARP broadcasts the ARP request on the local subnet. If ARP determines the destination address is remote, the ARP request is sent to the default gateway.

As you discovered in Chapter 4, Subnets and Subnetting, the subnet mask is used to determine whether the IP address is local or remote. So what happens if there is an incorrect subnet mask?

Well, if ARP decides wrongly that a remote machine is actually on the local network, ARP will generate broadcasts on the local network trying to resolve the address with the remote machine to no avail. Because the remote machine can never reply to a local broadcast, no communication can occur.

What if ARP mistakenly decides a local machine is on a remote network? ARP would send an ARP request to the default gateway, and then IP would start sending data to the gateway. The gateway, configured to forward data to remote networks, would not know where to send the data because the IP address is local. So communication would again fail.

ARP, in both examples, is useful in troubleshooting incorrect subnet masks.

For Review

- TCP/IP uses the *Address Resolution Protocol* (ARP) to resolve an IP software address to the physical hardware address of a network interface device.

- The first step ARP takes in resolving an IP address is to check the ARP cache.

- If the destination IP address is local, an ARP request containing the destination IP address is broadcast.

- If the destination IP address is remote, the ARP request will contain the default gateway of the source computer.

- Address resolution problems are often tracked to incorrect subnet masks.

- If ARP wrongly decides a remote machine is actually on the local network, ARP will generate broadcasts on the local network trying to resolve the address with the remote machine.

- If ARP mistakenly decides a local machine is actually on a remote network, IP would send data to the gateway, which would not know where to send the data because the IP address is local.

From Here

Friendly names must be converted to numerical IP addressing for network communication to occur. Several systems, such as HOSTS, DNS, LMHOSTS and WINS, provide host name and NetBIOS name resolution and will be discussed in the next few chapters.

CHAPTER 7

Host Name Resolution

R emember that song, *What's your name, what's your number?*
That could easily be the jingle to introduce this chapter.
Domain Name System (DNS) is the Internet service that makes
it possible for humans to use the Web.

People remember names far more easily than numbers. For
example, what would you remember more: *My Internet address is
18.181.0.29,* or, *My Internet address is* www.pill.com? Computers on
the Internet, as we learned in previous chapters, communicate with
each other through a complex numbering system: the IP address.
Computers hooked to the Internet read IP addresses in datagram
headers, and then call on ARP to find the physical MAC address of
the network interface cards or devices to which they send packets.

While many Internet gurus can work with binary or decimal IP
addresses, the majority of people on the Internet get along better in
this huge sea of technology by using name resolution systems.

TCP/IP, almost since the start of the Internet, is endowed with
the ability to allow applications to request a connection using a
name associated with an IP address. This name is an alias for the
actual IP address, and of course you can map any number of aliases
to the IP address. Common practice, as is the case with DNS, is to
give an address a formal name, such as SDA-SERVER = 209.213.45.6,

and then map a bunch of lesser aliases to the same number, such as APP-SERVER, FILE-SERVER, PRINT-SERVER, and MOTHER-SERVER. These so-called aliases were once known as nicknames in the early days of the Internet.

The Domain Name System

Back in Chapter 2, we touched briefly on the history of the Internet and of the standards authorities. One of the earliest objectives of the *Internet Activities Board* (IAB) was to create a system for resolving domain names and the names of hosts within their control. This was finally achieved in 1984, when the Domain Name System was introduced.

 What is the objective of the Domain Name System? First, it allowed the means by which a computer attached to the Internet could be uniquely referenced and corresponded with, no matter where it is installed. Secondly, DNS allows that name to be translated into the IP address of the computer so that it can be communicated with, as we have outlined in the previous chapters. All communications via TCP/IP depend upon knowing the IP address. Thus, DNS provides for the resolving of host names (derived from domain names) into IP addresses, and the resolving of IP addresses into host names.

The DNS can grow as large as necessary. It is not supported on any one computer but is instead a system of distributed databases installed worldwide. The DNS database keeps growing, because hundreds, and even thousands, of DNS servers are being added to the Internet every day.

But DNS is not only an Internet service. If you maintain a large organization and need to resolve many host names on a private network, a DNS server will be a far better option than huge HOSTS files that take time to parse.

How DNS Works

DNS not only allows IP addresses to be resolved into host names and vice versa, but it also has many other functions. For one, it can be used to identify daemons and services running on remote computers, identify network IDs, provide mailbox information and more.

The DNS is a hierarchical system similar to how the Windows NT registry is arranged. This hierarchy is borrowed directly from the UNIX file directory system. As illustrated in Figure 7.1, you have a high order of nodes representing parents and a lower, or devolved, order of nodes representing children and their siblings. Many like to think of the DNS as an uprooted tree standing on its head. The roots are at the top. The top level domains, the branches and the leaves are children. The branches eventually lead to a single host, and finally down to its IP address where DNS stops and IP takes over to resolve the IP address into the MAC (physical) address.

In Figure 7.1, *harvard* is a subdomain of the top level domain *edu*. The *harvard* subdomain is pictured to include a computer named *wizkid*. So, the *Fully Qualified Domain Name* (FQDN) for the pictured computer would be *wizkid.harvard.edu*.

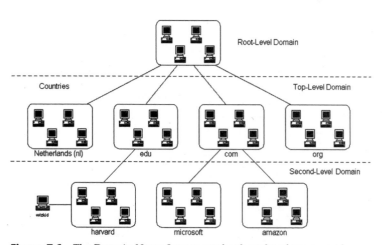

Figure 7.1　The Domain Name System can be thought of as an upside-down, uprooted tree.

The Internet DNS is, of course, a planet-wide system. Under the so-called roots of the DNS are the top-level domains, as illustrated in Table 7.1. These top-level domains are controlled by the Inter-NIC. Figure 7.2 further illustrates the top level of the DNS.

Table 7.1   The top level domains. According to the Internet Society, in July 1998 there were 186 *geographical,* top-level domains—only four examples are shown here.

Top-Level Domains	Description
.COM	Commercial organizations
.EDU	Educational organizations
.GOV	Government organizations (excluding military)
.INT	International organizations
.MIL	Military organizations
.NET	Network providers and network services
.ORG	All other entities and organizations
.CA	Geographical Canada Domain
.CH	Geographical Switzerland Domain
.DE	Geographical Deutschland Domain
.US	Geographical United States Domain

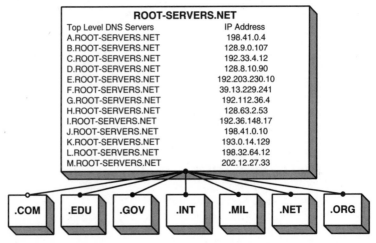

Figure 7.2   The root servers provide DNS service for the top-level domains.

Fully Qualified Domain Name (FQDN)

When referring to a host name on the Internet, we talk of a *fully qualified domain name*, or FQDN. The FQDN refers to the host name, the domain in which the host resides and any upstream domains until the top-level domain (see Figure 7.3 and 7.4). Dots or periods separate each level. For example, tekmatix.com is the FQDN of the Tekmatix company. The domain is *tekmatix*, and the top level domain of tekmatix is *.com*. We could add a subdomain to tekmatix.com, thus tekheads.tekmatix.com. *Tekheads* could represent a host within the *tekmatix* domain. DNS then resolves *tekheads* into an IP address.

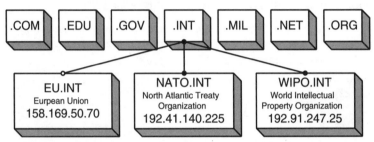

Figure 7.3 Each top level domain is comprised of many lower levels. The .INT top level domain contains three second-level domains.

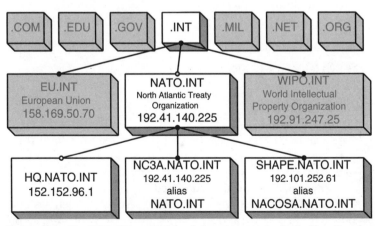

Figure 7.4 The NATO.INT second-level domain contains both Class B and Class C addresses represented at the third level.

Another example of a FQDN is www.cnn.com. Here we are referring to top-level domain *.com*, a second-level domain called *CNN* and a host name *WWW*, which identifies the host to humans as being a World Wide Web server.

The DNS is also occasionally able to perform reverse-address mapping. In other words, it can take an IP address and look up a domain name of a host.

As you are aware, Windows NT uses NetBIOS names that can confuse matters for DNS management; hence, the need for the *Windows Internet Name Service* (WINS), described in Chapter 10.

Resolving Host Names to IP Addresses

Below, we discuss the methods that can be used to resolve host names to IP addresses. Resolution of NetBIOS names to IP addresses is discussed in Chapter 9, NetBIOS Name Resolution.

 Here is the resolution sequence for a host to resolve a host name to an IP address:

1. Check to see if the name queried matches its own.

2. Search a HOSTS file.

3. Query Domain Name System (DNS) server(s), if configured.

4. Check the local NetBIOS cache.

5. Query WINS server(s), if configured.

6. Broadcast b-node queries.

7. Search a LMHOSTS file.

The HOSTS File

 The *HOSTS file* is a static text file located on a local computer. The HOSTS file is designed to map a computer's host name, such as www.microsoft.com, to an IP address. HOSTS files must be manually updated.

A HOSTS file offers a system of name resolving. Such systems become hard to manage as the network grows, however. And if you are dealing with a large file of host names, the process will suffer from the tedious effort of having to search through a huge file of mappings.

On a Windows NT 4.0 system, the HOSTS file is found in the folder

```
%Systemroot%\system32\drivers\etc
```

A sample HOSTS file is installed on Windows NT 4.0 with TCP/IP. Here are some typical host names:

- `www.3com.com`
- `marketing.foobar.net`
- `violet.flowering.org`

and a typical HOSTS file is shown in Table 7.2.

Table 7.2   Example HOSTS File

127.0.0.1	localhost	
10.0.1.21	server2	#BDC
10.0.1.60	server1	#PDC
199.170.88.90	mx2.io.com	#Outgoing E-mail
199.170.88.29	illuminati.io.com	#IO DNS Server
199.170.88.1	aus-gw-F0-0.illuminati.net	
199.170.88.5	pentagon.io.com	
199.170.88.6	xanadu.io.com	
199.170.88.7	bermuda.io.com	
199.170.88.8	atlantis.io.com	

HOSTS File Usage Rules

- Everything after a pound or hash sign is a comment.
- Fields are separated by white space, tabs may separate entries.

 If a computer using a HOSTS file is unable to connect to another computer using its host name, check the HOSTS file for a bad entry. It is also possible that the user is attempting to access a computer using an incorrect FQDN.

Microsoft has been known to ask several questions relating to the poundsign in HOSTS files. Remember that it is merely a symbol that indicates all text following it will be regarded as a comment and will be ignored by the computer.

DNS Server

When a computer is configured to use a DNS server, the computer will send a request to the DNS server to resolve the host name.

Resolving a host name using a DNS server is similar to resolving a host name with a HOSTS file. Rather than parsing the HOSTS file, the DNS server's database is searched for the host name.

Installing and configuring the DNS service on a Windows NT Server is discussed in Chapter 8, Microsoft DNS Server.

NetBIOS Cache

If a computer is unable to resolve a host name using DNS, the local NetBIOS cache will be examined. Maybe you are thinking, *But the NetBIOS cache doesn't contain host names. Why is it being used?* The NetBIOS cache is checked because host names and NetBIOS names can be the same. And when they are, a valid IP address can be obtained. See Chapter 9, NetBIOS Name Resolution, for more information on resolving NetBIOS names to IP addresses.

WINS Server

If the computer has been configured to use WINS, a request will be sent to the WINS server.

As with the NetBIOS cache, the WINS server provides NetBIOS name resolution. If the host name and NetBIOS name are the same, however, a valid IP address can be obtained.

Installing and configuring the WINS is discussed in Chapter 10, Windows Internet Name Service.

b-node Queries

A b-node broadcast is an attempt to resolve a NetBIOS name to an IP address. Similar to the NetBIOS cache and the WINS server, if the host name and the NetBIOS name are the same, the host name can be resolved to an IP address.

Details on b-node broadcasts are contained in Chapter 9, Net-BIOS Name Resolution.

LMHOSTS File

A LMHOSTS file is a static text file similar to a HOSTS file. While a HOSTS file maps host names to IP addresses, a LMHOSTS file maps NetBIOS names to IP addresses. When the same host name and NetBIOS name are used, then a valid IP address can be obtained.

The LMHOSTS file is discussed in Chapter 9, NetBIOS Name Resolution.

If after these seven steps a valid IP address cannot be obtained, the host name resolution process will end and an error message will be returned.

CAUTION
Remember, when you are troubleshooting name resolution issues, determine if the application is resolving a host name or a NetBIOS name.

For Review

- The *Domain Name System* (DNS) provides for resolving host names (derived from domain names) into IP addresses and resolving IP addresses into host names.

- If you maintain a large organization and need to resolve many host names on a private network, a DNS server will be a far better option than huge HOSTS files that take time to parse.

- The resolution sequence for a host to resolve a host name to an IP address is:

  1. Check to see if the name queried matches its own.
  2. Search a HOSTS file.
  3. Query Domain Name System (DNS) server(s), if configured.
  4. Check the local NetBIOS cache.
  5. Query WINS server(s), if configured.
  6. Broadcast b-node queries.
  7. Search a LMHOSTS file.

- The *HOSTS file* is a static text file located on a local computer. The HOSTS file is designed to map a computer's host name, such as www.microsoft.com, to an IP address. HOSTS files must be manually updated.

- If a computer, using a HOSTS file, is unable to connect to another computer using its host name, check the HOSTS file for a bad entry. It is also possible the user is attempting to access a computer using an incorrect FQDN.

- The pound sign in HOSTS files is merely a symbol that indicates all text following it must be regarded as a comment.

From Here

Chapter 8, next, covers DNS resolution; Chapter 9 covers NetBIOS name resolution; and Chapter 10 covers *Windows Internet Name Service* (WINS).

CHAPTER 8

Microsoft DNS Server

Microsoft first introduced the DNS service as part of the Windows NT Resource Kit for version 3.51. Today DNS is part and parcel of Windows NT 4.0. However, DNS Server is not automatically installed. DNS is added the same way as the other networking services, such as RIP.

Advantages to using a DNS server include:

■ UNIX-based systems, Macintosh, and other non-WINS-enabled clients are more easily integrated into your network. With DNS, these devices can be accessed using friendly names and the non-WINS-enabled computers can query the DNS server to locate Windows-based devices.

■ Name resolution on the Internet requires a DNS Server rather than a WINS Server. This functionality can be extended to enhance access to an organization's intranet.

In larger organizations, a DNS Server provides a hierarchical naming system across the entire network.

All DNS software today is based on the University of California at Berkeley's implementation of DNS, called BIND. BIND stands for *Berkeley Internet Name Domain* and was created to work with

Berkeley UNIX. In this regard, many people mistakenly think that BIND is an Internet standard. The Internet DNS standards are based on RFCs 974, 1034, 1035, and 1183. BIND is based on these RFCs, as is Microsoft DNS. For a review of how DNS works, see Chapter 7, Host Name Resolution.

The Bind Boot File

The BIND Boot File is used in the start up of DNS as a boot process. Microsoft has included support for this file to provide compatibility with BIND versions of DNS and/or DNS management utilities. BIND Boot files can be copied to Microsoft DNS Server as a boot mechanism.

The following outlines the records in the Bind Boot file:

- **Directory**. This entry refers to the location of the DNS files. For example: `directory c:\winnt\system32\dns`.

- **Cache**. This entry refers to the cache file (discussed later).

- **Primary**. This entry refers to the zone files for which the local name server is responsible. For example: `primary tekmatix.com tekmatix.dns`.

- **Secondary**. This entry refers to the zone files for the local name server providing secondary name resolving services. The entry also refers to the server that can provide the secondary with zone file updates. For example: `secondary ns2.tekmatix.com 209.215.182.6 tekmatix.dns`.

- **Forwarders**. The entry refers to the name server that can be contacted for recursive queries. For example: `forwarders 209.215.182.7`

- **Slave**. This entry is included with the Forwarders entry to force the local name server to use the forwarders to resolve a query. The slave entry follows the Forwarders entry. For example: `forwarders 209.215.182.7. slave`

Microsoft's DNS Manager can be a bit quirky, so seasoned UNIX DNS managers now running Windows NT may prefer to edit the zone files in a text editor. If this is what you prefer, then you will need to work with the Boot file options just described.

Zone Files

The DNS database is sorted into a group of files known as zones. Zones are essentially a means of dispersing the management of sections of a domain over multiple domain name servers. Zones make for easier management of the domain name space. (The term zone is very misleading. It would have been better to call these files domain files, or something similar. In fact, some DNS systems (even those running under Windows NT) do not use term *zone* at all.

Zones can also be copied from one server to another through an automatic replication known as zone transfers (which are essentially file transfers). Zone transfers allow an organization to maintain a group of primary and secondary name servers, while only managing one server.

Zone files contain the resource records for the domain or the portion of domain for which the name server is responsible. Windows NT stores these files in `\WINNT\SYSTEM32\dns`.

Three types of files are managed by Windows DNS:

- Database files
- Cache files ·
- Reverse lookup files

Microsoft's version of the DNS files have the .dns extension. UNIX and other Windows NT-compatible files frequently have the .db extension. The DNS file is nothing more than a text file with lines of data that are parsed by the name server. These files can be simply edited by hand in a text editor, or you can manage them with the Windows NT DNS Manager.

The SOA Record

The database or DNS files start with the SOA record, which means start of authority for the file. The SOA record specifies the primary server for the domain.

There are a number of labeling and layout conventions that you should be aware of in a zone file:

- The @ symbol refers to the local server and starts the SOA record.
- The *IN* refers to the record as being an Internet record.

- The brackets "( )" contain the SOA record if it is on more than one line.

- The ; is a comment. Anything to the right of the ; is ignored by the resolver.

- The serial number refers to the version number of the name server's database. DNS manager updates this number every time you update the records. If you edit zone files with a text editor, you will need to increment this number yourself.

- The refresh time in seconds is the time it takes for a secondary name server to check the primary for DNS record changes.

- The retry time is the time that will lapse before a secondary name server retries a zone transfer.

- The expiration (expire) time is the time at which old zone information is deleted.

- The time to live is when the server has to cache resource records from the database file.

Note after the name server name is the e-mail address of the administrator. This is the only place in any TCP/IP service where you will find the e-mail address devoid of the @ sign, which is part of the SMTP e-mail address convention.

The Name Server Record

The name server record in the zone file refers to collateral name servers that cater to the domain. This syntax is as follows:

```
<domain> IN NS <nameserver host>
```

or

```
@ IN NS ns1.tekmatix.com
```

The Mail Exchange Record

The mail exchange record refers to the name of the mail server that receives mail for the domain. You can list multiple mail servers for a domain and you can specify the order in which mail servers are used to process mail.

The Host Record

The host record refers to the actual IP address of a host. The syntax for specifying host records is as follows:

```
<host name> IN A <IP address>
```

For example:

```
Mail IN A 209.215.232.6
Web IN A 209.215.232.7
FTP IN A 209.215.232.8
```

The Local Host Record

The local host record refers to the loopback address of the name server:

```
Localhost IN A 127.0.0.1
```

The CNAME Record

The CNAME (for *Canonical Name*) record refers to the alias of the host name. In other words, this section enables you to provide more than one name for each host. The following syntax is required for CNAME entries:

```
<alias> CNAME <host name>
```

 By using CNAME, you can provide a name for each TCP/IP service running on a host. For example, the server below has a mail server, Web server, and FTP server all running on the same computer:

```
Server1 IN A 208.212.170.142
MAIL CNAME server1
WWW CNAME Server1
FTP CNAME Server1
```

The Named Cache File

Every DNS server environment includes a named cache file that contains information referencing the top-level or upstream servers of the Internet. This means that if for some reason a local name server cannot handle a query, it defers to the cache file to look for the upstream servers to resolve the name.

This cache file is provided by the InterNIC and can be accessed at: `ftp://rs.internic.net/domain/named.cache`

The Reverse Resolver File

Every DNS server contains a Reverse Resolver file that allows a name server to resolve an IP address into a host name. This process in known as *reverse lookup*. The following list represents the reverse lookup files:

```
Network ID     Zone File
36.x.x.x       36.in-addr.arpa
138.107.x.x.   107.138.in-addr-arpa
242.24.108.x  108.24.242.in-addr-arpa
```

The Pointer Records

The pointer records are the *reverse lookup* entries. The following syntax represents the pointer record entry:

```
<ip reverse domain name> IN PTR <host name>
```

This represents the following entry:

```
209.215.182.5.in-addr.arpa. IN PTR ftp.tekmatix.com
```

The Arpa-127.rev File

Every DNS server environment includes the Arpa-127 file. As you now know, this is the loopback address and provides the reverse lookup information for the local host.

Name Servers

A domain name server is a computer and operating system that is capable of running the DNS daemon or service. Before Microsoft supported DNS in Windows NT, the name servers of the world were UNIX computers.

Installing and Configuring Microsoft DNS

Microsoft's DNS Server service can be installed on a computer with Windows NT Server installed. This computer must be using the TCP/IP protocol and be configured with a static IP address. The following are the steps you need to take to install the DNS service.

1. Go to the Control Panel and double-click the Network icon.

2. Click the Services tab and click the Add button (wait for the OS to build a list of available services).

3. Select the Microsoft DNS Server service and click OK (see Figure 8.1).

4. Point the installation to the Windows NT distribution files (usually the i386 path).

5. Click your way out through the Close button and then restart the server.

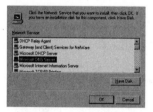

Figure 8.1 Add the Microsoft DNS service.

NOTE

If for any reason you must reinstall or remove Microsoft DNS, make sure to go to the %winroot%\system32\dns directory and delete it (just the \dns directory). The reason for doing this is the Microsoft service sees a boot file in the preexisting directory and assumes it is being asked to run as a BIND server. It will try to read the boot file and if it is not a valid file, it will fail. If this happens to you, check the Event Log to be sure it's a DNS problem, then remove the DNS server service, the \dns directory, and reinstall the service.

Do not attempt to run the DNS service at this point. After installation you need to go back to Networking and check some important information.

1. Go to the Control Panel and double-click the Network icon.

2. Go to the Protocols tab and select TCP/IP Protocol.

3. You can double-click TCP/IP Protocol or click the Properties button.

4. At the Microsoft TCP/IP Properties dialog box, select the DNS tab.

5. In the Host Name edit field, enter the host name of your name server, as you intend to register it with the InterNIC, (or perhaps it already is).

6. In the Domain edit field, enter your Internet domain that completes your FQDN for this name server.

7. Click your way out of the dialogs through the OK buttons.

Windows NT will warn you that your NetBIOS name, which is on the Identification tab of the Network dialog box, differs from the name you provided in the DNS dialog box. Trust me, you want that to be the case. What Windows NT is telling you is that your computer will be known by one name on the Internet and by another on your LAN.

I prefer that to be the case. For starters, if your server is being configured as a DNS server, then it needs an Internet host name becoming of a name server. MYCOMPUTER or THEPDC just does not cut it as an Internet host name in my humble opinion.

Secondly, you are likely going to change the NetBIOS name of the computer, or move it, some time in the future, so the host name you have registered with the InterNIC will eventually differ from that future NetBIOS server name. One name is a FQDN host name for an Internet service; the other is a name that only your LAN and Windows NT cares about.

Thirdly, if you are managing a network of many users (even 10 is a lot), they will be getting DNS service via the FQDN DNS name you give the Internet host, running on your computer.

Fourthly, DNS name servers on the Internet are commonly named ns1 or ns2, and so on. Unless you're inclined to name computers Goofy, Barney, Pooh, Wazu, or Flash, you will likely name your computer something like TEKMATIXPDC or SQLSERVER. Having these as name server host names not only looks silly, but you're also letting the Internet know what these computers are primarily being used for. Generally, the less conspicuous your computers are on the Internet the better.

The best name you can give a name server is simply according to the following syntax, `<ns1.domain.name>`. For example:

`ns1.tekmatix.com`

That name seems to be a lot of words for something that looks so simple. However, if you make the mistake of leaving the DNS host name and domain name fields blank or put a NetBIOS name in there, Windows NT will use it to set up the zone files via DNS Manager.

DNS Manager

After installation you will find that the service installation has added the DNS Manager (dnsadmin.exe) to the Administrative Tools menu. This is a smart tool that can at times seem a little quirky if you are using it for the first time. The tool allows you to manage multiple name servers from a single computer.

Let's start setting up your DNS server:

1. Go to the Start, Programs, Administrative Tools, DNS Manager menu option.

2. In the left tree pane, right-click Server List and select New Server from the drop-down menu, as illustrated in Figure 8.2.

3. Enter the IP address for the new server (make sure the server is assigned a static IP address and that it has the DNS service installed and running).

The server will appear as an IP address on the Server List tree. The DNS server now must be configured for the role it will play in your name server enterprise-wide services.

Figure 8.2 Add a new DNS server.

Server Roles

You will now decide what role your server will play. In other words, will it be a primary name server, a secondary name server, or a caching-only server?

 The name server can also be set up to act as an IP forwarder that can be used as a private resolver that passes queries it gets from users on a private network to name servers on a public network or one that is sitting outside the firewall.

Primary Name Server Setup

The first step to setting up a primary name server is to create a *zone* into which you will add records that enable computers on the Internet to resolve the IP addresses of your hosts or resolve the host names out of your IP addresses.

The following will step us through the process of setting up the zone files:

1. Right-click the server IP address and choose New Zone.

2. A dialog box will appear and allow you to choose Zone Type, Primary or Secondary. Choose Primary and then click the Next button.

3. In the next dialog box, enter the name of the domain (Zone Name) you are creating. Then hit the Tab button or click in the Zone File field. You can add an existing zone file into the Zone File field if you have one. If you do, you need to make sure it is in the `%winroot%\system32\dns` directory.

4. Click Next and then click Finish. Windows NT will build a zone file and automatically add the standard root resolver files (such as the loopback file) to the branch under the name server's IP address.

NOTE
By default, Windows NT 4.0 usually adds only the SOA record and the NS record to the zone file.

Creating Secondary Name Servers

Installing and setting up a secondary name server is essential if you are undertaking mission-critical responsibility for a domain, or several. In fact, it is not unusual to set up and maintain multiple backup name servers.

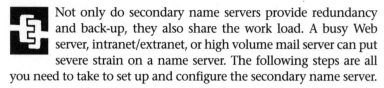 Not only do secondary name servers provide redundancy and back-up, they also share the work load. A busy Web server, intranet/extranet, or high volume mail server can put severe strain on a name server. The following steps are all you need to take to set up and configure the secondary name server.

1. Add a server (IP address) to the server list as you did when you created a primary.

2. Right-click the server and choose New Zone from the pop-up menu. In the new zone dialog box, choose Secondary.

3. Click the Next button and enter the zone file information as you did before. Windows NT will usually provide this information.

4. The next dialog box prompts you to identify the IP Masters for the zone. Again Windows inserts this information but allows overriding it with manual input.

5. Click Next to arrive at the Finish dialog. You are done.

Caching-Only Servers

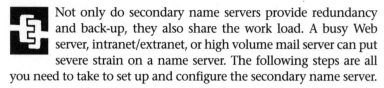 A caching-only server, as we discussed above, is a name server you will only use for resolving addresses. It cannot be a keeper or administrator of domains or zones. The `\%systemroot%\system32\Dns\cache.dns` file contains the root name servers that provide root-level name resolution in the United States and is automatically installed with DNS.

Caching-only servers do not host zones. You need only install the server and not enter any zone information.

IP-Forwarding Servers

The IP Forwarder (or query forwarder) is also a caching-only server. The main difference is you need to configure it with the IP address of another (authoritative) server. The following steps are all that are involved in setting up a name server to be an IP-Forwarder.

1. In DNS Manager, right-click the server and select Properties.

2. Click the Forwarders tab and check the Use Forwarders checkbox.

3. Select Operate as Slave Server only if the forwarder is using the services of the authoritative server to which queries are relayed.

4. Enter address of name servers to which queries should be relayed.

The SOA Record

We have already discussed the idea behind the SOA record. From here, however, you can load the record and change or update the values to suit your environment (of course, you can do all this manually, but that's another story). The following steps take us through changing or updating the SOA record:

1. Right-click the domain (zone) you wish to edit and choose Properties. Notice that on the General tab you can change the name server from primary to secondary or vice versa.

2. Click the SOA tab. The SOA fields will load default information. (Note this information is stored in the Windows registry, so editing the .dns file in the %winroot%\system32\dns will do no good. Manual editing is covered later in this chapter.) The following information can be changed:

   - **Responsible Person Mailbox DNS Name:** This is the e-mail address (the only one where you will NOT enter an @ sign). I made note of this entry first because 99.9 percent of the time it is the only entry you will initially change. Windows NT usually adds *"Admin"* to this field.

   - **Primary Name Server DNS Name:** This is the name you have registered as your primary name server with InterNIC. You need only enter the host name, because DNS Manager appends the domain name.

   - **Serial Number:** This is the version number that gets incremented every time you update the server data file (on the DNS menu). If you edit the zone files in a manual text editor, you will have to increment this number yourself.

   - **Refresh Interval:** This value tells the Secondary servers how often to check the serial number to perform a zone transfer. If you have a busy primary that is being changed a lot (adding new zones on a daily basis), you should set this value to something that will realistically keep the secondaries up-to-date. If you lose a primary name server and the zone files have not been transferred for some time, then clients depending on name resolving will not be too happy. In today's hectic Internet business climate, losing a name server for an hour can be like losing the phone system for an hour. The name servers at TekMatix.com are refreshed every 15 minutes.

- **Retry Interval:** Related to the above, this tells the secondary how long to wait before re-attempting to connect to a primary when a connection attempt failed. This could be left at default of 10 minutes.

- **Expire Time:** This is the time a secondary is still allowed to resolve old information despite being unable to connect to the primary for a zone transfer. The default is 24 hours.

- **Minimum Default TTL:** This is how long other name servers can maintain cached information about records that your primary resolves on their behalf.

3. Next click the Notify tab. These fields are for the benefit of secondary name servers. Here you will enter the IP address of your secondary name servers that you wish to notify in the event of a change. You can also check the option to *Only Allow Access From Secondaries Included on Notify List* to exclude certain servers from retrieving zone information.

4. Click OK and go to DNS | Update Server Data Files to bring the zone file in the \Dns directory up to date.

WINS Lookup

The last tab allows you to integrate DNS with WINS. This requires the host and NetBIOS names to be the same. The hosts and names also have to be registered with the WINS Server.

The following options can be set in the WINS Lookup tab:

1. **Use WINS Resolution:** Checking this box allows the DNS service to query WINS for queries that it for some reason fails to resolve.

2. **Settings only affect local server:** By selecting this option, you prevent sending WINS records during a zone transfer. This check box is available only for a primary DNS server.

3. **WINS Servers:** This entry allows you to enter the address of the WINS servers. You cannot leave this blank.

4. **Advanced:** Clicking this button loads the Advanced Zone Properties Dialog box. The fields to set include the following:

- **Submit DNS Domain as NetBIOS Scope**: This option allows you to use a domain name as a NetBIOS scope.

- **Cache Timeout Value**: This setting determines how long the DNS server is allowed to keep the information it gets from WINS.

- **Lookup Timeout Value:** This is how long the DNS server is allowed to wait for a result of a WINS query.

Creating a Reverse Lookup Zone

This should be your next task if you plan to resolve IP addresses against host names. This is the reverse of getting an IP address when you know the host name, but unless you create this first, you will not be able to create the PTR records for reverse lookup, described next. The process of creating the Reverse Lookup Zone is as follows:

1. Go to DNS, the first item on the menu, where most applications have File and select Update Server Data Files. This will save any new information you provided to the new zone files you created earlier.

2. Next you need to create a new Zone as you did earlier, but hold it—instead of giving it a name, you now must give it an IP address that excludes the host name. In other words, you must provide the network ID portion of the IP address (for the Class address space). If your network is 208.212.170.0, then this is the address you use, but you must reverse the order of octets. In other words the information you enter into the field is 170.212.208. Also add a final period to the third octet (170.212.208.).

3. Now add the value *in-addr.arpa* so that the complete zone name is 170.212.208.in-addr-arpa.

4. Next tab over to the Zone File field or click in the field. The zone file with the .dns extension is added automatically.

NOTE
If you already added hosts that require reverse IP address lookup, then you would either need to delete the host and re-enter it, or manually edit the text file or registry entry.

Adding Host Records

Your next task is to set up host records. Right-click the domain in the left pane in DNS Manager. The New Host dialog box will appear. All you need to do is enter the host name (without a trailing domain name) and its IP address.

You also have the option of creating the associated PTR record by checking the Create Associated PTR Record checkbox. This will fail, however, if you have not created the reverse lookup zone, described above.

Adding the Other Records

A number of additional record types can be used in the DNS for information lookup. For example, the emerging *Voice-over-IP* (VOIP) industry is using DNS records to allow voice gateways to resolve gateway IP addresses into an elaborate IP-telephone number-addressing scheme.

For the most part, however, you will use the New Record option to add aliases or *Canonical Names* (CNAME) to your zones. CNAMEs allow you to resolve more than one name to an IP address, as discussed earlier in the chapter.

These records include the following:

- **A**. The A record is the host entry record. This is the default record used when you select the New Host option.

- **AAAA**. This is the host A record type for Ipng or IP version 6, wherever it is.

- **AFSDB**. This record provides the address of an *Andrew File System* (AFS) database server or a *Distributed Computing Environment* (DCE) authenticated name server.

- **CNAME**. This is the canonical name, or alias, of the host.

- **HINFO**. HINFO allows you to enter CPU and OS information about the host.

- **ISDN**. This entry allows you to map an entry to an ISDN phone number. This entry is used with the *Route Through* (RT) entry discussed later.

- **MB**. This is an experimental record type associated with e-mail.

- **MG**. Also under experiment.

- **MINFO**. Also under experiment, this record is reserved for entering information about the party responsible for a Mail Record.

- **MR**. MR is an experimental record that allocates alias names to mail records.

- **MX**. MX stands for mail exchange. It has been around since the inception of DNS. MX records cater to inbound connections for mail. You do not need an MX record in order to participate in the e-mail community of the Internet. In the case where you are able to specify a mail server for a domain, connections can be made directly to the mail server. If the mail protocols are listening for mail on the well-known ports, the mail will be catered to, and there are several reasons you would use MX records:

  1. A host that is not directly connected to the Internet can have a server that is connected by its mail exchange agent.

  2. The MX record can redirect mail to another server when the primary or main server is down.

  3. The record provides the organization with a means of being able to deliver mail to a virtual host; and

  4. You can use MX records to exchange mail between mail servers on either side of a firewall.

- **NS**. This stands for Name Server record. This allows DNS to locate other mail servers in the domain,

- **PTR**. This is the pointer record that points to the IP address when the reverse lookup is used to query the IP address of a host.

- **RP**. This is the entry for responsible people for a domain the DNS is serving.

- **RT**. This is the route-through entry that provides information on how to reach a host through dial-up ISDN or X.25.

- **SOA**. As discussed above, this is the Start of Authority record.

- **TXT**. This is a means of tagging additional information onto the records. It can be used to provide additional information to the HINFO record.

- **WKS.** This lets querying agents known which well-known services are running on a certain host.

- **X25.** This entry lets you provide mapping of host names to X.25 names.

Creating Sub-Domains

For whatever reasons, you decide you want to break down your domains into sub-domains. DNS Manager allows you to set this up relatively easy. You need only select the parent domain under servers and right-click. Select New Domain from the menu and enter the new sub-domain name (without the upper-level domain).

If the sub-domain is resolved on the local computer, you simply enter the new domain. If you are resolving to a remote host, you must add the applicable records.

For Review

- UNIX-based systems, Macintosh, and other non-WINS enabled clients are more easily integrated into your network with a DNS server. They can be accessed using friendly names and the non-WINS enabled computers can query the DNS Server to locate Windows-based systems.

- CNAME is the canonical name, or alias, of the host.

- By using CNAME, you can provide a name for each TCP/IP service running on a host. For example, a mail server, Web server, and FTP server can be running on the same computer.

- The name server can also be set up to act as an IP forwarder that can be used as a private resolver which passes queries from users on a private network to name servers on a public network or one that is sitting outside the firewall.

- Secondary name servers provide redundancy and share the work load.

- A caching-only server is a name server used for resolving addresses. The `\%systemroot%\system32\DNS\cache.dns` file contains the root name servers that provide root-level name resolution in the United States and is automatically installed with DNS.

- The DNS database is sorted into a group of files known as zones, which are essentially a means of dispersing the management of sections of a domain over multiple domain name servers.

- Use WINS Resolution to allow the DNS service to query WINS for queries that it fails with for some reason.

- MX stands for mail exchange.

From Here

Our journey into name resolution and lookup is not over. Chapter 9 covers NetBIOS name resolution. Chapter 10, on WINS and how it interoperates with DNS, gets a lot of attention on the TCP/IP exam.

CHAPTER 9

NetBIOS Name Resolution

NetBIOS stands for *Network Basic Input/Output System*. It is the basic network connectivity service provided by Windows NT 4.0. NetBIOS is not a protocol—it is an *Application Programming Interface* (API) that allows the computer to participate in and use network services. The NetBIOS architecture is the basis of node addressing for Microsoft networking components. NetBIOS names identify computers on the network, accomplished by a unique naming system. NetBIOS names can be up to 15 characters in length and *cannot* contain any blank spaces or the following characters:

    / \ * , . " @

In addition to the 15 character name, a sixteenth invisible character is used to identify the kind of service being offered by the computer, such as the server or workstation service, or even identification as a domain controller. When a NetBIOS name is less than 15 characters in length, NetBIOS *pads* the remaining characters with blanks to reach the sixteenth character. So a NetBIOS name can be up to 15 characters in length with the sixteenth character reserved, and each NetBIOS name must be unique on the network.

The NetBIOS name is often what we consider the *friendly name* of the computer, such as Computer12, Corporate1, or even the user's first name. Any name can apply, as long as it is unique on the network and conforms to the standards above. NetBIOS names make it easy for *the users* to identify which computer is which.

Typical NetBIOS Computer Names

- Research1
- Research32
- ResearchServ1
- Sales1
- MarketingServ1
- Corporate1
- SGServer6
- Mary
- Billiesmac
- Albert

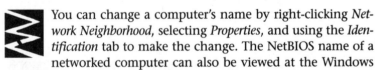 You can change a computer's name by right-clicking *Network Neighborhood*, selecting *Properties*, and using the *Identification* tab to make the change. The NetBIOS name of a networked computer can also be viewed at the Windows NT command prompt by entering `nbtstat -n`.

UNIVERSAL NAMING CONVENTION (UNC)

An issue that sometimes causes confusion in relation to NetBIOS names is use of UNC—Universal Naming Convention names. The UNC is simply a way to access a shared resource on a computer that already has a NetBIOS name. Think of the UNC as a postal address. A postal address always consists of a name and some kind of location information, such as a street address, city, state, and zip code. This is a uniform method for sending mail from one person to another. The UNC name is the same. It provides a uniform method for accessing computers and named shares located on those computers. So the NetBIOS name is the actual name of the computer and the UNC is simply a way to get to that computer. The UNC name is represented in the following manner:

```
\\computername\sharename
```

The UNC consists of the computer name and share name and is accessed via the run command in Windows NT and Windows 95/98. The UNC always begins with two backslashes and the computer's NetBIOS name:

```
\\computer6
```

In a NetBIOS network, entering `\\computer6` at the command prompt would provide the user with a list of all the resources that are shared and available on computer6. The command can be further refined if the user knows the name of a shared resource s/he would like to access. This increased specificity is accomplished by an additional backslash and the name of the shared folder or resource:

```
\\computer6\docs
```

In the above example, the folder *docs* is a shared resource on computer6. If the name of the actual document the user would like to access is known, the UNC can be further refined with an additional backslash and the name of the shared document:

```
\\computer6\docs\keynote.ppt
```

The shared PowerPoint presentation, `keynote.ppt`, can then be accessed directly by using the UNC name. UNC names allow quick access to network resources, especially familiar resources that are often used.

Of course, the UNC is only one way to access a computer and its share(s). Access to resources can also be accomplished through a GUI interface by using Network Neighborhood on Windows 95/98 and Windows NT machines.

Humans are language-based creatures. No matter how great our math skills, our brains function on a language basis. Computers, however, communicate through mathematical numbers, specifically binary math. Bridging this gap between humans and computers requires the conversion of NetBIOS names to mathematical addresses. So, NetBIOS names, though useful to us, must be translated to be mathematically based IP addresses.

Resolving NetBIOS Names to IP Addresses

 Several systems are available on a Windows NT network to resolve the NetBIOS names to IP addresses so that communication can continue on a network. A computer will attempt NetBIOS name resolution in the following order:

1. NetBIOS name cache
2. WINS Server(s), if configured
3. Broadcast b-node queries
4. LMHOSTS file
5. HOSTS file
6. DNS Server(s), if configured

NetBIOS Name Cache

This local cache contains the local computer NetBIOS names as well as computer names that have been recently resolved to IP addresses.

WINS Server

This service provides resolution of NetBIOS names to IP addresses. WINS is a server service that provides dynamic mapping of NetBIOS computer names to IP addresses. Installing and configuring the Windows Internet Name Service is discussed in Chapter 10, Windows Internet Name Service (WINS).

NetBIOS Broadcast

A broadcast packet is sent over the network requesting the resolution of a particular NetBIOS name. A computer that can resolve the NetBIOS name can answer the broadcast and help the broadcasting computer resolve the NetBIOS name to an IP address.

LMHOSTS File

This is a text file located on the local machine that maps the NetBIOS name to the IP address. LMHOSTS files are static files that must be manually updated, but they still provide necessary service in some networking circumstances. LMHOSTS files are useful in very small networks where each computer's four-octet IP address does not change frequently or in providing a name and address map to servers or other network devices that have permanent IP addresses. The LMHOSTS file is also discussed later in this chapter.

HOSTS File

This is a static text file located on the local machine that maps host names to IP addresses. This step only works if the host name and the NetBIOS name are the same. HOSTS files are discussed in Chapter 7, Host Name Resolution.

DNS Server

This server holds a database that maps host names to IP addresses. This step will only work if the host name and the NetBIOS name are the same. For more information on DNS Server, see Chapter 8.

NetBIOS Node Types

The order used to provide NetBIOS name resolution over TCP/IP is determined by the computer's name resolution node type. These types, as listed in Table 9.1, are defined in the *Request for Comments* (RFCs) 1001 and 1002.

Table 9.1
NetBIOS over TCP/IP Name Resolution Modes

Mode	Description
b-node (broadcast)	Uses broadcasts for NetBIOS name registration and resolution.
p-node (peer-to-peer)	Uses a NetBIOS Name Server, that is, WINS, for name registration and resolution. If the WINS server is offline, then name registration and name resolution will fail.
m-node (mixed)	This is a combination of b-node and p-node. First broadcast is used for name registration and name resolution. If name resolution fails, then the WINS server is queried.
h-node (hybrid)	This is also a combination of b-node and p-node. However, the WINS server is used for name registration and name resolution. If a name cannot be resolved by the WINS server, then broadcasts are used.
Microsoft-enhanced b-node	This enhanced b-node uses the LMHOSTS file for name resolution if efforts to resolve a name by broadcasts fail. When Windows NT is first installed, the node type is set as Microsoft enhanced b-node.

LMHOSTS File

The LMHOSTS file is a static file that maps NetBIOS names to IP addresses. A NetBIOS name for IP address mapping in the LMHOSTS file allows that NetBIOS name to be resolved for a remote computer that cannot respond to name query broadcasts.

When the LMHOSTS file was introduced, it could not be used to provide logon validation across subnets or when designing a domain that included multiple subnets. These limitations were removed by introducing a few keywords in the LMHOSTS file. The keywords and their functionality are described below.

Keyword	Description
#PRE	When #PRE is added after an entry, that entry is preloaded into the NetBIOS name cache. The entry stays in the NetBIOS name cache and does not time out.
#DOM:<domain>	When added after an entry, #DOM associates that entry with the domain specified by <domain>. This keyword affects how the browser and logon services behave in routed TCP/IP environments. To pre-load a #DOM entry, you must also add the #PRE keyword to the line.
#BEGIN_ALTERNATE	Gathers multiple #INCLUDE statements.
#END_ALTERNATE	Marks the end of multiple #INCLUDE statements.
#INCLUDE <filename>	Forces the system to seek the specified <filename> and parse it as if it were local. The #INCLUDE keyword allows you to use a centralized LMHOSTS file located on a server. In this way, a centrally maintained LMHOSTS file can be treated as though it were located on the local computer.

An example of an LMHOSTS file is:

```
131.107.2.5   server2                        #print server
131.107.2.7   server3                        #SQL server
131.107.2.2   server1 #PRE #DOM:domain1      #Domain controller
```

Use the # sign to mark text as comments. When the LMHOSTS file is used for name resolution, it is parsed one line at a time starting with the first line. To optimize the use of LMHOSTS, make the most frequently used resource the first entry, keep comments to a minimum, and list any entries with the #PRE keyword at the end.

The greatest limitation associated with using an LMHOSTS file is that it is a static file. Since it is static, entries have to be updated if the name or the IP address of the computer changes. This means updating the LMHOSTS file on each and every computer. An LMHOSTS file can be created or edited with any DOS editor and must be saved to %SYSTEMROOT%\system32\drivers\etc.

A sample LMHOSTS file (LMHOSTS.SAM) is saved to your hard disk when Windows NT is installed. It is located in %SYSTEMROOT%\system32\drivers\etc.

Configuring an LMHOSTS File

On each computer, in addition to an entry for the PDC, add an entry for each backup domain controller on the local network to the LMHOSTS file.

When configuring an LMHOSTS file for computers accessing multiple domains, add an entry for:

- the PDC in each remote domain
- each domain controller in the local domain

For Review

- Use nbtstat -n at the command prompt to view the NetBIOS name of the computer
- A computer will attempt NetBIOS name resolution in the following order:
  1. NetBIOS name cache
  2. WINS Server(s), if configured
  3. Broadcast b-node queries
  4. LMHOSTS file

5. HOSTS file

6. DNS Server(s), if configured

- The types of NetBIOS over TCP/IP Name Resolution Modes are:
  - b-node (broadcast)
  - p-node (peer-to-peer)
  - m-node (mixed)
  - h-node (hybrid)
  - Microsoft-enhanced b-node
- Keywords that can be added to a LMHOSTS file:
  - #PRE
  - #DOM
  - #INCLUDE
- A LMHOSTS entry using #PRE will be preloaded into the NetBIOS name cache.
- #DOM indicates a domain controller
- To optimize the use of a LMHOSTS file:
  1. Put most frequently used resource as the first entry.
  2. Keep comments to a minimum.
  3. List any entries with the #PRE keyword at the end of the file.
- On each computer, in addition to an entry for the PDC, add an entry for each backup domain controller on the local network to the LMHOSTS file.
- When configuring an LMHOSTS file for computers accessing multiple domains, add an entry for:
  - the PDC in each remote domain
  - each domain controller in the local domain

From Here

Chapter 10 next explains how WINS servers are used in Windows NT 4.0 TCP/IP networking.

CHAPTER 10

Windows Internet Name Service (WINS)

The *Windows Internet Name Service* (WINS) provides an easy way to resolve a NetBIOS name to the associated IP address.

A Windows-based computer that has been configured with the IP address of the WINS Server will register its NetBIOS name and IP address during startup in order to ensure that both are unique on the network. In this chapter we will cover how WINS handles NetBIOS name registration and name resolution.

WINS Clients

When the Windows NT operating system is first installed on a computer, the node type is set as Microsoft-enhanced b-node. This can result in a large amount of broadcast traffic that can have significant effects on the functioning of your network. In addition, in the segmented network, resources located across a router cannot be located without either an LMHOSTS file or a HOSTS file located on the local computer. Installation of a WINS Server to provide NetBIOS name resolution can greatly reduce the amount of associated broadcast traffic.

When a WINS client computer is configured to use a WINS Server, the client's node type is changed to h-node. Remember, b-node, which is the initial setting on a new Windows NT installation, relies on broadcasts exclusively. H-node is a combination of b-node and p-node so that the WINS Server is used first for name registration and name resolution. If a NetBIOS name is not resolved by the WINS Server, then the broadcast method is used. For more information, return to Table 9.1 in Chapter 9, NetBIOS Name Resolution.

A WINS client can be any computer running one of the following operating systems:

- Windows NT Server or Workstation 3.5 or later
- Windows 95/98
- Windows for Workgroups 3.11 running Microsoft TCP/IP-32
- Microsoft Network Client 3.0 for MS-DOS with the real-mode TCP/IP driver
- LAN Manager 2.2c for MS-DOS

The WINS client computer must be configured with the IP address of the WINS Server. The WINS client can be configured either dynamically via a DHCP server or manually. Figure 10.1 shows the WINS tab of the TCP/IP Properties box. Use this tab to manually configure the use of WINS for name registration and name resolution. Both a primary and secondary WINS Server can be entered.

If the primary WINS Server is offline, or if name resolution fails, an alternative WINS Server may be queried.

On Windows NT computers, to make the computer a WINS client you need only designate a DHCP server or a WINS Server. A WINS Server cannot also be a WINS client—the IP address of the WINS Server should be fixed, not dynamically allocated. On a Windows NT server with WINS Server installed, starting the Windows Internet Name Service in the Start | Control Panel | Services applet invokes the WINS Server—this same service is *not* needed for a computer to be a WINS client.

You can also configure a computer to use an LMHOSTS file for NetBIOS name resolution by checking the Enable LMHOSTS Lookup box. Use the Import LMHOSTS button to designate the location of an alternative file.

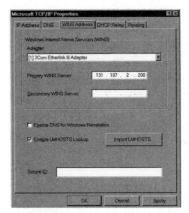

Figure 10.1 The WINS tab of the TCP/IP Properties dialog box is used to designate the WINS Server(s) each WINS client will use for name registration and name resolution.

When a WINS client starts, it registers its NetBIOS name and its associated IP address with the designated WINS Server. Because a computer can have more than one NetBIOS name, the registration process is repeated for each of the NetBIOS names that the computer must use.

Later, when the WINS client needs to communicate with another computer using that computer's name, the name query is sent to the WINS Server. The WINS Server, in turn, looks up the NetBIOS name in its database and returns the requested IP address to the WINS client making the request.

Name Registration

When a WINS client boots, it sends a Name Registration Request to the WINS Server. The WINS Server accepts or rejects the name registration by issuing a Positive or Negative Name Registration Response to the requesting node.

If the name does not exist in the WINS database, it is accepted as a new registration. The new name is entered in the WINS database and a Positive Name Registration Response is sent.

In a case where the NetBIOS name already exists in the WINS database but with a different IP address than that being requested, and the previous database entry has been released, the WINS Server treats the request as a new registration and a Positive Name Registration Response is sent.

If, however, the database entry is in the *active* state, the WINS Server sends a Name Query Request to the device already registered in the database. If the device still exists, it must send a Positive Name Query Response back to the WINS Server. The WINS Server then sends a Negative Name Registration Response to the computer attempting to register that name in duplicate—rejecting the name registration. If there is no response from the previously registered device, however, a Positive Name Registration Response is returned to the requesting computer and the name is registered in the database as a new registration.

Name Release

When a WINS client shuts down, it sends a Name Release notification to the WINS Server that originally issued that name registration. The WINS Server then marks the database entry as *released*.

WINS Server

The Windows Internet Name Service was designed to overcome the difficulties of using LMHOSTS files—thereby simplifying administration. A WINS Server is a dynamic database for registering and resolving NetBIOS names. The WINS Server is installed on a Windows NT server running TCP/IP and must have a static IP address. It may be a domain controller or a member server.

The WINS Server is installed using the Services tab of the Network Properties dialog box. Click the Add button and select Windows Internet Name Service. When you click the OK button, the appropriate files will be copied from the Windows NT server installation CD or the network share containing installation files. Reboot the computer and the WINS service should start.

The WINS Manager can be located under Start | Programs | Administrative Tools | WINS Manager. Use WINS Manager to configure and manage the WINS Server. WINS Manager can also be used to view the database containing the names and IP address of the WINS clients that have registered with it. Figure 10.2 shows the WINS Manager.

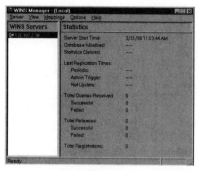

Figure 10.2 Use the WINS Manager for configuration and management of a WINS Server.

Since WINS is a dynamic service, as soon as it is started, entries are added to the database. These entries can be viewed by selecting Mappings | View Database from the WINS Manager menu. As clients register with the WINS Server, their NetBIOS names and associated IP addresses are added to the database. Figure 10-3 shows what the WINS database looks like.

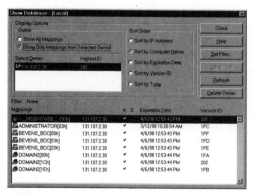

Figure 10.3 The WINS database contains the NetBIOS names and IP addresses for each computer that has registered with it.

Add Static Mappings

In order to provide name resolution for computers that are not capable of dynamic name registration, the WINS system also allows the registration of *static* names. WINS distinguishes between dynamic and static entries. This is accomplished using the WINS Manager by selecting Mappings | Static Mappings from the menu. The Add Static Mappings dialog box is shown in Figure 10.4.

Figure 10.4   Use the Add Static Mappings dialog box to enter static entries.

The types of static mappings available are:

- **Unique**— a unique name that allows one IP address per computer name. For example, a UNIX computer would be added to the WINS database as a Unique mapping.
- **Group**—specifies a normal group where addresses of individual clients are not stored. Broadcasts are sent to normal groups.
- **Domain Name**—specifies a group of Windows NT domain controllers, usually within a Windows NT domain.
- **Internet group**—includes user-defined mappings for grouping resources.

- **Multihomed**—specifies a unique name that can have more than one IP address.

TIP
Use static entries for any non-WINS computers, such as those running UNIX, to provide NetBIOS name resolution for requests from WINS clients attempting to connect to these resources.

Replication

With larger networks or networks that are segmented, you may wish to add additional WINS Servers to provide for more efficient NetBIOS name resolution and to keep name resolution traffic on the local segment. The disadvantage of multiple WINS Servers is that WINS clients may be using a WINS Server for name resolution that does not contain the address of the desired resource.

 To overcome this disadvantage of multiple WINS Servers, configure the WINS Servers to share their databases with each other. This process is called replication. Replication is configured using the WINS Manager as shown in Figure 10.5.

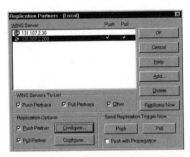

Figure 10.5   Select Server/Replication Partners on the menu of the WINS Manager to open the dialog box to configure replication.

There are two types of replication partners, Push Partners and Pull Partners. WINS replication can be configured using any combination of these such as Push/Pull, Pull/Pull, or Push/Push partnerships. Select the type of replication based on the speed of the connection between the two WINS Servers.

TIP
If the link between the two WINS Servers is a slow one such as a WAN link, use Pull replication rather than Push.

 With Push replication, replication occurs based on the number of changes that have recently been made to the WINS database. The default is 25 changes. Figure 10.6 shows the dialog box used to configure Push replication.

Figure 10.6 Enter the number of changes to occur before replication.

Pull replication is based on the amount of time to elapse before replication occurs and when replication is to begin. The interval is entered as hours, minutes, and seconds. Figure 10.7 shows the dialog box used to configure Pull replication.

Figure 10.7 Enter the amount of time to elapse before replication with a Pull Partner.

By using replication, each of the WINS Servers has the same information in its database as all others. This includes both dynamic and static entries. In this way, a computer that uses WINS Server1 is still able to successfully resolve names of computers registered with WINS Server2. All entries from WINS Server2's database are copied to WINS Server1 by the replication process.

WINS Proxy Agent

When dealing with the multi-platform network, provisions for name resolution must include the capability of non-WINS clients to resolve NetBIOS names. Non-WINS client computers such as UNIX and NetWare devices are not able to query the WINS Server for the IP address of a WINS client. The WINS Proxy Agent was designed to address this need.

The WINS Proxy listens for name resolution requests from the non-WINS clients. It then forwards these requests to a WINS Server. The WINS Server resolves the name to an IP address and sends this information to the WINS Proxy. The WINS Proxy then forwards this information to the non-WINS client making the request.

In order for a computer to be configured as a WINS Proxy, it must be a WINS client. This is accomplished by editing the registry entry:

```
HKEY_LOCAL_MACHINE\SYSTEM\CurrentControlSet\Services\Netbt
\Parameters\EnableProxy
```

The value type for this key is a REG_DWORD and can be set as 0 (false) or 1 (true).

TIP
A computer that is configured as a WINS Server cannot also be configured as a WINS Proxy agent.

The use of WINS Servers on your network has these advantages:

- There is a reduction of broadcast traffic associated with name registration and name renewal.
- Name resolution in the segmented network does not require LMHOSTS files on each computer.
- Browsing and logon validation can occur across the segmented network.

For Review

- A WINS Server resolves a NetBIOS name to IP address.
- A Windows-based computer that has been configured with the IP address of the WINS Server must register its NetBIOS name and IP address during startup in order to ensure that both are unique on the network.
- When a WINS client computer is configured to use a WINS Server, its node type is changed to h-node.

- A WINS client can be any computer running one of the following operating systems:

  - Windows NT Server or Workstation 3.5 or later

  - Windows 95/98

  - Windows for Workgroups 3.11 running Microsoft TCP/IP-32

  - Microsoft Network Client 3.0 for MS-DOS with the real-mode TCP/IP driver

  - LAN Manager 2.2c for MS-DOS

- The WINS client must be configured with the IP address of the WINS Server. The client can be configured either dynamically via a DHCP server or manually.

- The Windows Internet Name Service was designed to overcome the limitations of using an LMHOSTS files, thereby simplifying administration.

- Two of the five types of static mappings are:

  - **Unique**: a process in which a UNIX computer is added to the WINS database as a Unique mapping.

  - **Multihomed**: specifies a unique name that can have more than one IP address.

- In order to provide name resolution for computers that are not capable of dynamic name registration, the WINS system also allows the registration of *static* names.

- In order to overcome the disadvantages of multiple WINS Servers, configure the servers to share their databases with each other. This process is called replication.

- WINS Servers can be configured as a push or pull partner.

- Push replication is based on the number of changes that have been made to the WINS database before replication occurs.

- Pull replication is based on the amount of time to elapse before replication occurs and when replication is to begin.

- The WINS Proxy listens for name resolution requests from the non-WINS clients. It then forwards these requests to a WINS Server. The WINS Server resolves the name to an IP address and sends this information to the WINS Proxy. The WINS Proxy then forwards this information to the client making the request.

- In order for a computer to be configured as a WINS Proxy, it must be a WINS client.

From Here

Remember the TCP/IP exam will test you extensively on DHCP, DNS, WINS, and LMHOSTS and HOSTS files. Chapter 8, Domain Name System Server, covers the Microsoft DNS Server. Chapter 9, NetBIOS Name Resolution, explains use of LMHOSTS files. Chapter 11, Dynamic Host Configuration Protocol, explains Microsoft's implementation of the Internet's DHCP protocol.

CHAPTER 11

Dynamic Host Configuration Protocol (DHCP)

In order to run a TCP/IP network, each computer, networked printer, router, etc., must be assigned a unique IP address and a subnet mask. When TCP/IP was first implemented, the only way of accomplishing this was to manually configure and track all IP addresses. This method continues today. In order to ensure that no duplicate addresses are issued, the administrator must:

- Track all assigned addresses
- Manually configure each device that requires an IP address
- Maintain a list of unassigned addresses

This method can lead to problems with duplicate IP addresses being assigned. Troubleshooting duplicate IP address assignments can be an administrative nightmare. Although the client computer will provide a message that there is an IP address conflict, often the message identifies the conflicting computer by MAC address only. Since MAC addresses are seldom tracked, considerable time may be spent looking for the offending computer.

TIP
Microsoft will test you on how the DHCP, DNS and WINS services inter-operate. The three chapters, Chapter 8, DNS Server, Chapter 10, Windows Internet Name Service, and Chapter 11, Dynamic Host

Configuration Protocol are crucial and will account for a large portion of your score, in some cases over 50 percent of the exam.

Microsoft uses questions that involve all three services. A typical question would be one like this:

Your network has 15 UNIX computers, 8 Windows NT Servers, 100 Windows NT workstations and 75 Win95 PCs. What would you install to enable cross-network communications by computer name?

Be careful-all of the possible answers may appear correct.

Be sure you understand what is required to support DHCP across multiple subnets.

The *Dynamic Host Configuration Protocol* (DHCP) allows for the dynamic assignment of an IP address and subnet mask as well as other options such as the IP address of the default gateway. Using DHCP also makes administration easier. Some of these advantages include:

- Each DHCP Client is assigned a valid IP address

- Typographical errors are prevented

- Tracking of assigned and available IP addresses is simplified

- Fewer configuration errors mean less time spent in troubleshooting network problems.

Implementing DHCP on a network requires two components: the DHCP Client software and the DHCP Server. The DHCP Server and the DHCP Client must converse before an IP address is assigned by the DHCP Server and accepted by the DHCP Client. This process is referred to as address acquisition.

Address Acquisition

How does all this take place? How does a DHCP Server lease an IP address to a DHCP Client? The DHCP Client must first request an IP address. Then a DHCP Server must lease one to that client. This takes place in a four packet broadcast-based conversation. These packets which are shown in Figure 11.1 are

- DHCPDISCOVER

- DHCPOFFER

- DHCPREQUEST

- DHCPACK

These packets are a special type of broadcast packet. These four packets take about a quarter of a second with a total size of 1.368 bytes. These packets will be forwarded by a router that supports the BOOTP protocol as defined in RFC 1542. Even so, DHCP traffic does not pose a significant bandwidth problem. The overall effect of this traffic on your network is determined by the length of the lease and routers forwarding DHCP packets to other subnets.

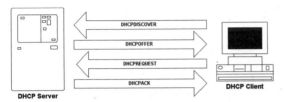

Figure 11.1 Address acquisition consists of a four packet conversation between the DHCP Client and the DHCP Server.

 If your routers do not support BOOTP, then there must be a DHCP Server on each subnet of your network, or you must install a DHCP Relay Agent on each subnet of your network that does not have its own DHCP Server.

When a DHCP Client boots, it broadcasts a DHCPDISCOVER packet, asking for an IP address. Each and every DHCP Server that receives this packet responds with a DHCPOFFER packet, which contains an IP address and subnet mask that is offered to the client.

The client responds to the first packet offer with a DHCPREQUEST packet accepting the offered IP address. The server then returns the DHCPACK packet to the client acknowledging assignment of the offered IP address. In addition, this packet contains any assigned options. These options are discussed later in this chapter.

Once the client has received the acknowledgement packet from the server, TCP/IP is initialized and the boot process continues. If the computer has multiple network adapter cards, this process is repeated for each network adapter card. A unique IP address must be assigned to each network adapter card.

Address acquisition will occur whenever a DHCP Client does not have an IP address such as

- When the client initializes for the first time, or reboots
- If the client is moved to another subnet
- If the network adapter card in the client is replaced

- If the IP address has been manually released using

  ipconfig /release

  and then either the client is rebooted or the

  ipconfig /renew

  command is used

Address Renewal

When a DHCP Client receives an IP address, the DHCP Server puts a time limit on how long the DHCP Client may use that address. This is referred to as a lease. Something like leasing an apartment. When your apartment lease expires, you renegotiate the lease with the landlord or find someplace else to live.

When the lease on an IP address expires, the DHCP Client must also renegotiate the lease. This lease or address renewal occurs via a two packet conversation with the DHCP Server. These two packets as shown in Figure 11.2 are

- DHCPREQUEST
- DHCPACK

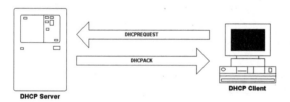

Figure 11.2 Address renewal consists of a two packet conversation between the DHCP Client and the DHCP Server.

These are the same two packets as the last two in the Address Acquisition conversation. If the address renewal takes place during the boot process, these packets are broadcast. However, directed packets are used when the DHCP Client requests a renewal based on the amount of time that has elapsed. At this time, the DHCP Client has TCP/IP up and running and knows the address of the DHCP Server that assigned its IP address.

Address renewal occurs whenever the DHCP Client boots and as a function of time based on the length of the lease. After 1/2 of the lease is expired, the DHCP Client sends a DHCPREQUEST packet to the DHCP Server that leased the address requesting to renew the lease.

If the DHCP Server does not respond to this request, the DHCP Client continues to use the same address—after all the lease has not yet expired. After 7/8 of the lease has expired, the DHCP Client again tries to contact the DHCP Server to request a lease renewal.

If the DHCP Server still does not respond, the DHCP Client waits until the lease expires and tries one more time to renew its lease. If the DHCP Server still does not respond, then the DHCP Client broadcasts a DHCPDISCOVER packet in an attempt to acquire a new IP address.

Once the lease expires, the DHCP Client no longer has an IP address and TCP/IP will no longer function. Another IP address must be leased before TCP/IP can be used again.

DHCP Client

 In order for a computer to be a DHCP Client, it must be running one of the following operating systems

Windows NT Server 3.5 or later

Windows NT Workstation

Windows 95/98

Windows for Workgroups 3.11

Microsoft Network Client 3.0 for MS-DOS

Microsoft LAN Manager 2.2c

 A DHCP Client is configured on the TCP/IP Properties dialog box as shown in Figure 11.3. As you can see, the client may be configured as either a DHCP Client or an IP address is manually assigned. If *Specify an IP Address* is selected, then this computer does not converse with the DHCP Server.

If *Obtain an IP address from a DHCP Server* is selected, you can still specify additional parameters on the other tabs of the TCP/IP Properties dialog box. These include assigning the address of a WINS Server or a DNS Server. If these entries are manually configured, they will override any options sent to the client by the DHCP Server.

Figure 11.3   Use the TCP/IP Properties dialog box to configure your computer as a DHCP Client.

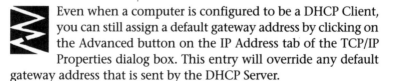 Even when a computer is configured to be a DHCP Client, you can still assign a default gateway address by clicking on the Advanced button on the IP Address tab of the TCP/IP Properties dialog box. This entry will override any default gateway address that is sent by the DHCP Server.

DHCP Server

The DHCP Server must be installed on a computer running Windows NT Server. This computer must be configured with a static IP address and subnet mask. The DHCP Server may be installed on a domain controller or a member server.

TIP
A DHCP Server cannot be installed on a computer that is a DHCP Client. In fact, after installing DHCP Server, the option to configure the computer as a DHCP Client is disabled.

DHCP Server is installed using the Network applet, Services tab. Click on the Add button and select Microsoft DHCP Server. When you click on the OK button, you will receive a message that all adapters must be assigned a static IP address. Once the necessary files have been copied from the installation share or CD-ROM, you must reboot your computer to finish the installation process.

After rebooting the computer, a new administrative tool is available—the DHCP Manager. When you first open the DHCP Manager, the DHCP Server is listed as Local Machine on the left side. In order to enable dynamic IP addressing, a range of IP addresses called a scope and a subnet mask must be configured. Figure 11.4 shows the DHCP Manager.

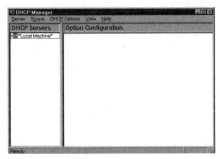

Figure 11.4   The DHCP Manager is used to configure and track the functions of the DHCP Server.

Scope

The scope is a range of IP addresses that the DHCP Server can assign to DHCP Clients. Each DHCP Server must have at least one scope which consists of the range of valid IP addresses and the associated subnet mask. Each DHCP Server may be configured to manage multiple scopes.

On the menu in the DHCP Manager select Scope / Create to display the Create Scope dialog box. Refer to Figure 11.5 to see the available fields that may be filled out.

Figure 11.5   The Create Scope dialog box is used to create a new scope.

First enter the *Start Address* and the *End Address* of the range of available IP addresses. You must also enter the appropriate subnet mask. All three of these fields are required fields.

The DHCP Server needs to know if any of the IP addresses in this scope have been manually assigned to a network device. These addresses must be excluded from the scope to prevent assigning a duplicate address. The DHCP Server tracks when it assigns addresses from this pool but does not verify whether an IP address is being used before assigning it.

Exclusions

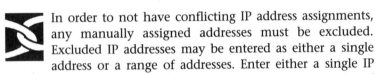 In order to not have conflicting IP address assignments, any manually assigned addresses must be excluded. Excluded IP addresses may be entered as either a single address or a range of addresses. Enter either a single IP address or the range of addresses in the *Start Address* and *End Address* boxes under *Exclusion Range*, then click the *Add* button. All excluded addresses will be listed in the *Excluded Addresses* box on the right. Multiple ranges of IP addresses may be excluded.

Lease Duration

The next section of the Create Scope dialog box defines the Lease Duration. The lease may be unlimited or set to a maximum of 999 days 23 hours 59 minutes. The default lease duration is three days.

The problem with unlimited leases is that if a computer is moved to a new subnet, the administrator will have to manually release the assigned IP address and have the computer acquire a new one. Although lengthening the lease period will decrease traffic between the DHCP Server and the DHCP Client, the length of the lease is best determined based on the ratio of available IP addresses to DHCP Clients.

If there are many more available IP addresses than DHCP Clients, the length of the lease can be lengthened. However, if the number of IP addresses is nearly equal to the number of DHCP Clients, then a shorter lease duration will guarantee availability of leases when needed.

The bottom section of the Create Scope dialog box has a place to enter a name for the scope and a comment. If a name is entered, it is displayed after the IP address in the DHCP Manager. Both of these fields are optional. Use the *Comment* box to enter text that will define the location of this scope.

When you are finished configuring the new scope and any excluded addresses, click on the OK button. You will then be presented with a message box asking if you wish to activate the scope. You may activate it at this time or wait until later. The scope must be activated before IP addresses from this scope may be assigned to clients.

Reservations

Computers such as domain controllers, print servers, file servers and application servers should usually have a static address assigned. These computers should not be DHCP Clients. The most common way of handling this is to manually configure the IP address on each of these computers.

An alternative method is to make these computers DHCP Clients that always receive the same IP address. The DHCP Server can be configured to reserve an address for a specific computer. This is called a Reservation. Reservations are configured by selecting Scope / Add Reservations from the DHCP Manager menu. This opens the Add Reserved Clients dialog box as shown in Figure 11.6.

Figure 11.6 Use the Add Reserved Clients box to assign an individual IP address to a specific computer.

In the *IP Address* box, type the IP address you want to assign to this computer. Enter the physical (MAC) address of the network adapter, without the hyphens, of this computer in the *Unique Identifier* box. Lastly enter the computer's NetBIOS name in the *Client Name* box.

The advantage to using reservations is that all IP address configuration is administered centrally making it easier to track what IP addresses have been assigned to what computer. However, this approach is not without its downside. The advantages of central administration must be weighed against the disadvantages. The most important consideration is the effect on your network if the DHCP Server is down and the client computer cannot renew its address.

If the lease expires and it cannot be renewed then one of two things will happen. First, the client will attempt to acquire another IP address. If another DHCP Server is not available, then TCP/IP will not be initialized and the computer will be unable to communicate on the network. In either of these cases, clients may be unable to access the resources associated with this particular computer.

DHCP Options

DHCP options are additional parameters that you wish to have assigned to all computers. These options may apply to a specific scope or client reservation, or be globally assigned. Options are actually TCP/IP parameters, most of which can also be assigned via the TCP/IP Properties dialog box.

The most common parameters that are assigned are:

- Default gateway or router address
- DNS Server addresses
- WINS Server addresses
- NetBIOS Node Type

The default gateway or router address is the address the computer uses to deliver packets to remote IP addresses, that is, addresses that are located on a different subnet than the computer. See Chapter 8, DNS Server for more information on the use of DNS Servers, Chapter 9, NetBIOS Name Resolution for information on NetBIOS node type, and Chapter 10, Windows Internet Name Service for information on WINS Servers.

Options are configured from the DHCP Manager and may be designated as Global or Scope Options. Select DHCP Options from the DHCP Manager menu as shown in Figure 11.7.

Figure 11.7 Select the type of options to configure from the DHCP Options selection on the DHCP Manager menu.

Global Options

Global scopes apply to the entire DHCP Server. In other words, these options will be sent to any client receiving an IP address from any of the scopes defined on that server. These options will always be used unless either Scope or Client options have been configured.

Scope Options

These options are configured to apply to a specific scope. Any client that is assigned an IP address from the scope will receive the options that are associated with it. If you have multiple scopes configured that are for separate subnets, then you should be sure to assign a default gateway for each of these scopes.

Scope options will override any Global options set for the same parameter. That is, if a WINS Server is configured as a Global option and a different WINS Server is configured as a Scope option, the WINS Server that is designated by the Scope option will be assigned to clients receiving an IP address from that scope.

Figure 11.8 shows the DHCP Options: Scope dialog box. In this instance, the 003 Router (Default Gateway) option has been selected. Its value has been entered by clicking on the Edit Array button.

Figure 11.8 The DHCP Options: Scope dialog box is used to select options to be applied to the scope. This is also the place to set the value for the selected options.

Client Options

Client options apply to a single client computer. These may either be configured at the client computer or as a client reservation. To configure client options, first define the client reservation as described above. Then under the DHCP Scope menu select Active Leases.

Select the client for which you wish to configure options, click on the Properties button. This will display the Client Properties dialog box as shown in Figure 11.9. Click on the Options button and select the options you want to configure.

Figure 11.9 Use the Client Properties dialog box to configure individual client options.

TIP

Any options that have been manually configured either at a client or as a client reservation will always override the options sent by the DHCP Server. In other words, if an IP address for the WINS Server has been entered at the client, when the DHCP Server sends an address for the WINS Server, it will be ignored. Remember this when troubleshooting why a specific option is not working.

How do you determine that an IP address and the appropriate options have been set for a client? Again, you use the utility ipconfig.exe, **which we discussed in Chapter 3 and in more detail in Chapter 14.**

When troubleshooting a TCP/IP configuration, the ipconfig utility provides a quick look at how it is configured. To get the full picture you can run the /all switch.

DHCP Relay Agent

The DHCP Relay Agent provides a way to forward DHCP packets from one subnet to another across a router that does not forward BOOTP packets. Computers running Windows NT Workstation or Windows NT Server can act as a DHCP Relay Agent.

The first step to install a DHCP Relay Agent is to install the DHCP Relay Agent Service. This is done through the Network Properties dialog box on the Services tab. After rebooting the computer, the DHCP Relay Agent is configured on the TCP/IP Properties dialog box using the DHCP Relay tab as shown in Figure 11.10.

Figure 11.10.   After installing the DHCP Relay Agent Service, configure the DHCP Relay Agent using the TCP/IP Properties dialog box.

 Each DHCP Relay Agent must be configured with the IP address of one or more DHCP Server(s). The DHCP Relay Agent then acts as a proxy to forward address requests from DHCP Clients to the designated DHCP Server.

Multiple DHCP Servers

 In the larger network, multiple DHCP Servers may be used to provide for load balancing. By installing two or more DHCP Servers, then clients will not have to wait as long to receive an IP address. Multiple DHCP Servers may also provide a measure of fault tolerance. If one DHCP Server should be offline, then the other DHCP Server would be able to respond to requests for IP addresses.

The most common method of configuring multiple DHCP Servers is to pair up two servers that are on different subnets.

 DHCP Servers on different subnets may be configured to provide IP addresses to DHCP Clients on either subnet.

For example, two subnets, A and B, each have a DHCP Server. To configure these servers to provide fault tolerance for each other, the available IP addresses should be split between the two. It is Microsoft's recommendation to configure a scope consisting of 75 percent of the IP addresses for the subnet that the server is on and another scope of 25 percent of the IP addresses for the other subnet.

 When splitting a scope between two DHCP Servers, be very careful that there are no duplicate IP addresses. Remember, a DHCP Server does not talk to other DHCP Servers. Also, a DHCP Server does not verify that another computer is not using an IP address before it assigns that address to a client.

In the above example, DHCP Server 1 on Subnet A would be configured with a scope that includes 75 percent of the available IP addresses on Subnet A. It would then be configured with another scope that consists of 25 percent of the available IP addresses for Subnet B.

DHCP Server 2 on Subnet B would then be configured with the other 75 percent of the available IP addresses from Subnet B and 25 percent of the available IP addresses from Subnet A.

With this arrangement, if DHCP Server 1 should be offline at the time that a DHCP Client from Subnet A requests an IP address, then DHCP Server 2 would be able to supply an appropriate IP address. In order for this to work, the router between Subnet A and Subnet B must be able to forward BOOTP packets.

The use of dynamic IP addressing can make one aspect of network administration less demanding. The DHCP Server provides an easy method to configure TCP/IP on client computers. The DHCP Server allows the administrator to better track assigned and available IP addresses.

For Review

- DHCP allows for the dynamic assignment of an IP address and subnet mask as well as other options such as the IP address of the default gateway.
- In order for a computer to be a DHCP Client, it must be running one of the following operating systems
  - Windows NT Server 3.5 or later
  - Windows NT Workstation
  - Windows 95/98

- Windows for Workgroups 3.11
- Microsoft Network Client 3.0 for MS-DOS
- Microsoft LAN Manager 2.2c
- A DHCP Client is configured on the TCP/IP Properties dialog box either as a DHCP Client or an IP address is manually assigned. If *Specify an IP Address* is selected, then this computer does not converse with the DHCP Server.
- The minimum configuration requirements for a DHCP Server are a range of IP addresses and a subnet mask.
- The range of IP addresses and its associated subnet mask is called a scope.
- In order to not have conflicting IP address assignments, any manually assigned addresses must be excluded. Excluded IP addresses may be entered as either a single address or a range of addresses.
- Reservations can be configured to have the DHCP Server assign a specific IP address to a specific DHCP Client.
- Global scopes apply to the entire DHCP Server. These options will always be used unless either Scope or Client options have been configured.
- Any options that have been manually configured either at a client or as a client reservation will always override the options sent by the DHCP Server.
- Use the ipconfig utility to verify the TCP/IP configuration.
- If your routers do not support BOOTP, then there must be a DHCP Server on each subnet of your network or you need to install a DHCP Relay Agent on each subnet of your network that does not have its own DHCP Server.
- Each DHCP Relay Agent must be configured with the IP address of one or more DHCP Server.

- When configuring DHCP Servers to provide fault tolerance, configure the scopes to contain 75 percent of the IP addresses from the home subnet and 25 percent of the IP addresses from the other scope. Be very careful that there are no duplicate IP addresses.

From Here

Chapter 8, DNS Server has information on the use of DNS Servers, Chapter 9 NetBIOS Name Resolution contains information on NetBIOS node type, and Chapter 10 Windows Internet Name Service provides information on WINS Servers.

The utility `ipconfig.exe` is discussed in Chapter 3 and in Chapter 14.

CHAPTER 12

Simple Network Management Protocol (SNMP)

The *Simple Network Management Protocol* (SNMP) is part and parcel of TCP/IP. It comes in various flavors from companies that specialize in TCP/IP protocols. It is, like DNS, a client-server service that uses the TCP/IP stack.

SNMP can be defined as a service that provides an interface for managing various TCP/IP devices on the network. For a more in-depth study of SNMP (it is a vast subject), you can consult RFC 1157, RFC 1212, and RFC 1213. SNMP is also covered in other RFCs and documents at the InterNIC and Internet Engineering Task Force (IETF) knowledge databases.

SNMP allows you to *probe* remote devices and to query their setup and configuration. SNMP can provide information on:

- The IP addresses of routers and gateways
- The amount of hard-disk space available on hosts
- The number of open files on hosts
- Host information, such as operating systems and memory
- Various networking activities and communications

SNMP works with, among other devices, the following:

- Routers
- Mainframe computers
- Hubs and bridges
- Windows NT servers
- Printers
- LAN Manager servers
- SNMP clients
- Terminal servers

SNMP is a distributed solution that is dispersed around networks.

TIP
Microsoft will test you on specifics related to Microsoft's implementation of the SNMP protocol and not about third-party SNMP products, such as the various SNMP agents and management products that abound.

SNMP Architecture

The SNMP is a simple architecture consisting of *Management Information Bases* (MIB) for each component of the SNMP protocol. A MIB contains information about manageable objects for a specific device.

A SNMP solution comprises a collection of management stations that communicate with network devices. Not all network devices support SNMP. Some network devices require the loading of software to run the management software. These management processes are also known as *agents*.

The other component in the SNMP picture is the management station. SNMP management stations can often be any computer or workstation running SNMP management software that can display information about the network devices being monitored or managed.

 In other words, a network must have at least one management station and Microsoft's SNMP (agent) service must be installed on each host that will be monitored.

The SNMP Management System

Every SNMP environment requires at least one management system to use the SNMP service. The management system is responsible for *probing* the device being monitored. The nature of the probing depends on the device being probed. You would not, for example, probe a printer about its hard disks.

The protocol itself defines five types of messages exchanged between the management station and the agent.

1. *Get-request:* This fetches the next value of one or more variables.

2. *Get-next-request:* This fetches the next variable after one or more specified variables.

3. *Set-request:* This sets the value of one or more variables.

4. *Get-response:* This returns the value of one or more variables. This message is returned by the agent to the manager in response to the above messages.

5. *Trap:* This notifies the manager that something occurred on the agent.

Figure 12.1 shows the five message operators in action between the SNMP manager and the SNMP agent. The ports used in this communication process are 161, for agent reception, and port 162 for manager reception or traps.

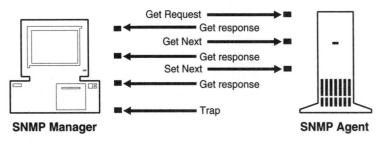

SNMP Manager   **SNMP Agent**

Figure 12.1   A SNMP conversation is sent between UDP ports.

The SNMP Agent

The SNMP agent receives requests from the management system and complies with responses to the manager. The agent is, for the most part, a passive software process that only responds to the queries. However, as indicated in Figure 12.1, the agent initiates the communication packet known as the trap.

The trap packet is a notification to the management system that an event has occurred on the network device being managed or monitored.

The Management Information Base

The *Management Information Base* (MIB) contains the information the manager requests from the agent. This is a list of questions the manager can ask of the agent.

MIBs are similar in structure to the Windows NT registry. The Microsoft SNMP service supports the following MIBs:

- MIB-II (RFC 1212 and RFC 1213)
- LAN Manager MIB-II
- DHCP MIB
- WINS MIB

MIB-II

MIB-II, as per RFC 1212 and RFC 1213, defines 171 *objects*. MIB-II (also known as Internet MIB-II) replaces the MIB-I. MIB-II is used for network monitoring, troubleshooting, and configuration.

LAN Manager MIB-II

This MIB defines a group of objects that refer to Microsoft Networks. The objects define questions related to information on a Microsoft Network such as users, logons, shares, sessions and so on.

DHCP MIB

The DHCP MIB contains objects that monitor the DHCP service on Windows NT. This MIB is installed when the DHCP service is installed. DHCP MIB contains 14 objects that monitor events such as the number of active leases and number of failures.

WINS MIB

The WINS MIB contains objects that can monitor the WINS service. Like the DHCP MIB, the WINS MIB is installed when the WINS service is installed.

WINS MIB contains objects that monitor items such as resolves, successes and failures, and items related to the WINS database.

Object Identifiers

An *object identifier* specifies an object in the MIB. This is known as an *authoritative identifier* because these identifiers are not assigned randomly. They are assigned by an organization that maintains the responsibility for the objects.

The actual identifier is a sequence of integers separated by decimal points. The tree structure is similar to DNS, which in turn was modeled on the UNIX file system1. Figure 12.2 illustrates the standard Internet MIB. Each node in the hierarchy is named for human readability. Note how the name corresponding to the object identifier 1.3.6.1.2.1 is iso.org.dod.internet.management.mibii. The Internet MIB also provides for vendor specific MIBs. These fall under the *1.3.6.1.4.1* identifier.

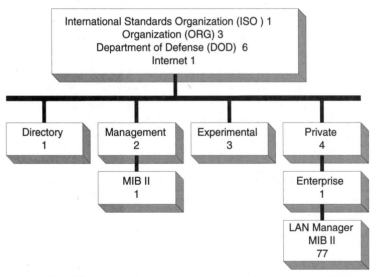

Figure 12.2 The SNMP Internet MIB tree structure is modeled on UNIX.

Installing and Configuring SNMP

The SNMP Service is installed for the following reasons:

- You want to check what is happening to TCP/IP with Performance Monitor. Note that SNMP must be installed on the host computer before using TCP/IP performance counters in Performance Monitor.
- You want to set up a computer as an SNMP agent.

The following are the steps you need to take to install the SNMP service.

1. Go to the Control Panel and double-click the Network icon.

2. Click the Services tab and click the Add button.

3. Select SNMP Service and click OK.

4. Point the installation to the Windows NT distribution files (usually the i386 path).

5. Click your way out through the OK buttons and then restart the server.

SNMP Security

After installation, you can set the SNMP service's security properties, as illustrated in Figure 12.3. Note the default community is named *public*. There are no passwords used in SNMP. Security is provided using community names.

The following security options can be set.

- *Send Authentication Trap:* Setting this option causes information to be sent back to the originator of the communication that the trap failed.

- *Accepted Community Names:* The list of community names to which the agent will respond.

- *Accept SNMP Packets from Any Host:* This means the service will accept packets from any host in a community.

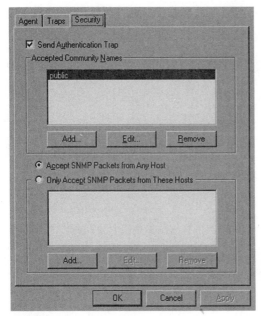

Figure 12.3 Setting up SNMP security properties.

- *Only Accept SNMP Packets from These Hosts:* The converse of the above. The service will accept packets only from those listed and prevents access from unauthorized hosts.

SNMP Traps

To set up a trap, at least one community name must be specified. The trap destination can be a host name, an IP address, or an IPX address (see Figure 12.4).

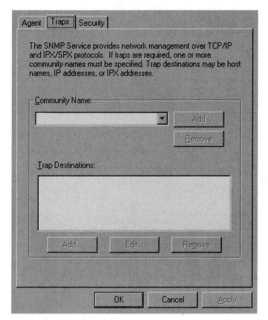

Figure 12.4 Set SNMP traps here.

SNMP Agents

Setting up agents allows you to specify devices you will monitor and allocate those responsible for the agents (see Figure 12.5).

Check the option for setting the contact name. This is the name of a person that needs to be alerted.

The SNMP Utility

The SNMP utility that ships with the Windows NT Resource Kit is named SNMPUTIL.EXE. It is a command line utility that can verify that SNMP is installed correctly and is working. Windows Help provides information on how to use the utility.

For Review

- SNMP can be defined as a service that provides a unified management philosophy for managing various TCP/IP devices on the network.

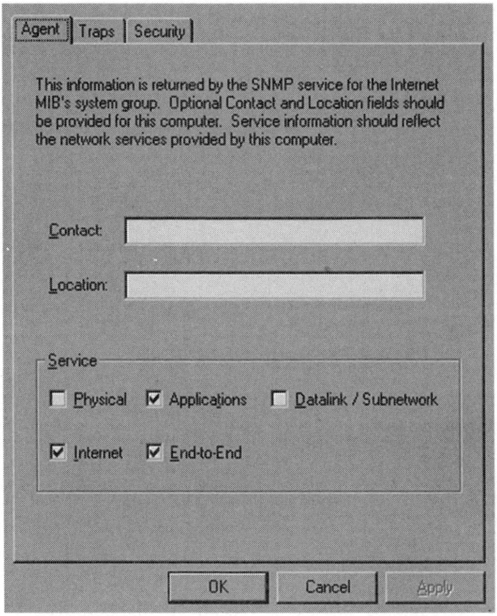

Figure 12.5   Set SNMP monitoring agents here.

- SNMP allows you to *probe* remote devices and to query their setup and configuration.

- Every SNMP environment requires at least one management system to use the SNMP service.

- Microsoft's SNMP (agent) service must be installed on each host that will be monitored.

- An SNMP solution comprises a collection of management stations that communicate with network devices.

- SNMP must be installed on the host computer before using TCP/IP performance counters in Performance Monitor.

- Select *Only Accept SNMP Packets from These Hosts:* for the service to accept packets only from those listed. This prevents access from unauthorized hosts.

- To set up a trap, at least one community name must be specified. The trap destination can be a host name, an IP address, or an IPX address.

From Here

SNMP is just one service that enables us to better manage and maintain a TCP/IP network and network services. Other TCP/IP services are discussed in Chapter 13, Internetworking Microsoft TCP/IP.

CHAPTER 13

Internetworking Microsoft TCP/IP

The world's networks and internetworks consist of a multitude of different technologies, operating systems, and platforms. TCP/IP provides a means of achieving connectivity between these platforms.

Microsoft TCP/IP has come a long way. It now provides a rich set of utilities and services that were not available a few years ago. These features include the following:

- **Remote Execution**: These utilities allow you to execute commands on remote computers, typically on UNIX systems. The commands include RSH (Remote Shell) and REXEC (Remote Execute). Both commands are typical TCP/IP commands that have been running on UNIX systems for some time.

- **File Transfer**: Microsoft Windows NT fully supports the FTP (File Transfer Protocol), as both a server through the *Internet Information Server* (IIS) and as part of the OS in client mode. The file transfer utilities also include RCP (Remote Copy Protocol).

- **Terminal Emulation**: Windows NT supports the Telnet client. Telnet provides terminal emulation for DEC VT100, DEC VT52, and TTY terminals.

- **TCP/IP Printing**: Windows NT provides a set of utilities to enable printing through TCP/IP. These include LPR (Line Printer Request), LPQ (Line Printer Query), and LPD (Line Printer Daemon).

This chapter concludes with a discussion of the *Remote Access Service* (RAS) and TCP/IP.

Remote Execution

These utilities enable you to execute commands on a UNIX host.

REXEC

REXEC allows you to connect to a remote host and start a process or service. You will be required to log on as a user and provide a password. Once validated, the host will start the process and later terminate the session.

RSH

RSH is similar to REXEC. UNIX validates the user login through the hidden rhosts file.

File Transfer

These utilities enable you to transfer files and data to and from Windows NT and remote hosts.

RCP

RCP is a file copy utility that allows Windows NT to copy files to a remote host.

FTP

FTP is one of the most popular utilities on the Internet. The protocol is extensive and robust, providing an important framework for transferring files to and from Windows NT and any host running an FTP service or daemon.

To use the FTP service, you must have an FTP client, such as the command-line version that is shipped with Windows. Many GUI-based utilities, however, are available to allow you to work with FTP servers in a File Manager- or a Windows Explorer-type environment.

TFTP

TFTP is similar to FTP for file transfer but coexists in a connection-less mode with TCP/IP. TFTP is much simpler to use than FTP, and is often much quicker. And unlike FTP, you cannot use TFTP with the command interpreter.

No TFTP server is currently being shipped with Windows NT, such as the FTP server that is bundled with IIS. TFTP is useful when dealing with non-Windows NT environments and devices, such as embedded systems (routers and so on). These machines cannot support full FTP servers and usually implement TFTP as means of unloading files and updating firmware.

Terminal Emulation

TELNET

Telnet is a utility that provides terminal emulation for DEC terminals VT100 and VT52 and TTY terminals. Telnet also uses the connection services of TCP/IP for data transfer between client and server.

Telnet allows a client to log on to a remote server and run applications located on the remote host.

The Telnet client is available on the Windows NT Server and Windows NT Workstation. The Telnet server service or daemon, however, is not provided with the Windows NT OS. A number of third-party Telnet servers for Windows NT are available.

After you have opened the Telnet client at the Run line or at the Command Prompt, you can connect to the Telnet server of your choice by entering settings in the Connect dialog box that loads when you click the Connect|Remote System option in the Telnet Connect menu item, as illustrated in Figure 13.1. The remote Telnet server connection can also be invoked as a command line switch—for example: `telnet io.com`.

Figure 13.1   Connect to a Telnet server for remote login from the Windows Telnet terminal client.

The options required are as follows:

- **Host Name:** Provide the name of the host or the IP address.
- **Port:** This is the port name supported by the Telnet environment. It can be Telnet, daytime, echo, qotd, or chargen.
- **Terminal Type:** Choose VT100, VT52, or TTY (ANSI).

Telnet can provide some security, in that a daemon can require a user ID and login password.

A good example of when Telnet comes in handy is looking up WHOIS information on the WHOIS database managed by the InterNIC. The code illustrates one such Telnet session looking up WHOIS information.

```
C:\WINNT
C:\WINNT>WHO IS iana.org

Registrant:
Internet Assigned Numbers Authority (IANA-DOM)
   c/o USC-ISI
   Suite 1001
   4676 Admiralty Way
   Marina Ddel Rey, CA 90292

Domain Name: IANA.ORG

Administrative Contact, Technical Contact, Zone Contact:
   Internet Assigned Numbers Authority (IANA) iana@iana.org
   (310) 822-1511
Billing Contact:
   Internet Assigned Numbers Authority (IANA) iana@iana.org
   (310) 822-1511

Record last updated on 06-Apr-98.
Record created on 05-Jun-95.
Database last updated on 1-Aug-98 05:48:04 EDT.

Domain servers in listed order:

VENERA.ISI.EDU          128.9.0.32 128.9.176.32
NS.ISI.EDU                  128.9.128.127

The InterNIC Registration Services database contains ONLY
non-military and non-US government domains and contacts.
Other associated whois servers:
   American Registry for Internet Numbers   - whois.arin.net
   European IP Address Allocations          - whois.ripe.net
   Asia Pacific IP Address Allocations      - whois.apnic.net
   US Military                             - whois.nic.mil
   US Government                           - whois.nic.gov
```

TCP/IP Printing (LPS)

This section on TCP/IP printing covers the UNIX-style inter-host printing environment known as *Line Printer Services* (LPS). Besides data and file transfer and host-to-terminal communications, Windows NT supports the use of LPS. In a multi-host, internetworked, heterogeneous environment, it is still relatively expensive to give everyone a print device. The print device will thus be the most-shared device in many environments.

LPS allows users to access the hosts that have print devices under their control and to redirect documents to the printer queues under the control of that remote host. LPS also allows print data to be directed from host-to-host or from print queues on one computer to print queues on another. In other words, LPS provides for a distributed printing environment.

The LPS consists of two components or processes: LPR and LPD. LPR is UNIX jargon for the client or machine requesting the printing services, and LPD is the server providing the line printer service or *daemon*. LPD accepts print output from an LPR on the network and routes the files into the print queue, on a host that is running LPD and is attached to a print device.

By now you might be asking, "*So what does this all have to do with TCP/IP?*" The answer is simple. LPS uses the LPR/LPD protocol, which uses TCP as its network transport mechanism.

The well-known port numbers for LPS are: LPD on 515 and LPR from 721 to 731. LPD listens for a connection request on port 515. LPD, once it receives a communication, can perform a number of management functions for the remote client, such as connecting and requesting printing services and determining the availability of print queues.

Microsoft TCP/IP supports the LPR/LPD protocol. Windows NT ships with the LPR utility. This utility allows Windows NT to send a print job to a host running the LPD daemon. For example, Hewlett Packard's HP JetDirect Print Server can run the LPD daemon, and thus Windows NT can redirect TCP/IP print jobs to the print device attached to the Jet Direct by addressing the print job and associated requests to the JetDirect printer's IP address.

LPD on Windows NT Server

 Windows NT can be set up as an LPD service or daemon, just like any UNIX host. The service you need to install is called *lpdsvc,* and it is added automatically when you add

Microsoft TCP/IP Printing in the Network applet. Figure 13.2 shows the beginning of the installation process, from

Start | Settings | Control Panel | Network | Services |Add

Figure 13.2 Microsoft TCP/IP Printing must be installed to use LPR.

You can test the installation by simply typing the following at the command line: *lpr -s <hostname> -p <printername> filename.* For example: *lpr -s ourpdc -p pdcprinter abigdoc.doc*

Creating LPR Printers

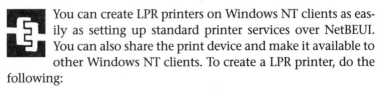

You can create LPR printers on Windows NT clients as easily as setting up standard printer services over NetBEUI. You can also share the print device and make it available to other Windows NT clients. To create a LPR printer, do the following:

1. Go to the Control Panel and select Settings/|Printers. Click on Add Printer and select My Computer. You are actually creating an LPR port, and the print device does not need to be connected to your computer as is usually the case. Click Next. See Figure 13.3 for the result.

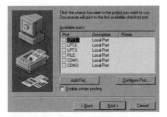

Figure 13.3 To create an LPR port on Windows NT, the first step is going to the My Computer printer wizard option.

2. Select Add Port and select the LPR Port option in the list box as illustrated in Figure 13.4.

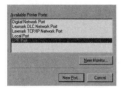

Figure 13.4 Add an IP address for the LPR service.

3. The next dialog box will ask you for the IP address of the host that is connected to the print device and the name of the printer or the print queue on that server, as illustrated in Figure 13.5.

Figure 13.5 Add an LPR port for the LPR service.

4. Now share the printer so that any computer can print to the new printer.

LPQ (Line Printer Query)

 By issuing the *lpq* command at a command prompt, a user can monitor the status of the print queue.

Remote Access Service and TCP/IP

Configuring TCP/IP on a RAS server is almost mandatory these days, because of Internet access and connectivity. Often a user may need to access the Internet via a remote site or from home. If the office network supports a high-bandwidth connection to the Internet, then setting up the RAS server makes sense.

Microsoft will test you on setting up TCP/IP on a RAS service in the TCP/IP exam. (General RAS and Dial-up Networking is covered in the Windows NT Server and the Windows NT Workstation exams.)

When the RAS server connects to an *Internet Service Provider* (ISP), the default gateway address on the RAS server should be blank. Because the RAS server acts as the access point to the ISP, the ISP will provide the gateway information to the RAS server. Local network clients, such as Windows 95 or Windows 98 computers, would then specify their default gateway address to be the IP address of the RAS server.

By default, RAS uses DHCP to assign remote TCP/IP client addresses. If you do not have or do not provide access to a DHCP server, however, then you must assign static addresses.

Point-to-Point Tunneling Protocol

The Point-to-Point Tunneling Protocol (PPTP) allows the use of the Internet to securely access your remote network. PPTP allows the use of IP, IPX, or NetBEUI over a TCP/IP network. It does this by encapsulating the data. PPTP also provides for data encryption. PPTP can support a *virtual private network* (VPN) over a public-switched telephone network (PSTN), ISDN, or X.25.

By enabling PPTP filtering, the RAS server will allow only PPTP packets to enter the local network. This increases security and gives only PPTP-enabled clients dial-in privileges.

The biggest advantages of using PPTP are lower costs and less administrative time involved in providing remote access. Since the Internet is used, a large number of modems are not required. In addition, no dedicated, leased lines are needed for a secure connection. Less hardware means less time spent managing access.

For Review

■ Microsoft TCP/IP includes a rich Internet protocol suite of utilities.

■ FTP server and FTP client services are fully supported by Microsoft TCP/IP, as is the TFTP.

■ Telnet allows a client to log on to a remote server and run applications located on the remote host.

- To set up Windows NT as an LPD service or daemon, install Microsoft TCP/IP Printing in the Network applet.

- For UNIX computers to send print jobs to a print device attached to a Windows NT Server computer:

  - Install TCP/IP Printing Service on the Windows NT Server computer.

  - Share the printer.

- Use the *lpq* command to check the status of a print queue.

- TCP/IP can be bound to Windows Client and Server Remote Access Servers, allowing dial-up modem users to gain access to an IP address pool and the Internet.

- Leave the default gateway address blank on the RAS server when the RAS server will be connecting to an ISP.

- Specify the IP address of the RAS server as the default gateway address on local network clients.

- PPTP can use IP, IPX, or NetBEUI over PSTN, ISDN, or X.25.

- Enable the PPTP filter to increase security and allow only PPTP-enabled clients dial-in privileges.

From Here

We learned in this chapter about the utilities that are now standard components of Microsoft TCP/IP. The next chapter wraps up our study of Microsoft TCP/IP with planning and configuration issues and troubleshooting exercises.

CHAPTER 14

Troubleshooting Microsoft TCP/IP

Today, more than any other network protocol, TCP/IP provides the fabric of the world's networks and internetworks. TCP/IP connects businesses, allowing them to connect to the Internet, to wide area networks, to metropolitan networking services and to internetworks, computers, monitoring devices, displays, printers, and more.

More importantly, TCP/IP is the key to the Internet. I consider the TCP/IP protocol a vital part of the life force of the Internet. Starving your clients or users of TCP/IP connectivity is akin to leaving a pet without air. Without this connectivity, businesses and individuals will suffocate.

With a working knowledge of TCP/IP, even Microsoft TCP/IP, you will be in a position to bring your clients and users up-to-speed with rapid computing and networking advances on the horizon.

With a full understanding of how TCP/IP works, a network engineer is able to provide the service that modern organizations demand. Without TCP/IP, a network engineer is like a surgeon unable to diagnose the patient's heart problems—unable to determine whether the patient needs a double, triple, or quadruple bypass or a heart transplant.

Microsoft TCP/IP management and troubleshooting is straightforward. The level of TCP/IP knowledge you need to pass the

Microsoft exam (and to begin work on today's TCP/IP networks) is offered in this study guide. Here, we are primarily dealing with network *planning, installing,* and *configuring.* For example, you are not required to know TCP/IP software development or to learn how software talks to sockets or listens on ports and so on.

Back in Chapter 2, you learned about how packets of data travel the TCP/IP network and make their way up-and-down the TCP/IP stack. In configuring and troubleshooting TCP/IP, we are primarily required to address configuration problems, setup, and resolving host names.

TCP/IP is widely adopted, popular and pervasive, and it is a routable networking protocol. When routing goes wrong, a TCP/IP network can be brought to its knees. The first hint of a problem with TCP/IP on a particular host usually comes from a user complaining that he is unable to receive e-mail or browse the World Wide Web.

TCP/IP Troubleshooting

TCP/IP troubleshooting follows a course of diagnosis and tests to determine and fix a problem. These tests can be performed with the various testing tools and utilities that come with Microsoft TCP/IP. Let's look at a list of testing procedures and stages.

- Step 1: Check the network cable and connection.
- Step 2: Check for a link light on the NIC.
- Step 3: Browse the network.
- Step 4: Ping the interface.
- Step 5: Ping the gateway address.
- Step 6: Ping an address on another network.
- Step 7: Tracert to an address on another network.
- Step 8: Ping the host name of a computer.

This chapter concludes with a discussion of two Windows NT monitoring tools: Network Monitor and Performance Monitor.

Step 1: Check the Network Cable

As ridiculous as it may seem, checking the network cable and connection is the first thing you should do. Too often, the problem is a network cable that has been unplugged from the card or the cable that has been yanked out of the interface connection. Yet, it still amazes me that some engineers do not check the cable first. It takes so little time and can save you so much aggravation.

Usually the cable is plugged back in, and that is all there is to it— your user is back in business. What if you do not check the cable? It only takes a few seconds. I remember once spending a whole day on a computer, and, finally, on day two we reluctantly called Microsoft and spent $195 on a support call. When I finally got over the 10 minutes of interrogation to set up the call, the support engineer first asked, "Have you checked your network cable? Is it plugged in?" It was not. Oops. Sorry, Bill says no refunds for dereliction of duty.

Step 2: Check for a Link Light

You can be sure that if there is no link light twinkling out the back of the NIC or on the interface device, you have a hardware problem. Check the cable again, only this time, check it at the hub and patch panel. If there is still no link light after patching into another hub and another patch-panel port, then the NIC or the motherboard is dead. Usually the NIC is the problem, because the problem is noticed only after Windows NT is running. Often, you will have link lights but little luck moving data and that could point to a hub and patch-panel problem.

Step 3: Browse the Network

If you get a link light, then it is time to turn to software configuration. At this point, you could look in the Event Viewer under System Log to search for a clue as to what might be wrong. I find that this compares to looking for the needle in the haystack in the beginning, because you do not really know what you are looking for and it takes time to trace the first error message that spawned the resulting errors. In any event, Windows may only report that a device attached to the system is not functioning. How nice it would be if Windows could report, "The NIC is not functioning because the network cable is not receiving data on pin two."

If you click on Network Neighborhood and can browse the network (see the list of other computers), then the problem is related to protocols or setup of TCP/IP. If, however, you cannot see the network, you need to look at the network settings because the problem is related to the OS. In other words, if Microsoft Networking is not working, then TCP/IP will not work.

3A. **Check Identification:** Go to the Control Panel and click on the Network icon. The Network dialog box appears. The first tab to look at is Identification. Make sure that you are trying to log on to the correct domain. Changing to the correct domain works better. Remember that you cannot have another computer in the same domain with the same name. These names are NetBIOS names and must be unique in a domain. If there is a conflict with NetBIOS names, the network will be unhappy. How do you know if the problem is the name? Check the event log—you will see.

#B. **Check Installed Services:** The Services tab in the Network applet lists the installed services. The first item in the list that you should look for is the Workstation Service. This service is not only essential for TCP/IP connectivity but also for just about everything related to communications. If the Workstation Service is missing, then a likely scenario is that the registry is corrupt or the service was not installed or was removed for some reason. First, try to install the Service by clicking Add. If this fails, the problem is in the registry. Reinstall Windows NT.

3C. **Check Adapters:** If you fly through steps one and two above and still cannot browse the network, or you get the dreaded *Unable to Browse Network* message, then the next Network tab to check is Adapters. (There is another school of thought that you should next check to see if the network protocols are installed. I feel you have to start at ground zero—at the hardware—to first get the network card in, then bind software to it, as discussed next.) If no network card or adapter drivers are installed, then that is where the problem likely lies.

Select the option to have Windows NT display the list of adapters it supports and then install a driver from the Windows NT Installation CD or from an install directory. If you have the latest Windows NT-compatible adapter driver on disk, then use it. If you have protocols installed, including TCP/IP, they automatically will bind to the adapter when you click to the next tab. This is another reason why I like to go to the Adapters tab first. Do not fail to check if the correct protocols are installed. If you are installing a generic (no-name-brand) adapter (such as Novell NE2000-compliant cards), you may be required to provide IRQ and I/O port information.

3D. **Check Protocols:** It is perfectly feasible to run a Microsoft network on TCP/IP exclusively and have all computers connected to the Internet, browsing the LAN, mapping drives, printing, and so on with a single protocol. On the other hand, NetBEUI is not a routing protocol, but it is fast and designed for a homogenous Windows LAN. If no protocols are installed at all, you have just found the reason why the computer cannot browse the network. The next protocol to install after NetBEUI is TCP/IP, if it is not already there. If TCP/IP was installed, you should have found that out already in Step 3, because the protocol would have automatically bonded to the adapter and prompted you for IP address information. One of the reasons to have at least one alternate protocol, perhaps NetBEUI, installed on all computers on the network is to get the network started. If NetBEUI is running, you will at least be able to map to network drives and browse and verify that the network is functioning—leaving you to concentrate on TCP/IP configuration. Also, when testing TCP/IP using the tools described later, you will have the comfort of knowing that the problems are related to TCP/IP and not the network hardware or the OS. Last, you never know when you will need to access another computer that does not have TCP/IP installed, to grab a file or check a configuration.

3E. **Check Bindings:** Bindings may have been installed and then disabled for some reason. If the bindings are in place and need to be enabled, then it is a simple procedure. If TCP/IP is critical to your business plan, you will want to raise it to a position higher in the binding order.

3F. **Check Services:** If after rebooting you still cannot browse the network and receive a link light, then it is remotely possible (but highly unlikely) that the services were disabled. Go back to the Control Panel and check the Services applet for startup information. If a critical service is not started, then start it up and make sure that the service's Startup Type is Automatic. If you can now browse the network, you can move onto TCP/IP configuration. If not, then you likely have a hardware failure— a bad cable, a bad NIC, or a bad computer. Replace each hardware part in the aforementioned order to resolve the problem.

Step 4: Ping the Interface

If TCP/IP is installed, you should be able to ping the local host or loopback address—127.0.0.1. Receiving the reply message, as shown in Figure 14.1, is an indication that

TCP/IP is installed and is bound to the interface correctly on the local computer.

```
C:\WINNT>ping 127.0.0.1

Pinging 127.0.0.1 with 32 bytes of data:

Reply from 127.0.0.1: bytes=32 time<10ms TTL=128
Reply from 127.0.0.1: bytes=32 time<10ms TTL=128
Reply from 127.0.0.1: bytes=32 time<10ms TTL=128
Reply from 127.0.0.1: bytes=32 time<10ms TTL=128

C:\WINNT>_
```

Figure 14.1 Ping the loopback adapter to verify that TCP/IP has been installed correctly.

The next step is to make sure that you have the correct IP address setup for the network adapter card.

Double-click the Network Icon in the Control Panel. When the Network dialog box appears, select the Protocols tab and highlight TCP/IP. You can either right-click on the entry or click the Properties tab. The Microsoft TCP/IP Properties dialog box will appear.

Make sure you have the correct setting here. If you are picking up an IP address from a DHCP server, then make sure that the option *Obtain an IP address from a DHCP server* is checked. Otherwise, check *Specify an IP address*.

Now, make sure that the static address entered is correct, that the subnet mask is correct, and that the default gateway is correct. A small typing error can prevent you from executing TCP/IP. Also ensure that the IP address and the default gateway have the same network ID.

Windows NT usually asks you to reboot at this point. As described above, after rebooting, ping the NIC IP address. If you receive replies from the ping in response to the NIC's IP address, then TCP/IP is now set up correctly on the computer.

Step 5: Ping the Gateway Address

The next step will help you determine if TCP/IP is correctly set up on other hosts. The first area to pay attention to is the gateway. Ping the gateway address. If the ping fails, there could be two reasons:

5A. The computer hosting the default gateway has not been set up correctly, or its hardware is faulty. Go to the gateway computer (possibly a router or a hub) and check the settings.

5B. The gateway address just installed in the local computer's TCP/IP configuration is incorrect. The best and quickest way to check this is by using the *ipconfig* utility.

Ipconfig quickly provides the IP address, subnet mask and default gateway for each NIC attached to the computer. *Ipconfig* lets you check TCP/IP configuration without having to run TCP/IP protocol options from the Network applet in the Control Panel. Figure 14.2 shows the results from running *ipconfig* on a Windows NT computer.

```
C:\WINNT>ipconfig

Windows NT IP Configuration

Ethernet adapter elnk31:

        IP Address. . . . . . . . . : 10.0.1.21
        Subnet Mask . . . . . . . . : 255.255.255.0
        Default Gateway . . . . . . : 10.0.1.60

Ethernet adapter NdisWan4:

        IP Address. . . . . . . . . : 0.0.0.0
        Subnet Mask . . . . . . . . : 0.0.0.0
        Default Gateway . . . . . . :

C:\WINNT>
```

Figure 14.2 Ipconfig displays the current TCP/IP configuration.

 The *ipconfig /all* command shown in Figure 14.3 provides a full display of the local computer's current TCP/IP configuration, including information on DNS, NetBIOS, WINS and DHCP settings.

```
C:\WINNT>ipconfig /all

Windows NT IP Configuration

        Host Name . . . . . . . . . : patrantsrv.Emissary
        DNS Servers . . . . . . . . : 199.170.88.29
                                      199.170.88.10
        Node Type . . . . . . . . . : Hybrid
        NetBIOS Scope ID. . . . . . :
        IP Routing Enabled. . . . . : No
        WINS Proxy Enabled. . . . . : No
        NetBIOS Resolution Uses DNS : Yes

Ethernet adapter elnk31:

        Description . . . . . . . . : ELNK3 Ethernet Adapter
        Physical Address. . . . . . : 00-60-97-62-A8-22
        DHCP Enabled. . . . . . . . : No
        IP Address. . . . . . . . . : 10.0.1.21
        Subnet Mask . . . . . . . . : 255.255.255.0
        Default Gateway . . . . . . : 10.0.1.60
        Primary WINS Server . . . . : 10.0.1.60

Ethernet adapter NdisWan4:

        Description . . . . . . . . : NdisWan Adapter
        Physical Address. . . . . . : 00-00-00-00-00-00
        DHCP Enabled. . . . . . . . : No
        IP Address. . . . . . . . . : 0.0.0.0
        Subnet Mask . . . . . . . . : 0.0.0.0
        Default Gateway . . . . . . :

C:\WINNT>_
```

Figure 14.3 Use *ipconfig/all* for a complete display of the current TCP/IP configuration.

Step 6: Ping an Address on Another Network

If the gateway address is correct and DHCP is working correctly, or you have the correct static address information, the problem now probably rests on the interfaces that lie on the other side of the gateway. Remember, the gateway is the exit for packets leaving the network. So, if you cannot ping an address on the other side of the gateway, especially the next IP address of the interface that lies upstream from your gateway, you have a routing problem.

There are two possibilities here. First, if you cannot ping the interface that sits immediately upstream from the gateway, then you have IP configuration and routing problems at the gateway. The gateway cannot relay the packets it is receiving onto the next network. Second, what if you can get to the addresses upstream from your gateway, but you still cannot ping an address on the Internet? Before we guess that the world has already ended outside of our known network, let's bring out the *trace route* utility.

Step 7: Tracert to an Address on Another Network

Trace route, or *tracert*, is an easy-to-use utility that can return valuable information where a route breaks down. The trace route can also return information indicating weak links in the routing chain. An example of a *tracert* is shown in Figure 14.4.

```
C:\>tracert 152.159.1.2

Tracing route to interlock.mgh.com [152.159.1.2]
over a maximum of 30 hops:

 1     *        *        *       Request timed out.
 2   221 ms   140 ms   140 ms   aus-gw-F0-0.illuminati.net [199.170.88.1]
 3   901 ms   140 ms   140 ms   WCC-GW.amap.waller.net [208.24.32.193]
 4   150 ms   150 ms   150 ms   aus1-core2-h1-1-0.atlas.digex.net [206.181.161.89]
 5   150 ms   150 ms   140 ms   dfw2-core2-pt4-0-0.atlas.digex.net [165.117.52.34]
 6   571 ms   180 ms   171 ms   lax1-core1-pt8-0-0.atlas.digex.net [165.117.50.25]
 7   250 ms   191 ms   200 ms   sjc4-core2-pt5-0-0.atlas.digex.net [165.117.53.74]
 8   191 ms   180 ms   200 ms   sjc4-core1-fa5-1-0.atlas.digex.net [165.117.244.1]
 9   200 ms   190 ms   190 ms   sjc2-core1-pos1-0-0.atlas.digex.net [165.117.56.82]
10   220 ms   201 ms   200 ms   f3-1.p221.t3.ans.net [140.223.12.130]
11   271 ms   200 ms   220 ms   f2-1.t12-0.San-Jose.t3.ans.net [140.223.12.129]
12   260 ms   230 ms   231 ms   h11-1.t68-0.Dallas.t3.ans.net [140.223.61.42]
13   281 ms   240 ms   240 ms   h14-1.t60-4.Reston.t3.ans.net [140.223.57.26]
14   260 ms   230 ms   241 ms   f3-1.t56-1.Washington-DC.t3.ans.net [140.222.56.121]
15   231 ms   260 ms   250 ms   f0.cnss61.Washington-DC.t3.ans.net [140.222.56.197]
16   320 ms   261 ms   240 ms   s0.enss3340.t3.ans.net [199.221.107.30]
17     *      261 ms   350 ms   interlock.mgh.com [152.159.1.2]

Trace complete.

C:\>_
```

Figure 14.4 Use tracert to find out the route a packet follows from source to destination.

Tracert can tell you exactly where the packets go off the proverbial edge.

If it is a computer on the ISP interface, upstream from your router's Ethernet and serial ports, then you can do little more than call the ISP and pray they can fix the equipment on the other side of the smart jacks or demarcations.

If the problem is on your organization's gateway computer or hub, then we will need to delve into the routing tables.

To display and edit static routing tables, use the *route* command. To view the routing table, specify *route print*, as shown in Figure 14.5.

```
C:\>route print

Active Routes:

   Network Address          Netmask  Gateway Address       Interface  Metric
         0.0.0.0          0.0.0.0       10.0.1.60      10.0.1.21       1
        10.0.1.0    255.255.255.0       10.0.1.21      10.0.1.21       1
       10.0.1.21  255.255.255.255       127.0.0.1      127.0.0.1       1
   10.255.255.255  255.255.255.255       10.0.1.21      10.0.1.21       1
       127.0.0.0        255.0.0.0       127.0.0.1      127.0.0.1       1
       224.0.0.0        224.0.0.0       10.0.1.21      10.0.1.21       1
  255.255.255.255  255.255.255.255       10.0.1.21      10.0.1.21       1

C:\>_
```

Figure 14.5 Use route print to display the routing table.

There will likely be many times when you need to add routes or manipulate routing tables. Refer to Chapter 5 for a more detailed discussion of routing.

It is possible to run your TCP/IP ship into a sand bank on physical address allocation problems. Although MAC addresses are burned into most NICs, there are some interfaces, especially in the mainframe world, that allow MIS people to *assign* MAC addresses. So MAC addresses can and are duplicated in the real world. This is bad.

The ARP protocol can be used to identify which host is actually assigned the IP address with which you are working. ARP was introduced in Chapter 2, "TCP/IP in a Nutshell." Figure 14.6 shows an example of resolving an IP address to a MAC address.

```
C:\>arp -a

Interface: 10.0.1.21 on Interface 2
  Internet Address      Physical Address      Type
  10.0.1.60             00-c0-6d-16-a2-1d     dynamic

C:\>_
```

Figure 14.6 Use ARP to resolve the physical address of a network interface device.

At this point, if you can route or ping to the router past any gateways or fire wall (if they let the packets bounce off the external interface), then TCP/IP on your Windows NT domain is working correctly. Remember TCP/IP does not work a little at a time or sluggishly, as some people have described. If you can ping or route packets, then TCP/IP is working. If there is packet loss, TTL expirations or intermittent failure, the problem is often related to network traffic or hardware—a router, hub, or other networking hardware.

Netstat and *nbtstat* provide additional methods of diagnosing networking problems.

NETSTAT

 Netstat will display protocol statistics and current TCP/IP network connections.

 To see the route table and current TCP/IP connections, use *netstat -r*, as shown in Figure 14.7.

```
C:\WINNT>netstat -r

Route Table

Active Routes:

Network Address          Netmask  Gateway Address     Interface  Metric
        0.0.0.0          0.0.0.0         10.0.1.60     10.0.1.21       1
       10.0.1.0    255.255.255.0         10.0.1.21     10.0.1.21       1
      10.0.1.21  255.255.255.255         127.0.0.1     127.0.0.1       1
  10.255.255.255  255.255.255.255        10.0.1.21     10.0.1.21       1
      127.0.0.0        255.0.0.0         127.0.0.1     127.0.0.1       1
      224.0.0.0        224.0.0.0         10.0.1.21     10.0.1.21       1
  255.255.255.255 255.255.255.255        10.0.1.21     10.0.1.21       1

Active Connections

 Proto  Local Address        Foreign Address         State
 TCP    patrantsrv:1074      ponlysrv:nbsession      ESTABLISHED
 TCP    patrantsrv:1098      ponlysrv:nbsession      TIME_WAIT
 TCP    patrantsrv:1101      ponlysrv:nbsession      ESTABLISHED
 TCP    patrantsrv:nbsession ponlysrv:2614           ESTABLISHED
 TCP    patrantsrv:1027      localhost:1031          ESTABLISHED
 TCP    patrantsrv:1031      localhost:1027          ESTABLISHED

C:\WINNT>
```

Figure 14.7   Use netstat -r to display the route table and current TCP/IP connections.

 To see Ethernet statistics, use *netstat -e*, as shown in Figure 14.8.

```
C:\>netstat -e
Interface Statistics

                        Received              Sent

Bytes                   5541565           3785003
Unicast packets           11377             11731
Non-unicast packets         421               172
Discards                      0                 0
Errors                        0                 0
Unknown protocols             0

C:\>
```

Figure 14.8   Use *netstat -e* to display Ethernet statistics.

The *netstat -s* command can be used to view protocol statistics, shown in Figure 14.9.

```
C:\>netstat -s

IP Statistics

    Packets Received                    = 11613
    Received Header Errors              = 28
    Received Address Errors             = 0
    Datagrams Forwarded                 = 0
    Unknown Protocols Received          = 0
    Received Packets Discarded          = 0
    Received Packets Delivered          = 11585
    Output Requests                     = 11854
    Routing Discards                    = 0
    Discarded Output Packets            = 0
    Output Packet No Route              = 0
    Reassembly Required                 = 0
    Reassembly Successful               = 0
    Reassembly Failures                 = 0
    Datagrams Successfully Fragmented   = 0
    Datagrams Failing Fragmentation     = 0
    Fragments Created                   = 0

ICMP Statistics

                            Received      Sent
    Messages                614           538
    Errors                  6             0
    Destination Unreachable 223           133
    Time Exceeded           325           0
    Parameter Problems      0             0
    Source Quenchs          0             0
    Redirects               0             0
    Echos                   17            388
    Echo Replies            43            17
    Timestamps              0             0
    Timestamp Replies       0             0
    Address Masks           0             0
    Address Mask Replies    0             0

TCP Statistics

    Active Opens                        = 74
    Passive Opens                       = 8
    Failed Connection Attempts          = 5
    Reset Connections                   = 13
    Current Connections                 = 5
    Segments Received                   = 10106
    Segments Sent                       = 10211
    Segments Retransmitted              = 84

UDP Statistics

    Datagrams Received      = 716
    No Ports                = 728
    Receive Errors          = 12
    Datagrams Sent          = 1023

C:\>
```

Figure 14.9   Use *netstat -s* to display protocol statistics.

NBTSTAT

 Nbtstat displays NetBT (NetBIOS over TCP/IP) statistics and current TCP/IP connections using NetBT.

 Use *nbtstat -n* to display the NetBIOS Local Name Table. This command, shown in Figure 14.10, can be helpful when trying to solve NetBIOS name resolution problems.

The *nbtstat -r* displays name resolution statistics. This command, shown in Figure 14.11, should not be confused with *nbtstat -R* discussed next.

```
C:\WINNI>nbtstat -n

Node IpAddress: [10.0.1.21] Scope Id: []

           NetBIOS Local Name Table

    Name              Type         Status
    ---------------------------------------------
    PATRANTSRU    <00>  UNIQUE    Registered
    EMISSARY      <00>  GROUP     Registered
    EMISSARY      <1C>  GROUP     Registered
    PATRANTSRU    <20>  UNIQUE    Registered
    EMISSARY      <1E>  GROUP     Registered
    PATRANTSRU    <03>  UNIQUE    Registered
    INet~Services <1C>  GROUP     Registered
    IS~PATRANTSRU..<00> UNIQUE    Registered
    PATRANTSRU    <01>  UNIQUE    Registered

C:\WINNI>
```

Figure 14.10 Use *nbtstat -n* to display the NetBIOS name cache.

```
C:\>nbtstat -r

NetBIOS Names Resolution and Registration Statistics
---------------------------------------------------------------
Resolved By Broadcast      = 0
Resolved By Name Server    = 9

Registered By Broadcast    = 0
Registered By Name Server  = 9

C:\>_
```

Figure 14.11 *Nbtstat -r* displays NetBIOS Names Resolution statistics.

 The *nbtstat -R* purges the NetBIOS name cache and reloads the LMHOSTS file. This command is shown in Figure 14.12.

```
C:\>nbtstat -R
Successful purge and preload of the NBT Remote Cache Name Table.
C:\>_
```

Figure 14.12 Use *nbtstat -R* to reload the NetBIOS name cache.

Step 8: Ping the Host Name of a Computer.

Finally, your TCP/IP problem may not be TCP/IP in general but rather a problem with the name resolution protocol, or DNS. If you are unable to resolve host names into IP addresses or IP addresses into host names, then you may have DNS problems.

Windows NT provides the ability to interact with a name server. Make sure you have one or more names in the TCP/IP configuration dialog boxes.

 A typical command from the command line is *nslookup*. *Nslookup* provides information that can help resolve host name resolution problems.

Monitoring Tools

Performance Monitor

Windows NT's built-in Performance Monitor, shown in Figure 14.13, provides a network administrator with a graphics tool to collect data regularly throughout each day, so trends can be determined through data analysis.

Figure 14.13 Use the *segments/sec* counter for the Object TCP to gather statistics on the rate at which TCP segments are sent or received.

Performance Monitor can be found on the Windows NT Workstation and the Windows NT Server in the Administrative Tools program group. Data from Performance Monitor can be viewed in real time, logged for future comparisons, and easily be used in charts and reports. The log files can also be exported for further analysis in other applications, such as Microsoft

Excel or Microsoft Access. Alerts can be set to warn the administrator when threshold values have been exceeded.

Performance Monitor collects data about system resources, called objects, and statistical information, called counters. Each object in Performance Monitor has many subcategories containing counters. A specific set of counters for an object can be selected depending upon your monitoring needs. For a specific counter definition, open the Add to Chart dialog box, select the counter and click on the Explain button.

To use the Performance Monitor counters for the following

- Network Interface (a NIC performance counter)
- TCP/IP
- Internet Control Message Protocol
- UDP

the Simple Network Management Protocol (SNMP) service and the TCP/IP network protocol must be installed on the computer you will be monitoring. SNMP is not automatically installed when TCP/IP is installed. To install SNMP, open the Control Panel, choose the Network Icon, select the Services menu, select the SNMP service, and click on Add. For more information about SNMP, see Chapter 12.

Network Monitor

Network Monitor is a software program that captures packets and provides information about the traffic sent and received by a computer on the network.

Network Monitor is installed through Control Panel | Network | Services. After installing Network Monitor (and rebooting Windows NT), the service can be accessed by Start | Programs | Administrative Tools | Network Monitor.

Figure 14.14 shows a Network Monitor capture window. The captured data can be reviewed on a packet-by-packet basis. Network Monitor filters can be set so that only the packets of interest are saved.

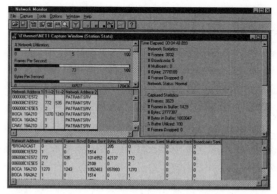

Figure 14.14 Use Network Monitor to capture data packets sent over the network.

For Review

- Troubleshooting TCP/IP can be a simple procedure, such as changing or replacing a network cable, or complex, such as manipulating routing tables.

- First, make Microsoft Networking functional if it is not before you try to troubleshoot TCP/IP.

- Ping the loopback address—127.0.0.1—to verify that TCP/IP is installed correctly on the local computer.

- Microsoft TCP/IP on Windows NT ships with a rich set of diagnostic tools for troubleshooting TCP/IP.

- The *ipconfig /all* command displays the local computer's current TCP/IP configuration, including information on DNS, NetBIOS, WINS, and DHCP settings.

- Use *tracert* to find out the route a packet follows from a source to a destination.

- To display and edit static routing tables, use the *route* command.

- Use ARP to resolve the physical address of a network interface device.

- *Netstat* will display protocol statistics and current TCP/IP network connections.

- *Netstat -r* displays the route table and current TCP/IP connections.

- *Netstat -e* displays Ethernet statistics.

- *Netstat -s* displays protocol statistics.

- *Nbtstat* displays NetBT (NetBIOS over TCP/IP) statistics and current TCP/IP connections using NetBT.

- *Nbtstat -n* displays the NetBIOS name cache.

- *Nbtstat -R* purges the NetBIOS name cache and reloads the LMHOSTS file.

- *Nslookup* provides information that can help resolve host name resolution problems.

- Data from Performance Monitor can be viewed in real time, logged for future comparisons and can easily be used in charts and reports.

- Network Monitor captures packets and provides information about the traffic sent and received by a computer on the network.

- Data captured by Network Monitor can be reviewed on a packet-by-packet basis.

- Network Monitor filters can be set so that only the packets of interest are saved.

From Here

We have explored a number of steps to diagnose and troubleshoot TCP/IP. If this is your last exam for your certificate, then good luck with the exam and your career as a MCSE.

Index

About the Author

Dave Kinnaman, MCSE, from Austin, Texas, has coauthored many books and articles about computers and the Internet. Dave is particularly involved in information-access issues, including Internet filtering software, disability access, and retirement issues on the Internet.

After more than 18 years as an underpaid state employee, Dave is exploring options in the private and not-for-profit sectors.

With spouse LouAnn Ballew, Dave operates several health-related Internet discussion groups—their three-year-old open discussion of allergies has more than 800 members in 40 countries.